1993

This study explores the problems faced by writers of the Enlightenment, who attempted to demystify all previous forms of knowledge by applying rationalist critiques that can in turn be applied to examine their own critical work. It focuses on the works of one of the best-known writers of eighteenth-century France, Denis Diderot, analyzing his experimentation with presenting critical knowledge. Playing close attention to the formal-poetic nature of Diderot's writing, his "art," it examines the interplay between critical knowledge and its representation, between epistemology and esthetics. Professor Brewer shows how Diderot's work in the areas of philosophy, science, the fine arts and literature pushed Enlightenment critique to its limits, and points to its remarkable similarity to aspects of modern critical theory.

Cambridge Studies in French 42

THE DISCOURSE OF ENLIGHTENMENT IN EIGHTEENTH-CENTURY FRANCE

Cambridge Studies in French

Recent titles in this series include

31 SARAH KAY
Subjectivity in Troubadour Poetry

32 GILLIAN JONDORF
French Renaissance Tragedy: The Dramatic Word

33 LAWRENCE D. KRITZMAN
The Rhetoric of Sexuality and the Literature of the French Renaissance

34 JERRY C. NASH
The Love Aesthetics of Maurice Scève: Poetry and Struggle

35 PETER FRANCE
Politeness and its Discontents: Problems in French Classical Culture

36 MITCHELL GREENBERG
Subjectivity and Subjugation in Seventeenth-Century Drama and Prose: The Family Romance of French Classicism

37 TOM CONLEY
The Graphic Unconscious in Early Modern French Writing

38 MARGERY EVANS
Baudelaire and Intertextuality: Poetry at the Crossroads

39 JUDITH STILL
Justice and Difference in the Works of Rousseau: Bienfaisance and Pudeur

40 CHRISTOPHER JOHNSON
System and Writing in the Philosophy of Jacques Derrida

41 CAROL A. MOSSMAN
Politics and Narratives of Birth: Gynocolonization from Rousseau to Zola

A complete list of books in the series is given at the end of the volume.

THE DISCOURSE OF ENLIGHTENMENT IN EIGHTEENTH-CENTURY FRANCE

Diderot and the Art of Philosophizing

DANIEL BREWER

Associate Professor of French, University of Minnesota

Published by the Press Syndicate of the University of Cambridge
The Pitt Building, Trumpington Street, Cambridge CB2 1RP
40 West 20th Street, New York, NY 10011-4211, USA
10 Stamford Road, Oakleigh, Victoria 3166, Australia

First published 1993

Printed in Great Britain at the University Press, Cambridge

A catalogue record for this book is available from the British Library

Library of Congress cataloguing in publication data

Brewer, Daniel.
The discourse of enlightenment in eighteenth-century France:
Diderot and the art of philosophizing / by Daniel Brewer.
p. cm. – (Cambridge studies in French: 42)
Includes bibliographical references and index.
ISBN 0 521 41483 0 (hardback)
1. Diderot, Denis, 1713–1784. 2. Enlightenment – France.
3. France – Intellectual life – 18th century. I. Title. II. Series.
B2017.B75 1983 92-25291 CIP
194 – dc20

ISBN 0 521 41483 0 hardback

To My Parents

Contents

Illustrations

Acknowledgments

"Lorsqu'on fait un conte," writes Diderot, "c'est à quelqu'un qui l'écoute." My own story too must begin by referring to several persons, to whom thanks are due.

I am especially grateful to Louis Marin for his gentle direction and generous contributions to this project from its earliest stages. My thanks go as well to Jean-François Lyotard, who was most patient regarding stories about "l'homme du dialogue." Many others too – friends, colleagues, and readers – have provided much assistance and encouragement along the way. I thank in particular Philip Lewis, Ross Chambers, Jack Undank, Georges Van den Abbeele, Nancy Miller, Walter Rex, and Christie MacDonald.

I am truly indebted to Timothy Murray for his unstinting and insightful comments concerning the manuscript. Finally, I express far more than indebtedness to Mária Minich Brewer, whose patience, confidence, advice, and knowledge made it possible to tell this story.

NOTE ON THE TEXT

Unless otherwise indicated, references to Diderot's works are to volume and page of the Hermann edition of the *Œuvres* (Paris: Hermann, 1970–). When necessary, reference will also be made to the Assézat-Tourneux edition of the *Œuvres complètes* (Paris: Garnier, 1875–77).

Introduction

In a short, programmatic essay written in 1784, Immanuel Kant asks the question, "What is Enlightenment?" His answer, condensed in the motto *sapere aude*, dare to know, is that Enlightenment comes about once the individual strives courageously to free herself or himself from the enslaving condition of ignorance. As Kant's essay suggests, this heroic struggle for liberating knowledge (Enlightenment) also characterizes the event of *the* Enlightenment, thus providing a way to understand Enlightenment in historical terms. It is tempting to believe, along with Kant, that ours is an age of Enlightenment, and that in inheriting the legacy of the past we free ourselves from what Kant calls its barbarism. This emancipation from the past means freeing ourselves from the immediacy of the event through a courageous act of cognition, the Kantian *sapere aude*. Historical understanding, then, would involve mediating the raw experience of the event and comprehending the past as such, as experience mastered by virtue of its being represented to consciousness.

Kant's *Was ist Aufklärung* marks an important moment in the history of European Enlightenment, wherever one locates its beginnings and ends (assuming it has ended and that the present belongs to a post-Enlightenment age). I do not propose to rewrite that history here. Instead I wish to ask whether the history of Enlightenment might not be unwritable insofar as Kant's question is unanswerable. Or rather, Enlightenment can be made into an event and its history written, but only by refusing to consider Kant's question as a philosophical one, involving the very conditions of possibility for critical knowledge, if not its limits. This at least is how it has been heard by Michel Foucault. Rather than answer the question, as so many have attempted to do, Foucault situates it, maintaining that philosophy has never been able to provide an answer to "what is Enlightenment?" Indeed, he defines modern philosophy itself as "the philosophy that is attempting to answer the question raised so imprudently two centuries ago: *Was ist Aufklärung?*"[1]

If the problem of defining Enlightenment critically marks the limits of modern philosophy, it is because philosophy can be modern only by becoming caught in what could be called the double bind of Enlightenment. To be truly liberating, to provide knowledge of self and world, philosophy must set about to produce a critical perspective so powerful that it calls into question any critique that could be produced, including that of Enlightenment and philosophy itself. The knots of this double bind begin to tighten as the eighteenth-century Enlighteners endeavor to free themselves from the fetters of what they call ignorance, superstition, and religious dogma. They attempt to produce knowledge at its most useful, insisting above all on the arbitrary status of any way of representing knowledge. Only thus can they arrogate for themselves the right and power to judge all representations of knowledge and to decide which shall be put to use. The entire project of rationalist critique is based upon the assumption that prior knowledge can be refuted only with knowledge. Light can dispel the shadows only by revealing that tenebrous knowledge does not know enough. Consequently, to challenge the authority of established truth discourses, the Enlighteners seek to produce more powerful truths. They do not claim to know things better or truly, however, just differently. Relying on the practice of reason (not acts of faith), stressing the role of the senses in the production of knowledge (and not the "innate ideas" of the Cartesian tradition), they insist on the empirical, experiential determination of knowledge. Quite willing to accept partial, provisional knowledge, they seek above all a useful and effective way to represent the world and the human subject's place in it.

The Enlighteners' entire project bears witness to the

conviction that reason cannot oppose power. It can only seek to be more powerful than what it sets itself against, which is to say that only one power can oppose another.[2] The Enlighteners wish to demystify all forms of knowledge by empowering knowledge in general. They reject the supposedly universal principles and timeless truths that had grounded the knowledge of a prior age, claiming that these express not the immutable essence of the divine, human or natural world, but rather the values of particular individuals or social groups. In the place of truth as a universal founding principle, the Enlighteners substitute values, which however powerful are ultimately arbitrary. Nowhere is this process more obvious than in the massive testament to Enlightenment that is the *Encyclopédie*. Hence this investigation of Enlightenment critique begins by considering the representation of knowledge in the encyclopedic text. Rephrasing Kant's question somewhat, I wish to consider not what Enlightenment is but how it represents.

I would suggest that Enlightenment can be examined not only as an historical period or philosophical concept, but also as a specific representational practice. In one sense, this means quite obviously that before saying anything concerning Enlightenment as period or concept, one must read Enlightenment texts. It is not enough though to invoke the commonplace of reading without at the same time seeking through reading to displace, rephrase or even refuse established interpretive paradigms or "master narratives." Failing to do so, one risks repeating and reactivating precisely the paradigms and narratives one wishes to comprehend and contest. Accordingly, as I use it here the term Enlightenment will not refer to what intellectual historians have already described in exhaustive detail, namely, a particular set of concepts or theoretical constructs belonging to such domains as epistemology, esthetics, ethics or social theory. By Enlightenment I mean a particular mode or art of producing knowledge as a form of representation, a specific set of techniques for figuring the relation between subjects and objects, people and things, and finally a way of inventing a critical relation to knowledge. The story I have to tell concerns how these techniques work and what effects they produce.

Although this story will relate a liberating Enlightenment, it must also consider the latter's limits. Enlightenment critique falls victim to entrapment and self-entrapment when it claims the knowledge it represents escapes the contingency of its representation. This claim amounts to an idealism designed to overcome the materiality of representations, the stubborn resistance to a conceptualizing, theorizing, idealizing drive that representations in their materiality continuously offer. The encyclopedic text provides a prime example of the consequences of this self-entrapment. Present in the words and images of the *Encyclopédie*, the Enlighteners' representational practice permits them to believe they can master knowledge without being mastered by it. However effective this practice may be, it risks infusing Enlightenment critique with the negative potential of power. Once the Enlighteners put their newly empowered knowledge to practical ends, reordering institutions and social practices according to the light of reason, Enlightenment begins to self-destruct. Once rationalism becomes a representational practice judged in terms of its effectiveness, productivity, and power, knowledge is instrumentalized. Nature, as well as human subjects, become yet other objects of knowledge, possession, and domination.[3]

This at least is the argument of those who caution against taking over uncritically one of the European Enlightenment's most appealing of legacies, namely, an abiding confidence in progress, in a meliorative, teleological view of history and the human subject's place in it. Max Horkheimer and Theodor Adorno argue in *Dialectic of Enlightenment* for example that in the empowerment of reason one witnesses the transformation of Enlightenment into myth, the conversion of a philosophy of reason into an ideology of rationalization and a technology of terrifying mastery.[4] In one of their more provocative examples, Horkheimer and Adorno present the Marquis de Sade's novel *Juliette* as one of the very emblems of Enlightenment, not a perverted Enlightenment gone amok, but rather pushed to its darkest and most violent limits.

The object of Horkheimer and Adorno's critique is not the eighteenth-century Enlightenment but modern culture. The question they raise is whether the most repressive, dehumanizing, and apparently irrational forms of modern thought and behavior are aberrant breaches in culture and history, or whether instead they reflect the inevitable development of rational philosophy and social practices. Their goal is not to reject Enlightenment and refuse reason, but to rid Enlightenment, if possible, of its accretion of myth, thereby restoring its authentic critical potential. What Horkheimer and Adorno do refuse is the story of a heroic and ultimately innocent Enlightenment, whose telling only mythologizes Enlightenment and mystifies precisely those values that should be able to free knowledge of mystification. Thus, while they would agree with Alfred Cobban when he refers to the "rebrutalization of contemporary life," they are far more cautious about calling for a return to what Cobban sees as the "ethical standards" of the Enlightenment.[5] Horkheimer and Adorno do not simply bemoan nostalgically the eclipse of Enlightenment. Their attempt to comprehend the consequences of Enlightenment, and keep them at bay, highlights the difficulty encountered in mounting a critique of Enlightenment, namely, that no "outside" to reason can be invoked that reason itself has not already always constituted. One can adopt no critical position that would not be articulated in precisely rational terms.[6]

This other story of Enlightenment makes it increasingly difficult to believe in a mythical Enlightenment in which the critique of authority somehow remains unaffected by the problem of the authority of critique. This other story reveals what a mythologized Enlightenment covers up, namely, its own double bind, the inability to prevent the critical practice of Enlightenment from turning or being turned back upon itself. If the eighteenth-century Enlighteners sought their freedom by refusing the paradigms and principles that unshakably grounded knowledge in religious and metaphysical terms, do they undo in the process the foundation of knowledge in general, including that of their own epistemological systems? If they reject the universals that underpinned the ethics, esthetics, and social theory of a prior age, what of the ultimate ground of their own theoretical enterprises in such domains? In the Enlightenment's rephrasing of truth as value, is the very foundation of rational thought lost (once again as always), and can any claim to have discovered the truth not be refuted, or at least deconstructed, as exemplifying a quite Nietzschean will to power? The Enlighteners produced a powerful critical discourse, yet one it would seem that must itself be subjected to a thoroughgoing critique. How then can one undertake a contemporary critique of Enlightenment if what one encounters are the limits of critique?

Kant's question is clearly a modern one, if not a postmodern one. And in asking it Kant is not alone in being imprudent, since critical theory in general is also trying to answer Kant's question. By the shorthand term of critical theory, I mean a self-reflexive, self-problematizing investigation into the real as it is produced in and by symbolic representation (such as texts and images, but also all other varieties of sounds and shapes). Critical theory has brought down disciplinary boundaries, questioning the paradigms relied on to interpret the world and make sense of it, and forging different perspectives onto events and values. What is contemporary about Enlightenment, then, as a representational practice, and which is highlighted by a thriving competition in the area of critical theory (theory of the subject, language, the artwork, the text, etc.), is that the present-day practice of representing knowledge continually and inevitably also confronts the double bind of Enlightenment. The discourse of critical theory, too, must not refuse to turn its critical power upon itself so to speak, even at the risk of questioning the very foundation of theoretical discourse and adopting a skeptical or at least incredulous attitude towards the latter's power to deliver up and reveal the truth.

A good deal of the debate concerning what is called the postmodern involves what value to grant to theory's admission of its constitutive double bind. Of course, to propose judging this double bind in terms of value is to decide the question in advance. There are those who argue that any critical theoretical discourse must be judged instead on the basis of its capacity to reveal truths. Refusing the possibility of such revelation, in such a view, would be tantamount to embracing inescapable relativism, skepticism or nihilism. The postmodern, for its most resolute of critics, is thus an antihumanism, a foundationless pluralism, an antifoundationalism that challenges the grounds for any kind of knowledge, moral action or esthetic judgment.[7]

The debate concerning postmodernism will not be resolved here. I would contend though that the distinctive feature of postmodern thought is a refusal to comprehend being and truth in metaphysical terms. Instead they are events, occurring in unique, nongeneralizable encounters that make up no History but designate a "post-history."[8] Furthermore, these events involve (an) art, and thus the crucial issue in the debate concerning the postmodern involves the place and function accorded to art. I must stress that by art I do not mean the object esthetic theory sets itself apart from in order to describe, regulate, and know. I mean rather the set of nongeneralizable techniques or working procedures for producing specific yet also unpredictable effects, only one of which may be knowledge. This definition of art not only questions the legitimacy of the domain of esthetics "proper." It also draws attention to theoretical discourse itself as a work of art, a discursive practice that enjoys no hierarchical superiority with regard to the various other cultural practices to which it refers or with which it may be linked.

One of the most extensive attempts to extend the range of art is found in the work of Jean-François Lyotard, which bears witness to his conviction that the time has come, as he puts it, to take leave of truth. In formulating things thus, Lyotard does not clear the way for a return to error or a descent into nihilism or irrationalism. He wishes rather to break with or at least reposition the particular genre of discourse he characterizes as theoretical. "La grande affaire est maintenant pour nous de détruire la théorie."[9] For Lyotard, theory is a particular genre among others, a specific way of phrasing, and thus it can be analyzed in pragmatic terms as an act or work of language. Underscoring the pragmatics of theoretical discourse as resulting from an artful *savoir faire* or know-how, Lyotard is quick to add that the destruction of theory cannot take place by criticizing it. "La critique est elle-même un *Moment* théorique dont on ne saurait attendre la destruction de la théorie."[10] Critique cannot break the double bind. Required instead are what Lyotard calls pseudo-theories or theory-fictions. These are not a stronger instance of theory, a better "perspective," "approach," "system" or "method." Rather, they work to destroy theory by doubling it parodically. Indistinguishable from theoretical discourse in terms of truth and falseness, theory-fictions unseat that master discourse by countering its claim to distinguish and separate the true from the false.[11] Theory-fictions do not aim to produce knowledge or *le savoir*, defined in terms of true and false. Rather they display and deploy a know-how, a *savoir faire*. This art or artful competence exceeds the criterion of true and false and works to escape entrapment by theory and the theorist. Theory-fictions delegitimate the discourse of theory by showing that it too exemplifies an art and is but a genre like many different others.

Lyotard's restaging of theoretical discourse and his sketching out of the pragmatics of its parody testify to his belief that ours is a postmodern age, one that can no longer believe in theory, just as it is incredulous towards all "master narratives" designed to produce knowledge and thereby govern social activity and representation.[12] This postmodern loss of faith in the regulative power of theoretical discourse may seem fairly far removed, both historically and conceptually, from the Enlightenment. Yet whether we classify these master narratives now in disarray as belonging to literature, philosophy or science, many of them began to emerge during the eighteenth century, when Enlightenment's epistemological goal was, as Michel Foucault puts it, to "faire tableau." In representing knowledge, the Enlightenment also "fait récit," telling the story (or becoming a story) about its own attempt to formulate theories capable of producing critical knowledge. Thus, the very act that constitutes the most powerfully critical aspect of Englightenment also displays (or fails to conceal) its art, its reliance upon a discursive pragmatics in order to present its critical knowledge. This is the art I wish to consider, and principally through the texts of one of the French Enlightenment's most brilliant and problematic of writers, Denis Diderot.

Few of his contemporaries sensed as acutely as Diderot the conflictual nature of the relation between a theory of knowledge and its practice, and none pursued that conflict more inventively by experimenting with the art whereby knowledge is produced. Emblematic of the Enlightenment's desire to establish a powerfully theoretical position that could account for all aspects of human experience, Diderot's writing possesses a scope that is properly encyclopedic. I propose no new synthetic reading of Diderot's thought though, no overarching reordering of the Diderotian corpus. I do wish to argue that only by attending to what I shall call Diderot's art of philosophizing can one grasp most directly and intensely how he grapples with the issue of presenting critical knowledge, as it involves both the text(s) of Enlightenment and contemporary acts of interpretation.

To come to terms with that art, my own readings both rely on and question a traditional division of intellectual and disciplinary labor characterizing studies on Diderot and the eighteenth-century Enlightenment in general. Intellectual historians have focused on the expository, more conceptual texts in order to describe Diderot's place in the broader context of eighteenth-century science, ethics, political theory, and esthetics. Literary interpreters on the other hand have attended to more formal, poetic issues, concerning themselves primarily with the fictional texts and describing Diderot's narrative craft in at times myopic detail. In Diderot's case, and most likely in general, this division of labor between intellectual history and literary interpretation is no longer productive. Not only does this division lead to miniaturization and fragmentation. It also perpetuates interpretive practices based implicitly on the assumption that linguistic categories such as idea and form, message and vehicle, signifier and signified, can be kept separate and distinct, something that is far from certain. In Diderot's case, this division between what could be called the conceptual and the poetic, or, in slightly different terms, the philosophical and the literary precludes presenting what is most powerfully pertinent in his writing, namely, his art of philosophizing. My operative assumption throughout will be that Diderot writes texts that are both literary and philosophical, texts that preclude determining in advance to which category they belong or even whether the distinction between such categories or genres can be maintained. A brief consideration of Diderot's best-known novel, *Jacques le fataliste* will make this point.

Novelistic conventions and the workings of narrative are foregrounded in *Jacques* to such a degree that it is extremely difficult to read it even as the esthetic version of a philosophical treatment of the concept of determinism. At the same time however, *Jacques* cannot be contained within the generic confines of the category of novel. This text is not simply another reworking (however innovative) of novelistic conventions, another stage in the evolution of literary form. Thus, neither intellectual nor literary history can adequately account for this text. A story above all about storytelling, *Jacques* sets up the category of fictive reader and it sets the real reader up, at least the one who desires knowledge of what the story is about and thus misses its point. As the most insightful readings of this self-reflexive text have shown, if *Jacques* is about anything it is about itself, the ways a text provides the material for a reader's desire to encounter, if not the real, then at least what can be taken to be the real. As Diderot's text also shows, this knowledge is gained only by overlooking or attempting to move somehow beyond the text's determining structures, its enabling conditions, its textuality or, as I would prefer to say, its materiality. To be sure, *Jacques* thematizes determinism as a philosophical concept. It also presents it as text, figured as "the great scroll up yonder." Finally, it stages determinism, performing it in the relation between Jacques and his master, narrator and fictive reader, and text and reader. Thus *Jacques* is about "aboutness" in a larger, self-reflexive sense, for it also stages reading as resulting from the desire for knowledge of what stories are about, a desire however that blocks grasping precisely how such metacritical knowledge is produced. What must be grasped is the matter of that production, the materiality of knowledge as representation. Hence, *Jacques* is less about the philosophical concept of determinism than about the material determination of philosophy, or of any instance of knowledge.

Materialism is also a major thread in the story I wish to weave. In one sense, this term refers to the theory of materialism elaborated by the eighteenth-century philosophers, and thus my story may resemble that told by Diderot's intellectual biographers, who trace his evolution from deism, skepticism, and sensationalism to an atheist materialism. This intellectual trajectory has the distinct advantage of neatly unifying the Diderotian corpus, and in such varied domains as epistemology, ethics, and esthetics. Such unity comes at a cost however, and I am not the first to note that the goal of synthesis is the least attainable in Diderot's case, and perhaps the least satisfying. To analyze how Diderot seeks to account for the material determination of knowledge, "another" materialism must be considered, or rather a materiality, which is excessive with respect to the opposition between idealism and materialism that is regularly invoked to contain it. Diderot's sensationalism or his theory of matter must be grasped in and through the material practice whereby he philosophizes about it, his philosophical art of phrasing what matters. Points of high intensity for this philosophizing are the subject of the body and the work of art.

Diderot's answer to the double bind of Enlightenment is not something that could go by the shorthand terms of a materialist esthetics. His art of philosophizing is neither an esthetics nor a materialism, however much it resembles them (just as theory-fictions resemble theory). Yet this material, artistic practice marks both an inaugural and a limiting moment in Enlightenment critique. In the acts of interpretation Diderot performs, critical discourse is pushed to its limits, coming to resemble a dramatic narrative, a powerful story of interpretation. In short, Diderot's critical discourse comes to resemble a work of art, which self-reflexively and artfully questions any privilege it might enjoy with respect to the object it proposes to interpret. However much he may be of the eighteenth-century European Enlightenment, Diderot's writing contains something uncannily contemporary in the critical art of philosophizing it displays. His work pushes Enlightenment critique to its limits. It is from this "excentric" position, to borrow a term from Georges Benrekassa,[13] that one can undertake as well as interrogate a contemporary critical enterprise. In the attempt to move, if not outside or beyond Enlightenment, then at least to its edge, to a common historical and theoretical border we share with it, one can most effectively ask whether the critical practice signalled by such a move in fact stands for a "post-Enlightenment" one. At any rate, this is the question and the wager of the present study.

CHAPTER I

Representing knowledge: reading the Encyclopédie

L'étrange machine qu'une langue.

Diderot

La Science n'est donc pas autre chose que la Grammaire, historique et comparée, afin de devenir générale, et la rhétorique.

Mallarmé

The utility of myths

Conceived initially in 1745 as a business venture consisting of a two-volume translation of Ephraim Chambers' *Cyclopedia* of 1728, the *Encyclopédie* project had already outstripped all original plans by the time the first volume of articles appeared in 1751. When completed a quarter-century later, this monumental work comprised twenty-eight folio volumes containing 71,818 articles and 2,885 plates. Five subsequent editions were printed in Switzerland and Italy before 1789; roughly one-half of these 25,000 copies went to readers in France. Judged in terms of its innovative approach to the compilation and transmission of knowledge, the financial and technical means marshalled, the size of its readership (some 4,500 subscribers), and the number of its eventual collaborators (over 150 identified), the *Encyclopédie* project stands as one of the greatest exploits in the history of French culture and modern capitalism.[1] The *Encyclopédie* is also the text most representative of the French Enlightenment, providing massive testimony to the Enlightenment belief in the value of unfettered inquiry into all sectors of human knowledge. Helping to consolidate the Enlightenment as a movement of intellectual and social reform, the *Encyclopédie* contributed as much to the change of ideas during the last decades of the *Ancien Régime* as to the exchange of capital.

A scale model of Enlightenment,[2] this monumental work is doubly representative of Enlightenment in that it constitutes an event that can be understood in both epistemological and social-cultural terms. Chief among the ideas the encyclopedists sought to change was that of knowledge itself, its origins and ends, its production and use. Moreover they reflect upon the type of knowledge that could make most comprehensible the social-cultural context in which their text appears. Thus, the encyclopedists' self-reflexive concern with encyclopedic form and the most effective presentation of knowledge marks a crucial moment in the establishment of Enlightenment critique: the empowerment of language so as to produce critical knowledge. The encyclopedists reject knowledge in and of itself as insufficient to eradicate unreason and bring about the reasoned reordering of values and institutions. Instead they present knowledge as representation, materially and inseparably linked to a process of production that is both linguistic-epistemological (the generation of ideas) and textual-discursive (the writing of the encyclopedic text). Only thus, the encyclopedists believe, can knowledge be empowered, acquiring the critical force necessary to found Enlightenment critique. The two editors of the *Encyclopédie*, Denis Diderot and Jean Le Rond D'Alembert, unhesitatingly characterize their age as "revolutionary,"[3] a term that refers in the case of their text to a restructuring of the relation between power and knowledge, exemplified in the encyclopedic representation of knowledge.

Signs of this shift occur well before mid-century. Emblematic of a first generation of Enlighteners or social critics, Voltaire tirelessly struggles against the power of institutionalized forms of knowledge, notably in the area of religion and idealist metaphysics. Making tactical use of an emergent new science, he repeatedly invokes Locke, Newton, and English empiricism to articulate a type of knowledge less concerned with knowing things in and of themselves than with experimenting with how they may be known. Just as Voltaire's Candide turns ultimately from questions of essence to that of practice ("il faut cultiver notre jardin"), Voltaire presents the writing of history in *Le Siècle de Louis XIV* as a practice involving the discursive production of (historical) knowledge. A second generation of Enlighteners, including Diderot, Condillac and d'Holbach, pursues this experimentation as they continue to contest the authority and legitimacy of idealist explanatory systems. Seeking a more limited working knowledge of the various parts of experience, working to eradicate residual idealism in philosophy, science, and ethics, this second generation produces programs of critical inquiry that redefine the object of knowledge and the human subject's relation to it. Resolutely more materialist, atheist, and utilitarian, these programs reflect the philosophes' desire to "demystify" knowledge. Relying on the practice of reason (not acts of faith), stressing the role of the senses in the production of knowledge (and not "innate ideas"), the philosophes insist on the empirical, experiential determination of knowledge. Willing to accept partial, provisional knowledge, they seek above all a useful, effective way to represent the world and the human subject's place in it.

The Enlightenment as a whole can be summed up as the conjuncture of knowledge and power.[4] This conjoining cannot be treated thematically or descriptively however. It must be grasped in the most direct and material of fashions by engaging the texts that produce it. To gauge the critical practice of the encyclopedic text in its empowerment of knowledge, especially in relation to Enlightenment critique, we must take up the question of reading the *Encyclopédie* and specifically the way it represents objects of knowledge, for whom, and to what ends. The question is not a simple one, for nothing guarantees that this text, any more than any text, provides direct access to meaning, to some encyclopedic "message." Such an assumption implies that the text's function is essentially descriptive, each article unproblematically representing its object by translating into language the ideas to which it refers and which together constitute an eighteenth-century Enlightenment "mind" or "mentality." This essentially reductive view of reading (the *Encyclopédie*) treats the *Encyclopédie* as a work and not a text, as an object whose sense would already be fixed once and for all, rather than as an ongoing process of signification unseverable from the act of reading.[5] Ultimately, taking the *Encyclopédie* as a classical work of the Enlightenment means treating it as an eighteenth-century artifact to be dusted off, framed by quotation marks, repaired by the web of commentary, and placed in the imaginary museum of literary and historical studies. This somewhat argumentative characterization of how the *Encyclopédie* is frequently read suggests that a less classical reading of encyclopedism must focus on the most performative, self-reflexive aspect of encyclopedic practice, namely, the foregrounding of knowledge as representation in order to produce effectively critical knowledge.

Marking a conjuncture between knowledge and power, the epistemological and the social, the encyclopedic text stems from a collective effort to delineate an effectively critical position from which existing forms of knowledge and discourses of order can be contested. The encyclopedists do not wish to totalize knowledge so much as to capitalize on the ordering principle underlying any form of knowledge. Through discursive and pictorial mechanisms that instrumentalize knowledge, the *Encyclopédie* contests other eighteenth-century discourses of order by showing them to be either inoperative or at least less efficient. By no means though does it undermine the concept of order, in either a political, economic or epistemological sense. Consequently, one should be wary of viewing the *Encyclopédie* as reflecting a "progressive" Enlightenment, a "liberal" and liberating approach to order understood in a negative, restrictive way. In this multivoiced "Tower of Babel" as Voltaire called it, certain articles break with existing principles, values, and institutions, while others inflexibly affirm the *status quo*. The *Encyclopédie* is hardly revolutionary, at least not in a narrowly political sense of the term. Yet it exemplifies a textual experimentation with representing knowledge and which involves a kind of discursive politics. This experimentation clearly helped the Enlighteners consolidate their own adversarial position as intellectual and social reformers. More important, it sharpened their understanding of how best to capitalize both philosophically and politically on the idea of order itself.

De Jaucourt's call for restructuring the power relations of the monarchical state, the proposals of Turgot and the Physiocrats for reorganizing economic relations in not yet industrialized France, and D'Alembert's genealogical portrayal of the human mind and his optimism concerning progress still to come – all these "ideas" traditionally taken to characterize Enlightenment testify to the attempt to substitute one order for another. At the same time, the "new" order of ideas the *Encyclopédie* presents and the critical power it seeks to exert result from a different relation to order itself. More significant than any "new" knowledge the *Encyclopédie* contains is its reflection on the enabling conditions of knowledge in general, a turning back or speculation upon how the encyclopedic text represents ordered knowledge and thereby produces desired effects. A prime example of this self-reflexive speculation on encyclopedic order is D'Alembert's *Discours préliminaire.*

On the face of things, the *Discours* presents a straightforward discussion of the encyclopedic text's structure and function. Dictionary and encyclopedia – its complete title being *Encyclopédie, ou dictionnaire raisonné des sciences, des arts, et des métiers* – this text displays a double structure, one alphabetical, the other epistemological. Thus it has two objectives.

> Comme *Dictionnaire*, il doit contenir sur chaque science et sur chaque art, soit libéral, soit mécanique, les principes généraux qui en sont la base, et les détails les plus essentiels, qui en font le corps et la substance ... Comme *Encyclopédie*, il doit exposer autant qu'il est possible, l'ordre et l'enchaînement des connaissances humaines.[6]

Seeking to compile and condense knowledge, to systematize it and display the interconnection of all its branches, the *Encyclopédie* proposes to order the sum total of knowledge. As D'Alembert notes, the order of the alphabet creates the most immediate of relations between articles, yet also the most arbitrary. Required is a supplemental ordering principle that ensures a more effective use of the knowledge the *Encyclopédie* contains, a principle that also provides a protocol for reading. The principle the encyclopedists select is grounded in epistemology, for they pattern their notion of an ideal interconnection between all articles ("l'ordre encyclopédique") after the way they believed ideas are generated in the mind ("l'ordre généalogique"). As Diderot explains it in the article "*Encyclopédie*," judgment (*l'entendement*) acts upon perception in one of three ways, by process of enumeration, examination or imitation. This results in ideas belonging to the three basic categories of thought: history, philosophy, and poetry. Subdividing these in turn, and continuing this mental and textual process of subdivision, the encyclopedists arrive at a complete "tree of knowledge." Reflecting a genealogy that is both epistemological and textual, the tree of knowledge figures the encyclopedic ideal of perfectly mimetic identity between mind and language, mental order and textual structure. Furthermore, this double order of ideas is related to a third, historical order, in that it displays the successive advancement of all branches of knowledge throughout the ages. The *Encyclopédie* thus contains three overlapping orders, textual order recapitulating both epistemology and philosophical history.

This preliminary, encapsulated version of Enlightenment designates the *Encyclopédie* as that place where text, knowledge, and philosophy are interwoven. The *Discours* describes that interweaving and performs it as well. A descriptive discourse *on* order, D'Alembert's text also contains a performative discourse *of* order.[7] Providing an explanatory model or scaled-down reflection of the *Encyclopédie*, the *Discours* amounts to a powerfully structuring act that channels interpretive force and brings it to bear upon the reading of the encyclopedic text. In the reading the *Discours* seeks to produce, any particular order of knowledge the *Encyclopédie* contains has less significance, less value, than the overarching ordering practice whereby knowledge is presented.

D'Alembert and Diderot explicitly thematize this practice in their discussion of the enabling conditions of epistemological representation. All models, they argue, for ordering knowledge are inevitably arbitrary. Consequently, any model may be selected (or rejected) according to values and criteria that do not belong intrinsically to the model itself, but instead are fashioned by the practitioner of knowledge. The encyclopedists lay full claim to the powerful right to determine themselves the criterion according to which knowledge will be represented. This claim marks a self-reflexive turn towards the practice that produces knowledge as representation, a turn that has been taken to characterize Enlightenment scientific discourse,[8] and that may well be the hallmark of "modern" epistemology and philosophy.

This empowering self-reflexivity is what marks the particular relation to knowledge the encyclopedists sought to establish. It also reveals how they would distinguish their own more experimental and experiential approach to knowledge from an earlier, more abstract and idealizing one. Critical of doctrinaire Cartesianism and its reductive *esprit de système*, the encyclopedists relied instead on *l'esprit systématique*.[9] Yet their work remains Cartesian in its valorization of useful knowledge, *utilité* becoming the prime criterion for representing knowledge. The encyclopedists too seek to realize Descartes' dream of putting knowledge to use, and not only to guarantee being irrefutably, as the philosopher of the *cogito* wishes to do, but also to ensure mastery and possession over the world ("nous rendre comme maîtres et possesseurs de la nature," as Descartes puts it in the *Discours de la méthode*). With the *Encyclopédie* this world of being explodes into a world of objects, a collection of things that must be ordered and put in place. The order of things in the *Encyclopédie* is determined above all by the status accorded them as belongings, by their usefulness to an ordering subject. Things in the encyclopedic text do not simply exist, they are meant to be used, and the products of their use are of value, which is one reason for the countless images of tools and machines in the encyclopedic plates.

Viewed thus, the *Encyclopédie* is less audacious yet far more effective than many of its commentators have been.[10] D'Alembert's narrative of Enlightenment as the historical and philosophical development of useful knowledge recounts no long march towards truth and light, but rather the story of acquiring useful and valuable goods. To be sure, the encyclopedists

1a and b. *Moulins à vent*, plates 1 and 2; unattributed engravings showing a windmill in elevation and in cross-section from the entry on *agriculture et économie rustique* in volume XVIII of Diderot's *Encyclopédie*, published in 1762.

reject the supposedly natural or divine models upon which other discourses of knowledge claimed to be founded. And clearly, in declining to discuss the ultimate nature of reality the encyclopedists effectively undercut the authority of these other discourses of knowledge and the legitimacy of sociopolitical institutions purporting to state the true and unchanging nature of things. The *Encyclopédie*'s emancipatory appeal notwithstanding, one must remember that if the encyclopedists lay no claim to knowledge in and for itself, leaving that understanding

to God and its pursuit to metaphysicians, it is because such knowledge is of little value to them. They desire only useful knowledge, relativized by being produced and ordered in relation to the human subject.

This *utilité* or usefulness, and the purpose of encyclopedism itself, should not be phrased in purely humanitarian terms. The encyclopedists' utilitarian epistemology institutes a notion of text that rationalizes and justifies a new relation between individual and world, subject and object, by presenting that relation as determined by representation. Encyclopedic knowledge is useful because it provides a way to imagine appropriating and mastering a world made into a set of represented objects. To know something through reading the *Encyclopédie* does not involve disinterested understanding, for value attaches itself inseparably to the knowledge the *Encyclopédie* produces. This valorization of knowledge makes it possible to imagine the acquisition of and absolute control over all objects the encyclopedic text makes knowable, knowledge guaranteeing possession through representation. I think therefore I have, or rather, I order so as to possess. Not by chance do the encyclopedists use the metaphor of the voyage to describe reading their text, and that of the map to figure how it structures knowledge. Like the maps used to chart the great voyages of discovery, the encyclopedic *mappemonde* too holds out the tantalizing promise of territorial expansion, power to be achieved, and wealth to be had. Like Wolmar in Rousseau's *La Nouvelle Héloïse*, a character who caricaturizes a kind of pastoral rationalism, readers of the *Encyclopédie* too can be masters of their well-ordered domain, playing with property and arranging things as they desire. An inventory of goods, the *Encyclopédie* establishes just such proprietary rights over the wealth of knowledge contained in the encyclopedic storehouse.

The notion of *utilité* D'Alembert and Diderot repeatedly invoke provides the cornerstone for an epistemological utilitarianism, a self-interested instrumentalization of knowledge. In this sense the *Encyclopédie* is a manifesto of capitalist epistemology, a founding document of bourgeois ideology. Not surprisingly another model for encyclopedic order emerges, one which is the most motivated, ideologically determined of models for structuring knowledge conceivable. "Pourquoi n'introduirons-nous pas l'homme dans notre ouvrage," asks Diderot, "comme il est placé dans l'univers? Pourquoi n'en ferons-nous pas un centre commun? . . . L'homme est le terme unique d'où il faut partir, et auquel il faut tout ramener" (VII, 212–13). Instituting the notion of "man" as creator and user of knowledge, the *Encyclopédie* lays claim to providing an index to the world by relating everything to this ideal and imaginary center. To do so though, it must control a number of referential slippages. "Man" refers in the *Encyclopédie* at times to a seemingly non-gendered universal subject of knowledge, while at others to the white, European male subject of privileges and the social order in which he takes his place. The term thus designates through a constitutive gesture of exclusion numerous "others" whose differentiation makes possible a more useful representation of "man." Such slippages, and the attempt to control them, suggest that the encyclopedic notion of "man," like the encyclopedic text, is a thoroughly ideological product, the knowledge it provides amounting to an imaginary representation of real conditions of existence.[11] The *Encyclopédie* reveals clearly that the Enlightenment's reformulation of values takes place most significantly and effectively in its revalorization of representations.

This does not mean the *Encyclopédie* can be denounced as a distortion of reality caused by the self-interested desires of a particular group. Perhaps no form of representation could escape such inflexible denunciation, least of all the denunciatory genre itself. The encyclopedists were a socially heterogeneous group of intellectuals, united perhaps least of all by class.[12] More important, the model of class and class consciousness enjoys no particular explanatory privilege over the encyclopedic text, and may in fact stem from a desire for critical knowledge quite similar to the desire to work in the encyclopedic text. An ideological work to be sure, the *Encyclopédie* also displays the work of ideology. If we take this text as the expression of a preexistent consciousness (be it bourgeois or not), yet fail to analyze precisely the work of ideology as representation, we cannot grasp how this text works to produce the meanings and images that would somehow reflect such a form of consciousness. The encyclopedists claim that knowledge of all things can be derived from and referred back to the central notion of "man." Yet their text does not so much reflect the enlighteners' idea of their own humanity as it sets in place a narrative, figural, and representational apparatus that rationalizes and naturalizes certain actions and institutions, beliefs and values. It does so especially by employing the powerfully centralizing concept of "man" as the driving force in the production of knowledge. In a striking metaphor, Diderot likens the *Encyclopédie* to a machine, suggesting a way to read that comes to grips with how this text proposes to represent knowledge. A knowledge machine, the *Encyclopédie* makes the self known by producing the self as representation, figured in the objects it is said already to know.[13]

This technologization of knowledge stems only partly from the increased importance the encyclopedists attribute to what is now called technology and then the "arts and trades." The *Encyclopédie* is part of a far larger epistemic shift involving the way knowledge comes into being. In an extended reflection on the meaning of the term "invention," Jacques Derrida provides a helpful framework for articulating this shift. Around the seventeenth century, Derrida notes, a semantic transformation or mutation occurs that makes it no longer possible to use the term "invention" to refer to existences or truths that are discovered or revealed for the first time by this art. Instead, sometime between Descartes and Leibniz:

> on ne parlera quasiment plus de l'invention comme découverte dévoilante de ce qui se trouvait déjà là (existence ou vérité) mais de plus en plus, voire uniquement, comme découverte productive d'un dispositif qu'on peut appeler technique au sens large, techno-scientifique ou techno-poétique. Il ne s'agit pas simplement d'une technologisation de l'invention. Celle-ci a toujours été liée à l'intervention d'une *teknè*, mais dans cette *teknè* c'est désormais la production – et non seulement le dévoilement – qui va dominer l'usage du mot "invention." *Production* signifie alors la mise en œuvre d'un dispositif machinique relativement indépendant, lui-même capable d'une certaine récurrence auto-reproductive et même d'une certaine simulation ré-itérante.[14]

This shift at the dawn of techno-scientific and philosophical modernity involves the "re-invention of invention," the articulation of another, "modern" relation to truth (and which for Derrida is coextensive with deconstruction). Insofar as the *Encyclopédie* belongs to the modernity Derrida refers to, in its own epistemic *teknè* and the particular art of knowledge it appropriates from the discourse of its time and invents, the *Encyclopédie* contains an art and poetics of knowledge that perhaps we can neither do without nor get beyond. We must attempt instead to discover (or reinvent) a technique for reading this text that allows us to represent anew and again its critical relation to truth, as well as our own.

Image and power

One place to begin (again) to read the *Encyclopédie* is in its margins, in the supplemental text of its plates. But what to say of these roughly 3,000 engravings that fill eleven folio volumes? Providing no strictly verbal message, these images of men and machines, complete scenes and fragmentary objects, contain no original discourse that can be quoted, commented upon or rephrased. The plates show more than they say and signify more than they tell. In speaking of the plates, the power of the visual image must be supplemented by a verbal discourse that can never totally succeed in doubling its object.

The theoretical issue of the relation between image and language became an increasingly knotty one for Diderot too. He remarks already in the *Prospectus*, written well before the plates were printed, "un coup d'oeil sur l'objet ou sur sa représentation en dit plus qu'une page de discours" (v, 101). Ideally, the plates would depict objects such as tools and machines by visually condensing explanatory discourse. Reading a page of words can be equivalent to looking at a plate or the object it depicts, yet only if there exists some kind of mimetic correspondence or reciprocal transparency between image, word, and thing. Initially the encyclopedists may have believed in such a relation. During the preparation of the plates however, practical and theoretical considerations made such a belief difficult to maintain. It soon became clear that images alone could not convey sufficient knowledge of their object. Instead, the various parts of scenes and objects had to be labelled, and each step in production processes explained. This practice suggests that word, image, and thing are not interchangeable and that the image could not adequately represent words because it could not adequately represent things.[15] Possessing its own logic, the image can always be viewed as depicting something other than what it refers to. Thus, in writing about the plates we inevitably risk diverting them from what they represent, perverting them and changing them into whatever we wish to see. These images' power would thus make any truly critical vantage point inaccessible. Yet the plates also contain the potential for setting up a critical viewing that contests their power less than it capitalizes on it. To let this power do its work, we must ask what there is to see in the encyclopedic image and then examine the effects produced by such a viewing.

From the eighty-three plates on agriculture to the one hundred and thirty-five plates on weaving, including engravings illustrating the manufacture of corks, candles and nails, the technique of glass blowing and silver plating, or the fine points of calligraphy, fencing and military maneuvers, the images of the *Encyclopédie* provide a compendious picture of the crafts and trades, the arts and sciences, practiced in mid-eighteenth-century France. Such a collection in itself was not uncommon, and Chambers' *Cyclopedia* too included plates illustrating heraldry, sun dials, geometry, algebra, and navigation.[16] The plates of the *Encyclopédie* do not merely complete Chambers' collection though. They begin where he left off, with a step-by-step description of a process of production. If the weakness of previous encyclopedias and technical treatises was that they were addressed either to a broad public of nonspecialists and thus explained little, or to a narrow public of specialists and thus taught only what was already known, the encyclopedists held to a middle course. The plates show technological knowledge, not so much a vast and virtual *savoir* as areas of an applied *savoir faire*, whose utility and value can be measured in its productivity. Addressed to both educated reader and specialist, the plates depict the relative place of each area of technological and scientific knowledge in the whole mechanism of economic and social life.

The techniques and expertise represented in the *Encyclopédie* had changed little since the seventeenth century. Yet the plates represent a far more material, technological way of conceptualizing and depicting the relation between human subject and world. Designed to bridge the gap between theory and practice, between conceptual knowledge and its application in and on the material world, the plates reflect the utilitarian

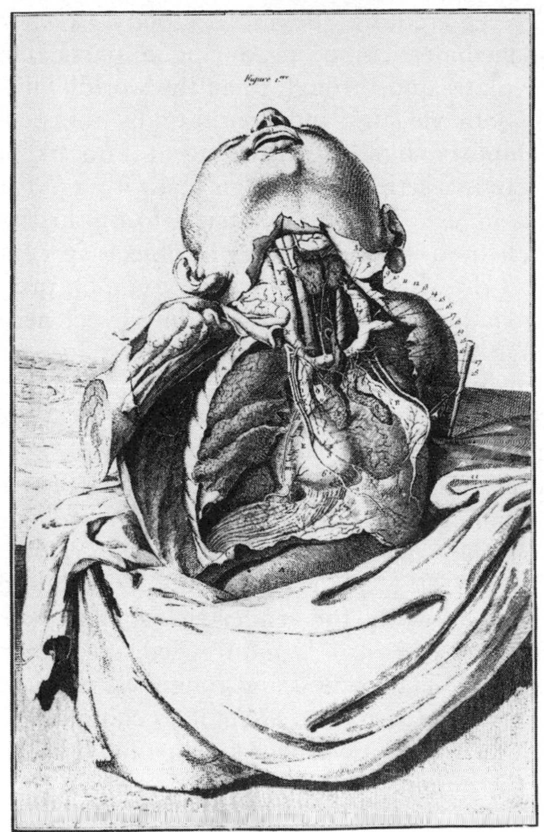

2. *Anatomie*, plate 18, engraving by Defehrt from volume xvIII of Diderot's *Encyclopédie* (1762).

rationalism, the sensationalist philosophy, and the experimental method that characterize Enlightenment philosophy and science. Yet they are more than a visual analogue of conceptual discourse, an illustration of Enlightenment thought. In graphic fashion the plates make manifest the representational apparatus whereby the text of Enlightenment presents what we take to be its ideas, concepts, and philosophy.

In the anatomical plates, for example, the instrument that slices through skin and bone to expose the workings of the body is not the surgeon's scalpel, nor even the artist's pen. Rather, this way of representing the human body as an object of knowledge mediates vision, producing a particular way of viewing the plates and through them the world. This encyclopedic gaze both visually and conceptually disassembles the body, machine or building, dividing it into its parts and ordering them in a series, whose logic leads from part to whole, from tool to its use, from raw material to finished product.[17] With the schematic representation of objects in cross section and assembly drawings, which became common practice only around the mid-eighteenth century, the viewer acquires not only an image of the object but also the rules of its composition, the key to its production and reproduction.[18] In viewing the object as presented in and through the plates, the viewer's own gaze is led by the logic and values the plates materialize. The viewer retraces the imaginary transformation of matter into objects and things into property, a visual and conceptual trajectory Barthes calls "le cheminement de la raison."[19] If, as Barthes suggests, the plates exemplify a "philosophie de l'objet," then the world the reader-viewer of the *Encyclopédie* comes to know is one entirely naturalized and humanized by the human hand, its fierceness and roughness mediated by the tool, which in shaping nature alters it so completely that it is recognizable only in its usefulness, known only in its productive relation to the human subject.

More significant than the technology represented in the *Encyclopédie* is the technique of encyclopedic representation. This technique determines the viewer's gaze, and hence knowledge of the object represented, through what is portrayed but also through what is not. A plate in the section *Manufacture du tabac*, for example, depicts four children seated on benches stripping tobacco. Yet as the number of empty benches indicates, the shop contains room enough for twenty-two children. Another plate in the same series shows tobacco presses. The accompanying explanation notes that "il y en a dans la fabrique de Paris jusqu'à soixante rangées le long des quatre faces d'une longue galerie. Vingt ou vingt-cinq ouvriers appliquent leurs forces à l'extrémité du grand levier de fer avec lequel on fait tourner les vis des presses." Once again though, instead of the twenty to twenty-five workers on each press, the artist depicts but one press which only two workers operate easily and expressionlessly. To be sure, the plates' cost would have increased drastically had the artist added the figures required to make them accurately depict actual working conditions. But the real values involved in encyclopedic representation are not just financial, given that the plates are designed to show a process of production (of objects and knowledge) rather than some exterior reality. Cautioning against viewing the plates in mimetic, referential fashion, Jacques Proust argues that they create "une sorte d'interférence qui interdit au lecteur de considérer [la planche] comme la transcription naïve de la réalité . . . Entre l'objet de référence et l'œil de l'observateur [se trouve] l'écran d'une conscience et d'une volonté, celles de l'encyclopédiste, soucieux de témoigner non pas de ce qui était, mais de ce qui pouvait ou devait être."[20] The desire to make things knowable is what drives the representational apparatus of the *Encyclopédie* as it screens out what will remain invisible or at least unrepresented, and thus supposedly insignificant. At the same time, this desire for knowledge also produces a screening, which does not so much explain what is seen as it rationalizes what has been screened out.

The explanatory text accompanying the section *Epinglier* indicates just what the encyclopedic plate screens out.

> L'ouvrier peut . . . donner soixante-dix coups de ciseaux par minute, c'est par heure quatre mille deux cents; et comme il coupe douze moulées à chaque coup de ciseau, cet ouvrier peut couper cinquante mille quatre cents têtes de menues épingles en une heure (les grosses étant plus difficiles), ce qui serait néanmoins un travail forcé, parce qu'il n'est point déduit de temps pour les reprises dans ce calcul; mais en y ayant égard, un ouvrier peut communément couper trente milliers par heure . . . Il ne pourrait pas . . . continuer sur ce pied toute la journée, parce que la vue fatigue beaucoup à cette fonction, mais il peut en couper quinze douzaines de milliers, grosses et menues, par jour.

The eerie calm hanging over the industrious world of the encyclopedic plates results from the desire to rationalize

3. *Métier à faire du Marli* (Marly loom), plate 1; engraving by Lacotte under the direction of Benard from entry on *Marli* in volume XXVIII of Diderot's *Encyclopédie* (1772).

production, to reduce labor to the mechanical and technical principles behind a given operation. The operation's other aspects, notably the temporality of the production process, remain invisible, and not only because the image cannot represent the passage of time. A kind of fascination with rational(ized) form reworks temporality, arresting a process and redirecting the forces there at work.

Encyclopedic representation operates its filtering not only on the space and time of work, but also on workers' very bodies. The general image of the worker in the plates is that of a body reduced to its hands. The individual carding cotton or weaving fish nets has no visible existence beyond the wrist and hand performing a task. The plates graphically portray the "manualization" of labor that informs Diderot's definition of the trades. A *métier*, he writes, is "toute profession qui exige l'emploi des bras, et qui se borne à un certain nombre d'opérations mécaniques, qui ont pour but un même ouvrage que l'ouvrier répète sans cesse." Elsewhere Diderot criticizes the long-standing prejudice against trades and craftspeople.[21] Here however this "manualization" of the worker suggests that the encyclopedists' defense of the mechanical arts may in fact stem from the desire to rationalize production. Proposing a principle for determining the superiority of one method of manufacturing over another, Diderot continues, "tel ouvrier ne fait et ne fera de sa vie qu'une seule et unique chose; tel autre, une autre chose: d'où il arrive que chacune s'exécute bien et promptement, et que l'ouvrage le mieux fait est encore celui qu'on a à meilleur marché" (v, 508). Not only must work be subjected to the order of reason so as to capitalize on techniques that will increase quality, profitability, and efficiency. The notion of the anonymous, interchangeable, manualized worker ("tel ouvrier," "des bras") is required to rationalize production and evaluate the production process rationally.

The plates' depiction of artisans and workers, together with the valorization of the mechanical arts to which they bear witness, cannot be explained in terms of the encyclopedists' intellectual curiosity or humane liberalism. Such a view is inconsistent at best with the political and economic doctrine of mercantilism the *Encyclopédie* expresses and with the notion of work and worker that derives from it. The prevalent economic theory in mid-eighteenth-century France, mercantilism is based on the view that a nation's wealth can be measured by the amount of gold and currency it possesses. Since the importation of foreign products effectively robs a country of its riches, industry must be allowed and encouraged to raise capital and develop techniques of production that permit domestic products to compete favorably with foreign goods.[22] The plates clearly have their own role to play in the consolidation of an emergent socioeconomic discourse. Despite their emphasis on economic productivity, however, they do not simply stem from or visually translate mercantilist theory, which is in fact a relatively small element in that larger socio-economic discourse. More significant is the plates' representational productivity, which we should take care not to characterize in anachronistic terms and according to values they in fact rework.

One example of such a characterization is found in Arthur Wilson's claim that the plates may have been the most subversive part of the *Encyclopédie* even though contemporary readers took them to be the least controversial. Undermining reigning aristocratic, monarchical values in the name of more democratic, nationalistic ones, the plates introduce humanist values into the economic domain, Wilson argues. "Nothing in fact could disseminate more efficiently than they the subversive doctrine that the daily routine of socially useful labor has inherent dignity and worth."[23] The plates certainly do represent how value becomes attached to work. But the plates' valorization of work can be explained by a less humanistic paradigm than the one Wilson suggests. "Nothing could disseminate more *efficiently* . . ." Two paradigms collide here – "inherent dignity" and "worth," timeless humanism and an emergent techno-capitalism. The two are governed, both syntactically and conceptually, by a third, that of "efficiency." Consequently, most subversive in the plates is not their valorization of technology in the name of human values and their "inherent" meaning, but rather the art or technique of encyclopedic representation that empowers the values it presents. Human values become operational in the *Encyclopédie*, the result or rather the products of this knowledge machine. This suggests that perhaps no exclusively human values can be relied on to judge this text's workings. The plates mark the beginnings of an uncannily familiar technologization of values, an epistemic shift towards a kind of techno-humanism that extends to the postindustrial, cybernetic age. Reading this process in pretechnological terms or in solely humanistic ones provides the comforting solace of anachronistic nostalgia. Read in more present-day fashion, the plates bear witness to the encyclopedic empowerment of knowledge by revealing the *Encyclopédie* to be quite literally a knowledge machine, a representational apparatus geared up to produce a powerful view of the world and the human subject's place in it.

But just what kind of machine is this text? The mid-eighteenth century has been characterized as a "remarquable période de transition entre l'atelier corporatif et ce que Marx appellera, dans le *Capital*, la 'machino-facture,' époque où l'ouvrier qui conduit les machines se double encore, le plus souvent, d'un artisan, au sens actuel du terme."[24] Prior to this transition brought about by the Industrial Revolution,[25] the machine was understood primarily as a more perfect tool. It was an extension of the hand, increasing its speed and accuracy. The corresponding notion of work was that of an artisanal activity, governed by human needs and desires. Work was an essentially human signature upon the material world.

Another notion of the machine supplanted this one around the time of the *Encyclopédie*. Diderot's discussion of the worker's role as mere agent performing a small task within a larger process of production suggests the beginnings of this shift. Later, with industrial capitalism, labor no longer would be a creative act uniting workers with each other and the world, but instead an alienating activity that acquires value only in being exchanged. By the mid-eighteenth-century, "the gilded legend of craftsmanship" that Roland Barthes claims the plates recount may have been no more than that, a myth and already tarnished. Even though the innumerable machines figured in the plates seem to be tools operated by the craftsperson's hand or foot, a less humanistic and more energetic viewing is equally possible, as well as a differing understanding of work and worker.

Nothing in fact prevents these workers' bodies from being viewed as an extension of the machine, and not the contrary. In this sense the machine is not a tool but a mechanism for productively and efficiently transforming energy, the source of which in the majority of the encyclopedic plates is the human worker. Like the most complicated machine of the time, the stocking-weaving machine Diderot discusses in the well-known article "*Bas*," the machines of the *Encyclopédie* are based on a system of levers and pulleys, moved in almost all cases by workers' hands and feet. This reliance on the worker as energy source explains those plates in which the individual is *not* reduced to two hands. Instead of being manualized, he or she is instrumentalized and mechanized, represented not as the machine's master but merely as one of its necessary parts. Thus, the encyclopedic plates contain two conflicting representations of worker and labor, one of the creative, independent, and individual craftsperson, the other of the mechanized, anonymous, and interchangeable worker. The coexistence of these mutually contradictory representations in the encyclopedic text bears witness to tensions caused by the emergence of a "new," more "modern" socioeconomic discourse on production.

On first viewing, the plates of the *Encyclopédie* depict a well-ordered world where industrious individuals exist in harmony with nature, and where human skills and knowledge are used to their fullest to reap great rewards. This view of the world and the human subject who dwells in it is an empowering one. It stems from the tangible desire that informs and invests the encyclopedic images, the desire to know, yet also, through knowledge, to acquire, possess, and control. Deploying a representational mechanics, this desire operates by means of certain positionings, filterings, and exclusions. The techniques of this desire need not be understood in exclusively human terms, which are perhaps inadequate for accounting for the *teknè* of epistemic desire located in the encyclopedic knowledge machine. Consider the following remark concerning what the plates depict and what they perform. "Nous les avons restreintes," explains Diderot in the *Prospectus*, "aux mouvements importants de l'ouvrier, et aux seuls moments de l'opération qu'il est très facile de peindre et très difficile d'expliquer. Nous nous en sommes tenus aux circonstances essentielles, à celles dont la représentation, quand elle est bien faite entraîne nécessairement la connaissance de celles qu'on ne voit pas" (v, 102). In this gap or disparity between vision and language, the plates of the *Encyclopédie* perform their epistemic work. Clearly visible in the plates, yet difficult to explain, is the process whereby representation leads to knowledge. Finally, the most powerful knowledge the plates produce, the most "essential circumstances" of the encyclopedic machine(s), lies in the working of the encyclopedic image, the poetics or performativity of encyclopedic representation. If Diderot affirms that the encyclopedists have limited themselves to depicting these essential circumstances, it is as if he senses that the limit of what can be represented in the plates is also the enabling condition for the most powerful way of representing knowledge. Only by reflecting upon the mechanisms of representation itself, the manner in which it makes things knowable, can the discourse of encyclopedism claim to challenge other forms of knowledge.

At least one concern remains, however, and one not easily dispelled. The plates bear witness to the Enlightenment's attempt to empower representation, to contest the power of other discourses of order by laying claim to power in its own right. By reading the plates in this fashion, we can successfully describe their productivity, the technique or *teknè* whereby they deploy their power. But does such a deployment constitute a critique? Is critique no more than a collision of forces, a power play? Phrasing the question slightly differently, can critical knowledge be attained in and through the poetic, performative potential of representation? Does the Enlightenment's self-reflexive turn towards the enabling conditions for representing knowledge constitute a truly critical act? Or does this self-reflexive turn carry with it the risk of self-entrapment, a movement towards mythologization and mystification? In the latter case, the Enlightenment's self-perpetuating myth consists of the alluring story of power it tells, and which, however much we may wish to counter it, we can only retell, playing out yet once again the power that resides in representations of Enlightenment.

Marking the limits of Enlightenment, these questions should not be resolved too abruptly. They will remain audible as we consider a second instance of Enlightenment's self-reflexive empowerment of representation, contained in Diderot's most significant contribution to the encyclopedic enterprise, his article "*Encyclopédie.*"

The language of knowledge

One of the major manifestos of French Enlightenment, the article "*Encyclopédie*" provides a detailed picture of the philosophical, social, and ethical context in which the encyclopedists situated their project, the ideals they sought to realize, and the criteria and strategies adopted to achieve their goals.[26] By nature of the object to which it refers, Diderot's article occupies a metadiscursive position in relation to the *Encyclopédie* as a whole. The most explicitly self-referential, self-reflexive entry in the entire work, Diderot's article confronts head-on the problem of representing knowledge, both thematically and discursively. Even more directly than in the plates, we encounter here the performative self-reflexivity of encyclopedism, in terms of which Enlightenment's attempt to critically empower representation can be gauged.

Reference to language provides an initial entry into Diderot's article. Not just one of the many objects of human knowledge represented in the *Encyclopédie*, language occupies a privileged position in the encyclopedist's conception of this text. Describing the beneficial impact a well-made encyclopedia would have on future generations, Diderot unhesitatingly affirms "la connaissance de la langue est le fondement de toutes ces grandes espérances . . . et cet objet est le premier de ceux dont il convenait à des encyclopédistes de s'occuper profondément" (VII, 188). This "knowledge of language" involves the clarity of definitions, accessibility of style, and other practical issues relating to the encyclopedic writer's craft. But practical issues are constantly doubled by theoretical ones in Diderot's article. This self-reflexive turn towards the language of encyclopedic representation also refers to the "knowledge of language" provided by Enlightenment linguistics, the theory of language that held sway in France for roughly a century following the appearance in 1660 of a short treatise on language written at the Jansenist enclave of Port-Royal.

Port-Royal grammar theory is founded on the claim that reason, not usage, determines the workings of language. "Encore que l'usage soit le maître des langues pour ce qui est de l'analogie," writes Lancelot, "le discours n'étant néanmoins que l'image de la pensée, il ne peut pas former des expressions qui ne soient conformes à leur original pour ce qui est du sens, et par conséquent qui ne soient fondées sur la raison."[27] Accepting the Cartesian definition of mind as the seat of innate and immutable reason, and of the idea as an immaterial substance that is part of mind, the language theorists of Port-Royal ascribe to language the primary function not simply of communicating ideas but representing thought. Language represents thought analytically moreover, in that syntactical order makes manifest the set of logical relations constituting the rational order of thought. The word is the sign of the idea, linguistic order reflecting with luminous clarity mental order.

"La Grammaire est l'Art de parler. Parler est expliquer ses pensées par les signes, que les hommes ont inventés à ce dessin," write Arnauld and Lancelot.[28] If thought precedes language, and being is anterior to its representation, then grammatical knowledge can provide direct access to mind. This linkage is made explicit in *La Logique de Port-Royal*, written two years after the *Grammaire générale*.[29] Figuring the origin of general grammar as all origins are figured, after the fact, *La Logique* establishes the principles relating language and mind, speech and thought, that grammarians and philosophers alike will repeat for more than a century as they interweave language theory and epistemology in a common representational matrix. "La grammaire a une liaison nécessaire avec la science des idées et du raisonnement," writes the eighteenth-century grammarian Du Marsais, "parce que la grammaire traite des mots et de leurs images, et que les mots ne sont que les signes de nos idées et de nos jugements."[30] Similarly for Condillac, "la grammaire est comme la première partie de l'art de penser. Pour découvrir les principes du langage, il faut donc observer comment nous pensons: il faut chercher ces principes dans l'analyse même de la pensée. Or l'analyse de la pensée est toute faite dans le discours."[31] Grammar becomes so inseverably linked to eighteenth-century epistemology that Beauzée the grammarian can ask somewhat defensively, "mais pourquoi croirait-on la métaphysique déplacée dans un livre de grammaire générale? La grammaire en effet doit exposer les fondements, les moyens généraux, et les règles communes du langage; et le langage est l'exposition de l'analyse de la pensée par la parole. Or il n'y a rien de plus abstrait et de plus métaphysique que cet objet."[32]

In many respects Diderot's own "knowledge of language" expressed in the article "*Encyclopédie*" is freely borrowed from the eighteenth-century grammarian-philosophers. He accepts their definition of language as synonymous with usage, the ways a society employs spoken signs to represent its thoughts (Douchet, "*Langue*, " XIX, 548). He also understands grammar as the science that makes comprehensible the workings of spoken and written language (Beauzée, "*Grammaire*," VII, 841). Despite his principled distrust of linguistic laws, "l'habitude bien fondée que j'ai de suspecter toute loi générale en matière de langue" (VII, 194), he subscribes fully to the founding principle of general grammar: the analogy or identity between language and mind. Like the grammarian Beauzée, who claims that "la parole est une sorte de tableau dont la pensée est l'original" ("*Grammaire*," VII, 841), Diderot too maintains that language constitutes an "image rigoureuse et fidèle de l'exercice de la raison" (VII, 197). "Image," "painting," "original" – these privileged metaphors of eighteenth-century linguistics and epistemology, together with the notions of anteriority and derivation, origin and reproduction they imply, constitute the warp and woof of the Enlightenment understanding of representation.

If Diderot ascribes such importance to the "knowledge of language" provided by linguistic theory, it is because the encyclopedists understand the workings of their text according to the same representationalist matrix the Enlightenment grammarian-philosophers invoke to explain the role of all language. Just as the grammatical and epistemological function of language is to represent thought, providing an image of its original, so too the *Encyclopédie* should supply an image of its own original, the sum total of all human knowledge: "un tableau général des efforts de l'esprit humain dans tous les genres et dans tous les siècles" (*Prospectus*, V, 87). Like language, the encyclopedic text should represent thought analytically, its encyclopedic, genealogical order providing a textual syntax that displays the interconnection of all forms of knowledge produced by the human mind. Consequently, the encyclopedists believe that while other encyclopedias may be instructive, their models for dividing up knowledge, by discipline for instance, are less powerful than the encyclopedists' own model based on the logic of reason.[33] In the encyclopedists' grand, overarching design, their text represents both the process of thought, the generation of ideas, as well as the taxonomy of thought, the order of ideas thus produced. This is why in figuring their text's relation to knowledge, the encyclopedists employ metaphors involving a dynamic temporality. The encyclopedic "*tableau*," for instance, portrays knowledge the way a flow chart designates a dynamically productive process. This "*mappemonde*" charts the labyrinth of knowledge, mapping an epistemological space and marking a path through the text and the genealogical history of ideas it represents. Finally, the "*arbre des connaissances*" figures how the *Encyclopédie* presents both a static, taxonomic portrayal of human knowledge as well as its dynamic linkage, "*l'enchaînement des connaissances.*" This powerful image holds out the promise of access to all regions of knowledge by figuring the encyclopedic understanding of knowledge, and thus the activity of reading the *Encyclopédie*, as a potentially continuous circulation on a vast epistemological chain.[34]

The encyclopedists' metaphors for their text testify to the desire not simply to provide a static reflection of the rational order of thought, but more important to represent the very work of reason, the dynamic, temporal process that produces such order. Read self-reflexively, these metaphors also signify the attempt to develop a notion of language and text that would make such representation possible. In the process, they push the question of encyclopedic representation to the limits – if not beyond – of what a restricted mimetic theory of language and text can account for. At one point in his article Diderot states, "chaque chose étant ... dans l'*Encyclopédie* ce qu'elle est en soi, elle y aura sa vraie proportion" (VII, 215). The "truth" of encyclopedic representation would lie in a mimetic adequation between text and world, a seamless correspondence between language and its referent. Yet this version of "truth" elides the question of both mind and language, the two models for the encyclopedic text invoked to explain how things can be known "in themselves" and how they acquire "being" as representation. When Diderot confronts this double question more directly, things become increasingly problematic in the encyclopedic text and the knowledge of language that supposedly provides its theoretical underpinnings.

One instance of this confrontation occurs in Diderot's discussion of the temporal, historical nature of language. All the while subscribing to the principal tenet of general grammar, namely, that language functions as the mirror of mind, Diderot also wishes to consider this reflection in diachronic, historical terms. Representing more than a timeless logic, as a social and cultural product it also provides a yardstick of human progress.[35] For Diderot, words are vessels laden with knowledge from other times, memory traces of past cultures. Language becomes historicized, made into what Sylvain Auroux calls "un monument pour qui l'histoire n'est pas le lieu de son existence, mais la trace du temps en lui."[36] In Diderot's desire to see language as reflecting a universal mental order and as providing a measure for philosophical, cultural, and technical progress, he collapses the distinction between nominal and objective definitions. "Les définitions de noms ne diffèrent point des définitions de choses" (VII, 177). This distinction, essential for Port-Royal grammar, allowed for a dialectical understanding of the relation between usage and rule, between the arbitrary, mediated nature of speech and the absolute representational function of language, and between the temporality of linguistic usage and the timeless representation of thought. Without such a distinction, time once again becomes problematic. The temporality and materiality of language in its use inevitably encroach upon the linguistic theory of the classical age, which would sever language from its use and somehow place representation beyond time and history.

As editor, Diderot foresees the consequences this encroachment of the dynamic vicissitudes of time and history may have regarding the encyclopedic representation of knowledge. He wishes fervently to believe that the fruits of Enlightenment are cumulative and will serve to make future generations wiser, happier, and more virtuous. The *Encyclopédie* plays this ideal role in a history of continuous progress, the gradual comprehension of an eternal, seamless pattern. Yet he readily admits that nothing guarantees this optimistic view of historical change. The materiality of history may impinge upon encyclopedic representation and render this ideal unachievable. Glimpsing a far darker future, Diderot cannot exclude the possibility some "great revolution" would halt scientific and technical progress and plunge the world back into the shadows. The *Encyclopédie*'s most glorious moment, he adds, would be after such a "temps de troubles," when this text, unable to advance knowledge, at least would have been able to preserve it from the ravaging vicissitudes of the historical.

The Enlightenment's greatest fear was a return to an age of darkness, the springing forth of an unreason it could neither extirpate nor silence. The "*troubles*" to which Diderot refers are not located exclusively outside the encyclopedic text, however, in a social-political history of events. Most troubling for the encyclopedists is the temporality and historicity of knowledge, an epistemological field they perceive to be not linear and continuous, but marked by folds, breaks, and sudden shifts.[37] Through the historical materiality of language itself, temporality impinges upon the encyclopedic representation of knowledge.

The problem of inevitable and uncontrollable linguistic flux is one that Diderot, as editor of the *Encyclopédie*, cannot avoid. Bearing witness to a people's technological and intellectual advancement, language will always receive new words to refer to new discoveries, techniques, and ideas. Noting that the French language of 1750 no longer resembles what was spoken even ten years earlier, Diderot fears the inherent temporality of language may make the *Encyclopédie* outdated even before its completion and thus incomprehensible to future generations. Consequently, linguistic flux must be arrested or at least regulated.[38] The *Encyclopédie* must be more than a collection of articles. It must also be a well-made dictionary, supplying the proper definitions of all its terms and thereby contributing to the formation of a truly philosophical vocabulary and the ultimate fixing of meaning. Were language finally taken in charge, Diderot maintains, this new philosophical language would outstrip the present state of knowledge and bring about even further advances, simply by forcing philosophy to keep up with it.[39] If the encyclopedists can produce such a work, they will guarantee the transmission and advancement of knowledge, which for them rests on establishing once and for all the necessary and true relationship between word and idea, sign and referent.

For the relation between sign and referent to be univocal and immutable, however, the temporality of language must be eliminated from encyclopedic representation. Consequently models for language proliferate. Diderot advises his contributors to frame their definitions according to an unchanging nature, and not people's constantly changing conventions and beliefs. He also proposes the symbolic system of geometry as another model for linguistic permanence. Less developed than human language, this set of univocal signs, "des unités pures et simples," nevertheless permits of total and perfect representation, thus realizing the ideal of the classical age's theory of representation.[40] A language of space, a form of knowledge that knows no time, geometry provides the model for an "idiome commun," a universal language Diderot rhapsodically praises for its capacity to spatialize representation entirely and abolish time absolutely.[41] Thoroughly utopian, these linguistic models collapse time into the space of an eternal present. They also reveal an essentially reductive aspect of general grammar, which seeks to restrict the linguistic sign to univocal and immutable representation by excluding the temporal and historical dimension of linguistic practice.

It is evident why the encyclopedists would found their entire project upon this "knowledge of language." Like the perfectly mimetic language of general grammar, the stable and static language of geometry, or the universal language of philosophical truth, their text too would collapse all human knowledge into one timeless space. It would also ideally provide a perfect and monumental representation of knowledge. This at least is the story Diderot wishes he could tell. It is not, however, the only story the article "*Encyclopédie*" contains. The metadiscursive, self-reflexive position Diderot establishes here cannot be accounted for by a mimetic theory of representation, which suggests that the representation of knowledge in the *Encyclopédie* cannot either.

Grammar's other

Diderot is no grammarian-philosopher. His article "*Encyclopédie*" is not written in the theoretical genre adopted by Du Marsais, Beauzée, and Douchet, who supplied most of the *Encyclopédie*'s technical articles on language. In a sense this article represents another instance of Diderot's fulfilling his editorial responsibilities by supplying articles on topics not covered by other contributors, "filling the gaps" as he puts it. Yet the gap here concerns what he saw as the most serious one in the *Encyclopédie*, its weakest part, the treatment of language. In the initial encyclopedic plan, he writes, "le côté de la langue est resté faible (je dis de la langue, et non de la grammaire)" (VII, 188). This distinction between language and grammar is crucial, for it suggests that general grammar, together with the theory of representation that subtends it, cannot account for the encyclopedic representation of knowledge, which is the particular instance of linguistic practice Diderot's entry addresses. This is why Diderot must turn away from grammar and an abstracting, idealizing linguistic theory in order to describe this practice and, more significantly, to engage in it.

For long, Diderot's commentators minimized his involvement with linguistic theory by taking his remarks on language to be essentially disconnected observations, either peripheral or redundant with respect to a more consolidated, theoretically coherent eighteenth-century linguistics. And if Diderot is marginal in relation to the linguistic theory of his time, the latter itself has been marginalized, if not written off as prescientific and prehistorical.[42] To be sure, only much later than the eighteenth century would the study of language become rigorously scientific, in the modern sense of the term. Without the following century's "discovery" of Sanskrit as the source of all Indo–European languages, a truly general grammar could not be elaborated. And only following the Saussurean distinction between *langue* and *parole*, language and speech, would linguistic theory succeed in bracketing the questions of linguistic diachrony and usage in which earlier writings on language seem hopelessly entangled. From a present-day standpoint, eighteenth-century language theory appears vexingly limitless, continually shading off into psychology, theology, rhetoric, speculative logic, and metaphysics.

Understandably enough, to establish linguistics as a consolidated theoretical discourse and an institutionalized discipline, its links to a murky past had to be severed, at least by linguists. Yet philosophers, historians of epistemology, and even literary critics have returned to these "premodern" writings on language with far more seriousness, critically questioning the very notion of language upon which contemporary linguistics is founded.[43] These returns have shown that the Enlightenment may have failed to develop a full-fledged *science* of the linguistic sign, nevertheless it did produce a particular kind of *savoir* concerning language, a knowledge or know-how that grants it a double status. Not only an object to be known, language for the Enlightenment is also a thing to be used. This is why the Enlightenment texts that take up the question of language most insightfully engage not only in theoretical speculation but also in a social, political practice,[44] however contradictory or conflictual these two manners of treating language at times appear, in both Enlightenment texts and present-day ones.

This insight is precisely what determines Diderot's turn from grammar to language in the article "*Encyclopédie*." The article presents general grammar as a consolidated theory that treats language as a translucent, idealized object, severed from its practice and absolved of its historicity. It also marks the limits of this linguistic theory though, by foregrounding the aspects of language that linguistic theory either dismisses or seeks repeatedly to get around. These limits concern the will or desire to represent, a powerfully performative force that drives the practice of language and determines its effects. Only by turning from grammar to language, by situating himself on the margins of linguistic theory, can Diderot articulate these limits in terms of another "knowledge of language," a different kind of technique or *savoir faire*, and one which is at work in the encyclopedic representation of knowledge.

Diderot's turn towards the practice of language in the article *Encyclopédie* begins with a brief discussion of the origin of language. Like Condillac and Rousseau, he locates the historical origin of language in *le besoin*, that is, in primal or primary affects. Originally, ideas were expressed with imagination, force, and exactitude since pictures, not words, made up this first and natural form of communication. "L'art de transmettre les idées par la peinture des objets, a dû naturellement se présenter le premier" (VII, 193). Unlike Condillac and Rousseau however, Diderot does not elaborate a genealogy of affects figured in and through language. Given to neither nostalgia nor alienation, he phrases his fascination with an historical and affective origin of language in terms of the latter's figural power, its capacity to represent pictorially.

For Diderot and the Enlightenment in general, the model or metaphor of painting provides a suggestive explanation of language's original or primary function. Grammarians call language a painting whose original is thought, esthcticians judge poetry according to the dictum of *ut pictura poesis*, and the encyclopedists liken their work to a *tableau* of human knowledge.[45] These references to pictoriality tend to collapse painting and language within a common matrix of representation. Less precipitous, Diderot focuses on an irreducible difference separating them, their respective capacity to represent temporal processes such as actions or thought.

Whereas language represents dynamically, he claims, its syntax reflecting the order or process of thought, painting does not. "La peinture n'atteint pas aux opérations de l'esprit" (VII, 193). Pictorial representation is static, its temporality that of an eternal present. Even the spatial arrangement of figures on a canvas is not an analogue of linguistic syntax. Consequently, because painting can show only a single moment, whenever it attempts to represent even the simplest movement it becomes obscure. Taking the example of a painting depicting a king over whose head a crown is held, Diderot asks how one can know whether the crown is being put on or removed. "C'est à l'histoire à lever l'équivoque," he adds. Only contextual knowledge can dispel this uncertainty. Painting's attempt to represent continuous actions will always give rise to the problem of discontinuity; there will always exist gaps ("des vides"), which only the viewer can fill. Pictorial representation must be made complete through spectatorial response, through a linkage to *l'histoire* – the historical context or a simple story – the viewer reads into or branches onto the painting.

Although painting immobilizes the temporal and thus represents incompletely, it is immediately comprehensible since its elements mimetically double the object they represent. "Les peintures des êtres sont toujours très incomplètes; mais elles n'ont rien d'équivoque, parce que ce sont les portraits mêmes d'objets que nous avons sous les yeux." The linguistic sign, on the other hand, signifies not by resemblance but by convention. "Les caractères de l'écriture s'étendent à tout, mais ils sont d'institution; ils ne signifient rien par eux-mêmes." Usage is determined by a "pact" among speakers, an arbitrary agreement that can never be fully explained since the process of signification cannot be made totally explicit. Certain linguistic signs, if not all, have a degree of indetermination, and thus their meaning can never be entirely established or codified. The attempt to comprehend language, to read and interpret the text, will always encounter "des nuances délicates qui restent nécessairement indéterminées."

Diderot's fascination with linguistic indeterminability, which today one would call the connotative, poetic function of language, reappears throughout his writings. He refuses to view language simply as communication, and the word as the luminous sign of thought. On the contrary, he senses that the very condition for the practice of language is linguistic indeterminability. He is well aware moreover that this linguistic indetermination risks jeopardizing the entire encyclopedic project. Designed to provide a complete and continuous representation of human knowledge, the *Encyclopédie* was to be a closed, self-defining work, an epistemological *tableau* that would also be the most perfect of dictionaries. Yet certain words cannot be defined, Diderot notes, nor should they be. These *radicaux* or *termes primitifs*, the most basic elements of language, refer to "les propriétés générales des êtres," such as "âme, espace, courbe, existence, étendu, pensée, sensation, temps" ("*Dictionnaire*," IV, 959). These primary terms of being(s) prevent the encyclopedic grid of definitions from being filled; the encyclopedic portrait of knowledge must remain a discontinuous one, the *radicaux* corresponding to the "intermediary moments" that escape representation.

The *Encyclopédie*'s gaps and spaces, the "nuances délicates" that can be sensed but not defined, make the encyclopedic representation of knowledge analogous to painting after all, yet in a problematic sense. As Diderot's coronation example suggests, the temporal gaps of pictorial representation can be filled and a kind of syntax formulated. (The viewer can decide, for instance, that the king is being crowned.) But in this act that completes representation, a shift occurs from painting to language, from the figural to the discursive, from the act of viewing to that of producing an interpretive narrative. If in the case of painting the viewer's judgment (or desires) must be relied on to fill pictorial gaps, in the case of language does it fall to the reader of the *Encyclopédie* to supply his or her own definitions? Can the truth of encyclopedic representation, to say nothing of its effect, be assured?

Diderot confronts this issue by way of an analogy, likening the natural world to a huge machine made up of so many interconnecting pieces that it can be described and figured in an infinite number of ways. "L'univers soit réel soit intelligible a une infinité de points de vue sous lesquels il peut être représenté, et le nombre des systèmes possibles de la connaissance humaine est aussi grand que celui de ces points du vue . . . Il est donc impossible de bannir l'arbitraire de cette grande distribution première" (VII, 210–11). If any system of knowledge, any figuration of the natural world, is but one of several "points of view," then encyclopedic representation cannot avoid the arbitrariness of epistemological perspectivism. The *Encyclopédie* will never be an absolute and perfect systematization of the phenomenal world,[46] for the relation between the object of representation and the object represented will always be one of noncoincidence, marked by gaps or *écarts*. The arbitrary nature of epistemological systems, coupled with the indeterminacy of language, leads Diderot to envisage the *Encyclopédie* project's ultimate failure. "Nous voilà donc arrêtés dans notre projet de transmettre les connaissances, par l'impossibilité de rendre toute la langue intelligible . . . Est-ce la peine d'écrire pour les siècles à venir, si nous ne sommes pas en état de nous en faire entendre?" (VII, 194). The encyclopedic representation of knowledge cannot escape the indetermination, flux, and discontinuity characterizing the quotidian, individually mediated practice of language.

Yet this admission of defeat is only tactical. "Résolvons ces problèmes," continues Diderot without hesitation, proceeding to supply not one but two solutions to the problem. The first somewhat ingenious solution involves using so-called dead languages to establish the meaning of the basic, otherwise undefinable terms of a spoken language. Since ancient languages exist only as texts, for Diderot they are necessarily static, univocal, and perfectly translatable, thus offering one way to immobilize living language and thereby to represent. A more interesting solution (and a less dubious one) involves the encyclopedic system of *renvois* or cross-references, which Diderot calls the most important part of encyclopedic order. Making explicit the common principles and analogies joining one article with another, the *renvois* mark out the path the reader may follow to retrace the "genealogical tree of knowledge." Reflecting the *Encyclopédie*'s ideal structural and epistemological unity, the *renvois* establish the truth of encyclopedic representation, a truth resulting though from the deployment of power and from conflicting forms of knowledge.

> [Ils] entrelacent la branche au tronc, et donnent au tout cette unité si favorable à l'établissement de la vérité et à la persuasion . . . Ils opposeront les notions; ils feront constater les principes; ils attaqueront, ébranleront, renverseront secrètement quelques opinions

ridicules qu'on n'oserait insulter ouvertement. Si l'auteur est impartial, ils auront toujours la double fonction de confirmer et de réfuter; de troubler et de concilier (VII, 221).

An integral part of the encyclopedic machine, the *renvois* show how a work expected to be a harmless piece of collective erudition became a discursive *machine de guerre*, redoutable to both religion and the state. By linking one article presenting traditionally accepted views and beliefs with another containing a more "enlightened" critical view, the *renvois* introduce an invasive, subversive irony into the entire text.[47] More important, the *renvois* exemplify the particular practice of language the encyclopedists invent and deploy to realize their objective of "undeceiving" people, not just by replacing one view, one truth, one form of knowledge with another, but by reshaping entirely the reader's relation to knowledge in general. Making manifest the impossibility of presenting any "point of view" as natural, anonymous or absolute, the *renvois* contest the authority of texts and discourses that would conceal the authored, contextual, institutional determination of knowledge. Foregrounded in the system of cross-references is the material, discursive apparatus of encyclopedic representation, which constantly mediates the reader's access to existing knowledge. Moreover, encyclopedic representation locates the production of knowledge in the act of reading, a productive relation to knowledge the encyclopedists wish to empower as a truly critical practice. Ideally able to situate all forms of knowledge without being situated absolutely by any, this critical practice would possess the self-legitimating potential to (re)produce itself anew in each and every interpretive act.

This practice is not a hermeneutical one that reveals the ultimate meaning of things. When Diderot cautions "[qu']il faut lire l'article avec précaution, et en peser exactement tous les termes" (VII, 224), he refers to the inescapably conflictual nature of interpretation, and which no critical practice can fully eliminate. Possessing "une force interne et une utilité secrète, dont les effets sourds seraient nécessairement sensibles avec le temps" (VII, 221–22), encyclopedic representation results from a technique or *savoir* concerning knowledge, an interpretive know-how that Diderot's self-reflexive article passes on to the reader of the *Encyclopédie.* If Diderot suggests that the most powerful "effects" of the encyclopedic representation of knowledge will become palpable "with time," it is because the *Encyclopédie* establishes an empowered relation to knowledge and situates that practice in interpretation, in the moment of every future act of reading that instantiates the potential of an empowered practice of knowledge.

The encyclopedists of course do not inaugurate this critical relation to knowledge. Bayle's *Dictionnaire historique et critique*, to take a notable example, stages interpretation as an essentially conflictual act by mobilizing the subversive force of citation, as does Montaigne in his *Essais.* Yet the effective power of critique in these cases is counterbalanced by the seductions of skepticism, an ironic relation to knowledge based on the claim to know its limits. Voltaire too deftly dances between these two poles in the hope of striking a safe balance between public and private, the social and the individual, knowledge and critical thinking. No such balance is sought in the *Encyclopédie.* The encyclopedists cast aside the protection of skepticism and irony in order to realize a more effective relation to knowledge and its representation, as well as a more political one.

Jacques Proust has argued that insofar as all Diderot's articles, whatever their subject, are designed to modify opinion, all are political.[48] In a broader sense, not only are Diderot's politics fundamentally discursive, the discursive practice of encyclopedic representation seeks to empower the reader's relation to knowledge in a political way. To be sure, one cannot ignore just *what* the encyclopedists proposed in the way of changed opinions. But a descriptive, thematic reading cannot grasp how the encyclopedic knowledge machine performs the empowerment of knowledge, especially the knowledge relied upon to read this text. What is called the Enlightenment cannot be presented simply as a set of principles, a collection of ideas, somehow independent of the discursive practice that produces them. To be truly effective, and in a way that goes beyond politics in a narrow sense, any knowledge of an historical period and its products, as well as the role, value or effect this knowledge can have in the present moment, cannot be severed from the technique or know-how involved in producing that knowledge. This is why the encyclopedists turn self-reflexively to the practice of representation, and why it is more productive to ask not *what* one reads in the *Encyclopédie* but *how* one reads it and to what ends.

Herein lies the ultimate significance (or effect) of Diderot's self-reflexive turn from grammar to language, from a theory of representation to its practice. Only by leaving aside a linguistic theory that reduces language to the role of mimetic sign can Diderot articulate how signs work. This does not mean he rejects language theory or the theoretical genre in general; rather, he marks its limits. He willingly maintains that the word is the material representation of the idea, and that language is in some sense determined by thought. Of far greater pertinence for him though are the ways thought is acted upon by language, a problem traditionally demeaned, circumscribed or excluded by grammarians and philosophers alike. Diderot's turn to the practice of language plays out a broadly constitutive tension within the linguistic and epistemological theory of the classical age, a conflict between signification and intentionality, meaning and motivation, representation and interpretation, text and reader.

In this turn, linguistic theory of the classical age comes up short. Founded on the assumption that the gap between words and things can be bridged, this theory of representation would reduce language to a purely nominative function.[49] Ultimately though such a reduction destroys the very object linguistic theory seeks to contain. Once the word is uttered, once language becomes the place of absolute and unmediated representation, language must be absorbed by the word and disappear. The word as absolute name ultimately puts an end to speaking, to a use of language mediated by the individuality of speaking subjects, as well as by the materiality of language, the contextuality of the discursive situation, and the temporality of the historical.

In the writings of the Enlightenment grammarian-philosophers, this unified theory of language and mind begins to break up as a different linguistic *savoir* emerges, a discourse whose concepts had to be invented.[50] By the eighteenth century, the rationality that earlier had been ascribed to language was taken to mean not only that language expresses an original, universal, and timeless reason, but also that linguistic reality is governed by laws that can be discovered through observation and empirical analysis. Port-Royal grammar theory loses its explicative authority as grammarian-philosophers redefine the meaning of the term "language." Beauzée, for example, may sound like his predecessors of the previous century when he affirms that language reflects the "lois de l'analyse logique de la pensée [qui] sont invariablement les mêmes partout et dans tous les temps" ("*Grammaire*," VII, 841). Yet Enlightenment linguistics and epistemology seek access to the experience of primary perception through a language analyzed in all its phenomenal, material texture. Reversing the hierarchical relation between idea and word steadfastly maintained by Port-Royal grammar, the Enlightenment grammarian-philosophers place themselves in a theoretical double bind. They wish to demonstrate their belief in the essential rationality of language as the transparent representation of thought, yet they choose to do so through empirical observation of the raw materiality of language. This confrontation with an opaquely arbitrary practice of language leads to a kind of eighteenth-century linguistic explosion. The grammarians' knowledge of language must treat far more than the syntax of the phrase, whose logic doubles that of the mind. Descriptive rather than normative, it must also be concerned with numerous other instances of linguistic practice, such as phonetics, etymology, metaphor, and synonyms.

This shift within language theory signifies a far larger reformulation of representational practices in the Enlightenment, and which occurs in exemplary fashion in the *Encyclopédie*. Situated between a way of representing knowledge that is static and spatial, nominative and mimetic, and another that is dynamic and temporal, discursive and narrative, the *Encyclopédie* participates in both epistemological paradigms and representational practices. The encyclopedists seek to capitalize on this conflictual situation by turning what seems to be an impediment to representing knowledge into its very condition. This explains why they readily admit that the only system of knowledge whose order is absolute, nonarbitrary, and possesses unquestionable authority would be "le système qui [existe] de toute éternité dans la volonté de Dieu" (VII, 211). Yet they recognize that such an ideal form of representation is unattainable. More important, it runs counter to the goals of encyclopedism. For instead of increasing knowledge of the world, ideal encyclopedic representation would be just as difficult to understand as the world itself.[51]

Ultimately, the arbitrary nature of encyclopedic representation causes the encyclopedists little concern. What they seek to realize is a representational practice that however arbitrary and mediated presents knowledge most powerfully and productively. Representation may indeed occur at one remove from the object represented, yet the gap between signs and their referent can nonetheless be gauged, if not bridged, by imposing an arbitrary order upon the world, by overlaying the referent with its representations. Capitalizing on these gaps, the encyclopedic text mobilizes and channels the power of knowledge as representation. Unable to escape the arbitrary, the encyclopedic text figures an *arbiter*, marking out the reader's place in the interpretive act, demanding his or her participation, indeed justifying and legitimating it. And with this intervention, the fixed geometric point that previously grounded representation becomes plural. That single point, occupied by the transcendent observer of the Cartesian eye/I, multiplies into an infinite number of points of view. This is why the encyclopedists invent the crucial notion of *enchaînement* or linkage, a way of representing knowledge continuously, both as product and as process of production, the linkage occurring in the act of reading.

Paralleled in eighteenth-century literature by the invention of different narrative forms and the emergence of other reading sensibilities, or in art by a changed understanding of spectatorship, the *Encyclopédie* exemplifies a particular representational and interpretive practice that produces knowledge symbolically as representation. No longer a passive spectator of representation before whom the total meaning of all signs is played out, the reader of the *Encyclopédie* becomes an integral part in this machine's production of narratives of knowledge. In the name of "man," in other words the interpreting subject and practitioner of knowledge, the *Encyclopédie* stakes its claim to empowered, critical knowledge in the desire to forge new discursive, epistemological, and social orders.

To be sure, the encyclopedic representation of "man" is as arbitrary as the plates' representation of a rationally mechanized world, and just as mediated by the desire for powerful, masterful knowledge. Just as certainly the encyclopedic knowledge machine holds the potential to entrap its readers, luring them into believing that the *Encyclopédie* truly reflects a preexisting reality and that the world is structured the way it is represented. In short, the encyclopedic machine is a thoroughly ideological one. At the same time however, the *Encyclopédie* reflects on the enabling conditions of such representation, presenting self-reflexively a representational performativity that can be taken as the critical limit of Enlightenment critique. If it is not pushed to such a limit, Enlightenment knowledge remains powerless to contest effectively "irrational" or less "enlightened" forms of knowledge. And taken beyond this limit, Enlightenment knowledge itself falls victim to self-entrapment, bereft of the means to distinguish itself from these less self-reflexive forms of knowledge.

Situated on this self-reflexive cusp of Enlightenment critique, the encyclopedic text and its images display a powerful performativity, a *teknè* or technique of knowledge that finally must be accounted for in any reading of Enlightenment texts. Enlightenment's self-reflexive turn towards the enabling techniques of knowledge as representational practice results in the seductive and liberating sense of being able to master knowledge instead of being mastered by it.[52] Yet as is visible in the encyclopedic plates, this mastery potentially takes the form of constellations of power, instrumentalized knowledge, the self-interested rationalization of beliefs and values. This explains why the encyclopedists' work helped undermine an old order, and why its continuation, the *Encyclopédie méthodique*, helped establish new orders, serving equally well the interests of monarchy, revolution, and republic. The encyclopedists intended indeed to fashion a useful relation to knowledge. Yet their practice of representing knowledge inevitably escapes their intentions, revealing the critical means to expose the arbitrary, motivated, and ideological use to which their text and knowledge in general can be put. The Enlightenment is a shifting, multi-layered object, a product of the last two hundred-odd years of inventing stories to tell about the Enlightenment. The production of these stories has always been mediated by specific desires, political motivations, and ideological imperatives. The strength and effect of further rereadings of the *Encyclopédie* will be measured by the extent to which they help gauge this mediation. Only by refusing to separate language from the will and desires of those who put it to use can one come to grips with the social, historical, and ideological pressures and powers at work in narratives about the Enlightenment and its texts.

CHAPTER 2

Enlightenment critique and Diderot's art of philosophizing

As witnessed in the encyclopedic text, critical discourse of the Enlightenment seeks to empower knowledge. Restructuring the relation between subject and object, the practitioner of knowledge and the thing represented as knowable, critical discourse implements powerful techniques for producing knowledge, in such varied domains as moral philosophy, natural science, esthetics, and political theory. Intellectual history is the discipline that proposes to describe this knowledge and evaluate it in an historical perspective. So long as it remains a history of *ideas*, however, intellectual history may not be the most effective idiom for articulating the practice I claim produces this knowledge in that it overlooks the relation between the idea and the representational practice that presents it as such, as something knowable. The intellectual historical idiom remains an idealizing one insofar as it severs its object from the material practice that produces it, and above all from the practice of intellectual history. While it makes comforting sense to believe that terms such as the Enlightenment "mind," "thought" or "spirit" refer to some grounding source or governing cause exterior to the practice of knowledge, I would argue these terms refer instead to *effects* of a representational practice, constructs that are an intrinsic part of it. Insofar as the discourse of intellectual history fails to articulate how knowledge results from particular idioms or practices of knowledge (including its own), these practices will remain ungraspable, invisible, unknowable.

For quite some time the need has been felt to "rethink intellectual history," to write a "new literary history" or found a "new historicism."[1] In such "returns" to history, the crucial issue involves the relation between (historical) knowledge and the enabling conditions of its coming into being, which I shall call the material practice of its presentation. Various terms and models have been invoked to explain this process: the discursive event, rhetoric, text, narrative, etc. Each in its own way indicates a critical reworking of the paradigms with which knowledge is understood. These varied attempts to resituate knowledge in relation to the tangible practice that produces it signal at least the desire to achieve critical understanding, if not of the real then at least of a constructed reality.

If this self-reflexive turn towards representational practices constitutes the chief trait of a "(post)modernity," the latter dates from the Enlightenment. One of the Enlightenment's most powerful legacies, this reflection concerning the practice of producing knowledge suggests that the relation to knowledge the Enlightenment establishes is its most "modern" achievement. By this I mean that the Enlightenment relation to knowledge is familiar, one we recognize to a certain extent as our own. One way to gauge the modernity of the Enlightenment's practice of knowledge is through Diderot's article "*Art.*"

The term "art" refers here initially to the mechanical arts. This is the sense in which Diderot contrasts art and science, defining the two according to the relation between subject and object each involves. If the object is worked on, the rules governing this activity constitute an art, whereas if the object is only contemplated, this speculative activity falls under the heading of science. This distinction suggests other familiar ones, such as between eye and hand, thought and labor, viewing and doing, theory and practice. Breaking with a longstanding tradition that related these pairs hierarchically, Diderot refuses to subordinate the mechanical arts to the "nobler" activity of science. Following Francis Bacon, he instead places them on equal footing with science. Significantly, in attempting to rehabilitate the mechanical arts Diderot undermines the very principle that distinguishes art and science, thereby suggesting an understanding of art itself as a kind of knowledge.

Art consists of two aspects, Diderot claims, "la connaissance inopérative des règles de l'art" which he calls speculation, and "l'usage habituel et non-réfléchi des mêmes règles" which he calls practice. Displacing the traditional boundary separating science and art, this definition also reformulates the meaning of each. Instead of being distinct from art, and thus able to enjoy speculative exteriority, science exists in art as well. This science is not the removed contemplation or abstract, speculative reasoning Diderot criticizes in *De l'interprétation de la nature*. Rather it is a form of knowledge ("une connaissance"). "Inoperative" in that it pertains to art's "rules" or pure potentiality, this knowledge realizes its potential in the practice of art. No longer must art be taken in charge by knowledge of another order, for in elevating art to epistemological status, Diderot locates there a kind of technical, productive knowledge that already combines speculation and practice. "C'est à la pratique à présenter les difficultés et à donner les phénomènes; et c'est à la spéculation à expliquer les phénomènes et à lever les difficultés: d'où il s'ensuit qu'il n'y a quère qu'un artiste sachant raisonner, qui puisse bien parler de son art" (I, 714). Speculative and practical knowledge cohabit in art.

Enlightenment philosophes leave books and libraries in search of knowledge, and venture into the studio and laboratory, even the factory and workplace. They do so because Enlightenment epistemology restructures the field of knowledge, which appears in many places besides the mind of the speculative philosopher. Diderot's article testifies to a semantic shift undergone during the Enlightenment by the term "art," which comes to refer to an activity at once theoretical and practical, and in itself constitutes productive knowledge. The art in question here is no longer a mute, un-self-reflexive practice the philosopher desiring knowledge must make comprehensible. Rather, the art to which Diderot refers already produces that knowledge. The intelligent artisan ("l'artiste sachant raisonner") can himself speak knowledgeably about his art. This figure of the artist also stands for the practitioner of knowledge in general. Enjoying a status equal to that of the experimental scientist described in *De l'interprétation de la nature*, the "artiste sachant raisonner" engages in an artistic, artisanal practice designed to produce knowledge. Including the artisan, the artist, the scientist and finally the Enlightenment *philosophe*, the "artiste" here figures a form of knowledge concerning the rules, techniques, and performative practice of knowledge, a self-reflexivity that founds Enlightenment epistemological representation.

Diderot's reformulation of art bears witness to a wide-ranging epistemological shift characterizing Enlightenment philosophy in general. As Jacques Chouillet puts it, Diderot's definition implies

> qu'il existe un raisonnement sur les choses (ce que Diderot appelle une "métaphysique") aussi difficile, aussi abstraite que le raisonnement sur les idées ... Renonçant à l'introspection cartesienne, qui fonde la connaissance sur la réflexivité du moi pensant, la philosophie des Lumières va au-devant des choses. La nature extérieure, saisie par l'expérience, est le lieu de toute vérité. Il faut sortir de soi pour la posséder.[2]

Enlightenment philosophy shifts focus from an introspective subject, who pursues the truth of universal, abstract nature through speculation, to an "ex-centric" subject, constantly drawn outside itself through its empirical, physical experience of a particularized, material nature. In the broadest of terms, the Enlightenment's critical response to the idealism it inherited lies in this shift from ideas to things which results from what Chouillet calls a "raisonnement sur les choses."

Chouillet's phrase is suggestive. It also reveals how the intellectual historical idiom can recontain the most powerful aspect of the critique it identifies. For by reducing Enlightenment to a type of reasoning, an idea, however new, concerning the self and nature, this idiom elides the critical issue of the Enlightenment's *practice* of knowledge. The Enlightenment's formal experimentations with the enabling conditions for critical knowledge will inevitably be idealized, and thus misapprehended, so long as attention is focused on the idea of Enlightenment and not its texts, on thought and not the materiality of representational practices.

Enlightenment philosophy does not simply come up with "new" ideas, such as that of an empirical, material, particularized nature as the place of ultimate truth. Like the knowledge machines they are, Enlightenment texts instead *produce* such a nature, as well as a subject that can come to know itself in and through that process of production. Consequently, to judge these *effects* of Enlightenment, one cannot disregard the representational practice, the art of knowledge, that produces them. Enlightenment philosophy may in fact represent nature as "*le lieu de toute vérité*" as Chouillet puts it, and which can be known through experience. Yet the real place of truth lies in the representational practice the Enlightenment engages in, the art of knowledge it deploys, and the techniques it invents for determining under which conditions that which is said (but also thought, seen, felt . . .) can be called true.

Few Enlightenment writers were more passionately and daringly inventive in this regard than Diderot. To grasp what is most crucially at stake in the Enlightenment practice of knowledge, we can adopt the perspective suggested by his encyclopedia article and consider his writings as artworks. As I use the term here, it does not mean objects that reflect the attempt to express, attain or give form to some ideal such as beauty. The art at work in Diderot's texts is of another nature. The artwork I shall consider here is that product, that work of words (but also of sounds and shapes) resulting from specific techniques, rules, and means that are skillfully employed to achieve certain effects. By reading Diderot's texts as artworks, his artistic, even artisanal experimentations with the materials of his craft – particular techniques, genres, and models of writing – can be related to the discursive production of critical knowledge. Diderot's texts artfully rework the question of knowledge, which they displace and resituate through a powerful practice. This practice's critical power lies precisely in this displacement, which produces a different kind of knowledge, at once more critical, self-reflexive, and artistic.

Translating interpretation: "the real Diderot"

One of the earliest works of a thirty-two-year-old beginning writer, the *Essai sur le mérite et la vertu* of 1745 is a translation of Shaftesbury's *Inquiry Concerning Virtue and Merit.* The *Essai* faithfully presents Shaftesbury's argument for a religious, ethical, and philosophical position located on a middle ground between all extremes. For Shaftesbury, knowledge of what is good and true cannot be derived from divine revelation, arbitrary authority or opinions. Instead, it must be based on a "natural" law, a harmonious universal order to which all reasonable persons should conform by virtue of an inherent sociability. This common-sense deist rationalism clearly appeals to Diderot. In the *Pensées philosophiques*, *Promenade du sceptique*, *Suffisance de la religion naturelle*, and *Lettre à mon frère*, written immediately after the *Essai*, the critique of sectarian fanaticism, superstition, and the authority of divine revelation recalls the English moralist. Eventually though, Diderot leaves the model of Shaftesburian deism behind him, as he turns from metaphysics to science, from the universalizing, idealizing notion of "man" towards more empirical, physical, and material ways of critically addressing the epistemological, ethical, and social problems this notion entails.

The creation of the blind geometer Saunderson in Diderot's *Lettre sur les aveugles* marks a decisive break with the Shaftesburian notion of perfect harmony between God and the individual, nature and society. Quite literally, Saunderson embodies the sensationalist hypothesis concerning the causal relation between thought and the senses. Forced to sense his own monstrous and unjust abnormality, Saunderson remains both physically and philosophically blind to any divine principle of order and goodness. His melodramatic deathbed monologue on a heavenly emptiness his eyes cannot fail to see anticipates Diderot's future experimentations with other models for producing knowledge, models that would better account for how a body senses, views, and grasps things. Ultimately, Diderot turns from the common-sense compromise of Shaftesburian deism towards a more materialist critique of social and ethical values. This turn occurs in and through an artistic experimentation with other models for representing knowledge, such as the character Saunderson, models better able to account for the physical, material determination of knowledge. Diderot leaves Shaftesburian deism behind him, not simply because his ideas change, but because this particular critical model is insufficiently powerful.

The issue, then, the *Essai* raises concerns the relative power of critical models. Diderot's commentators, and his editors especially, have sensed this, yet typically they recontain their intuition by phrasing the problem in a negative, reductive way. Jules Assézat for instance, editor of the 1875 edition of the *Œuvres complètes*, claims that in the *Essai*, "nous n'avons ... pas, dans cet écrit, le vrai Diderot" (AT I, 7). In one sense of course, Assézat means simply that if "the real Diderot" is absent here, it is because the *Essai* is a translation. Whoever Assézat's "real Diderot" might be – presumably the one the introductions and notes to his edition reveal, and which joins the countless other Diderots fashioned during the nineteenth century – the "I" of the *Essai* is far more English than French. Assézat includes the *Essai* in his edition, yet almost against his better judgment and only to represent a short-lived yet important influence on Diderot's thinking. Assézat's denial of one model is made in the name of another, his own notion of "the real Diderot." This model is that of the thinker whose ideas must be traced back to sources and influences through the interpretive work of the positivist editor as he seeks to comprehend the intertextual relation between the *Essai* and the *Inquiry*.

More a writer than an editor, Diderot senses most acutely how one text can rejoin and rewrite another, perhaps even unbeknownst to the writer. "Nous empruntons nos expressions, nos idées des personnes avec lesquelles nous conversons, nous vivons" (AT VII, 125). Invoked by those critics who accused Diderot of having few original ideas of his own, the remark suggests more pertinently that no idea can be claimed to be original, one's own, for it is already spoken or written by another. Diderot "pense sur et à partir d'une autre œuvre, jamais sur et à partir de lui-même," as Yves Benot puts it,[3] suggesting an "intertextual thought" as work in the *Lettre sur les sourds et muets* (a critique of Charles Batteux's *Les Beaux-arts réduits au même principe*), the *Réfutation d'Helvétius* (a commentary of *De l'homme*), *Sur les femmes* (a review of Jean Thomas' work), the *Supplément au voyage de Bougainville*, the *Eloge de Richardson*,

Jacques le fataliste (whose fictional editor calls it an imitation of Sterne's *Tristram Shandy*) . . . The list continues indefinitely, since for Diderot "un discours s'enchaîne à un autre discours, qu'il continue, qu'il complète, qu'il développe, qu'il peut même développer indéfiniment, au risque, à chaque instant, de l'infléchir en le faisant déborder vers on ne sait quelles questions et régions étrangères au sujet."[4] The legend of Diderot the writer-*causeur*, spontaneously digressive and unable to compose a well-ordered text, need not be rejected entirely in the name of a more writerly, less dispersive Diderot.[5] For the legendary model suggests that Diderot "himself," his "thought," and above all the "Diderot" that thinks it, must be understood textually, in other words *as a text*, linked without exception to anterior texts it prolongs and rewrites, or to posterior texts whose writing it anticipates. Diderot's translation of the *Inquiry* is not unique after all, for the *Essai* poses the problem of all (Diderot's) texts, namely, the linkage that joins one to another. What interpretive model might account for this linkage?

The editors of the Hermann edition of Diderot's complete works suggestively raise the question of critical models by entitling the volume in which the *Essai* appears "le modèle anglais." The term refers in one sense to English philosophical thought, whose formative influence on the young Diderot has been amply demonstrated.[6] More pertinently, "model" also implies the existence of imitation, as if Diderot's early encounter with English thinking resulted in somewhat derivative works of lesser interest than the more original, authentic, and French works written later, works that better portray "the real Diderot." In a third and more interesting sense, the term "model" suggests a trait of all Diderot's thinking and writing, his constant and manifold experimentations with the technical means of producing critical knowledge. In the case of the *Essai*, this experimentation takes place in the margins of the French translation of the *Inquiry*, that is, in a preface and notes Diderot provides. Here he directly raises the question of critical models, their function and their force, by staging three different scenes of writing and reading. If there exists any "real" Diderot in this text, it can be located in this self-reflexive experimentation with models, in Diderot's "manner."[7] This experimental manner pertains not only to the intertextual relation between Diderot and Shaftesbury, the *Essai* and the *Inquiry*, but also to the interpretive models that produce the knowledge one can have of (Diderot's) texts.

A first scene of writing is staged in the translator's preface that frames the *Essai* proper. "J'ai lu et relu [Shaftesbury's *Inquiry*]: je me suis rempli de son esprit, et j'ai, pour ainsi dire, fermé son livre, lorsque j'ai pris la plume. On n'a jamais usé du bien d'autrui avec tant de liberté" (I, 300). Diderot is presented here as Shaftesbury's most faithful of readers, so open to the other that he becomes the perfect receptacle for the other's thought. Shaftesbury speaks through this Diderot, the *Essai* being a frictionless conduit through which the "esprit" of the English deist passes intact. As editor of the *Encyclopédie* too Diderot will make "free use of another's property."

The interpretive model that can be derived from this first scene of writing presents a fairly familiar Diderot, for whom all speech is interlocution, all discourse dialogical, all writing intertextual. In the *Salons* as much as in *Le Neveu de Rameau* or *Le Rêve de D'Alembert*, in the *Encyclopédie* as much as in *Jacques le fataliste* or *Ceci n'est pas un conte*, Diderot's writing consistently favors *discours* over *récit*, always subordinating the tale to its telling, foregrounding *énonciation* over the *énoncé*. Whether he addresses an historical interlocutor (Melchior Grimm, Catherine of Russia, Sophie Volland) or a fictional one (entering into dialogue with a painted figure in the *Salons*, speaking to posterity in the *Encyclopédie* or *Le Pour et le contre*), indeed even in his most "intimate" and apparently monological texts, such as the *Essai sur les règnes de Claude et de Néron*, Diderot is never alone when he writes.

The standard interpretation of this dialogical instance results from the model of being that can be derived from this first scene of writing. Jean Starobinski, for example, finds in all Diderot's writing an "interior dialogue" that reflects a "scissiparité subjective."[8] Georges Daniel refers to an "impulsion organique," a "besoin vital de [la] nature expansive et dominatrice [de Diderot] qui lui impose la fiction de l'autre." This other need not be a specific individual, an autonomous presence distinct from Diderot, but rather may be "une direction, une ouverture de son esprit, son esprit lui-même immobilisé sous forme d'obstacle ou prolongé dans son écho."[9] Georges Poulet suggests most succinctly how this linkage between self and other is grandly constitutive of being. For Diderot, "être, c'est devenir un autre; le moi n'est moi que parce qu'il diffère sans cesse de lui-même."[10]

Such formulations imply an understanding of writing as the privileged medium of access to a consciousness of self or self-reflexive knowledge. However desirable such knowledge might be, it comes at a price. To read Diderot's texts as standing for a subjective, psychological, ontological entity, a figure of consciousness called "Diderot," interpreters must dematerialize writing, collapsing the distinction between language and self, writing and being. Writing must be only a "moment," in Poulet's terms, of an ideal consciousness, not a material practice that produces the idea of such consciousness by constructing a self made knowable in and as representation. To be sure, Diderot's text refers repeatedly to writing. Yet these references are part of a larger self-reflexivity that marks his experimentation with the material of his craft, an experimentation that a simply thematic approach to writing can only essentialize.[11] As if to mark the limits of such an approach, the *Essai* returns to the question of writing by branching a second scene of writing onto the first. This second scene proposes another way to understand the relation between writing, being, and self-knowledge.

> On n'a jamais usé du bien d'autrui avec tant de liberté. J'ai reserré ce qui m'a paru trop diffus; étendu ce qui m'a paru trop serré; rectifié ce qui n'était pensé qu'avec hardiesse; et les réflexions qui accompagnent cette espèce de texte, sont si fréquentes, que l'Essai de M. S. . . . qui n'était proprement qu'une démonstration métaphysique, s'est converti en éléments de morale assez considérables (I, 300).

In this second scene, Diderot's *Essai* establishes linkage not with Shaftesbury's spirit but with the *Inquiry*, a text. Staging the act of writing as a stylistic, material practice, and not the expansion of (self-)consciousness, this model suggests that the other in question is a construct of words, contained in a book, or rather produced in the act of rewriting it. That book not only can be closed before writing begins, it must be. The other's voice must be silenced; the passivity of a receptive reading must be replaced by an active, forceful writing that transforms the apparently autonomous exterior presence of the other into an alterity produced by the act of referring to it. The passive, receptive reader does not write, which is to say that the dialogical harmony and unity of consciousness suggested by the first model is ultimately an imaginary one.

Diderot can translate Shaftesbury only by putting aside the book and taking up the pen, by transforming Shaftesbury into a text. This transformation also involves reforming – or deforming – Shaftesbury's thought and text. The *Inquiry*'s "démonstration métaphysique" becomes "éléments de morale" in the *Essai*. This reference to Diderot's rewriting of Shaftesbury in moral terms exemplifies his constant concern with the ethical implications of any idealist metaphysical system. The translator's formal, stylistic work bears the mark of Diderot himself, whose irrepressible reflections in the form of notes frame his translation of Shafesbury's text and even invade it to the point of freely recasting it. Stylistic analysis of the translation reveals just how Diderot redirected Shaftesbury's thought. At the same time though, this second scene of writing short-circuits the interpretive desire to derive Diderot's intellectual portrait from his style. Opening up a space of uncertainty within the *Essai*, Diderot the translator notes he has tightened what was loosely argued and lightened what was densely formulated. Introducing an ironic dimension, this kind of translating presents the secondary, derivative text as an original, which (re)produces the text of Shaftesbury anew. Thwarted in the search for the subject behind his words, how can one locate Diderot in this invasive, excessive practice where the signs of his presence are everywhere and nowhere? Turning to the English text provides only the illusion of an answer.

A third scene of writing returns us to the problem of *this* text. This scene is staged in notes placed *around* or *beside* the French version of the *Inquiry*. As Diderot explains, "de crainte que des préventions fondées sur la hardiesse de quelques propositions mal examinées n'étouffent les fruits de cet écrit, j'ai cru devoir en préparer la lecture par un petit nombre de réflexions, qui suffiront avec les notes que j'ai répandues partout où je les ai jugées nécessaires, pour lever les scrupules de tout lecteur attentif et judicieux" (I, 295). Farthest removed from the *Inquiry*, these "reflexions" belong apparently to the most authentic Diderot, writing now in his own voice. But does this marginal commentary reflect Diderot's interpretation of Shaftesbury? Perhaps, yet these marginal comments serve additionally, as Diderot puts it, not to convey his reading of the *Inquiry* but to prepare the reading the *Essai* will receive. This scene of writing is staged to counter a potential adversarial response, which suggests that interpretation is not a harmonious enterprise but a highly conflictual one.

Many Diderots are at work in the *Essai*. Assézat was correct in claiming the "real Diderot" cannot be found here, but not because the *Essai* is a translation in which Diderot cannot speak exclusively with his own authentic voice, and still less because of any intellectual differences between Shaftesbury and the later, more mature Diderot. As these three intersecting scenes of writing suggest, any understanding of the "real Diderot" results from a representational practice and is produced in the reading of his text. No objective, authoritative presence presides over the *Essai*, except the one constructed through reading conventions and interpretive assumptions, in other words critical models concerning language, subjectivity, and self-knowledge. Staging multiple scenes of writing in one text, the *Essai* foregrounds the productive instance of knowledge about *the* text. At the same time, Diderot's playing with these scenes marks the limits of the knowledge that interpretive models alone can claim as their own. This play or slippage displaces the place of knowledge from writing to reading, from the text that refers to the object of knowledge to the practice of producing text and knowledge.

This displacement shows that seemingly natural concepts such as "author," "self," and "subject" are interpretive conventions, arbitrary models invoked to impose meaning upon things. The argument has become somewhat familiar (although its critical implications continually risk being recontained). It is also the cornerstone of the structuralist critique of apparently value-free, neutral (but in fact valorizing and neutralizing) interpretive models.[12] Arguably, this critique continues a critical strategy set in place by the Enlightenment. By shifting the privileged place of knowledge from the object known to the discourse that represents it as knowable, Enlightenment (as well as structuralism) presents a different way of knowing things. Neither better nor more objective, this other practice of knowledge does provide for a more powerful and self-reflexive evaluation of the mechanisms producing any form of knowledge.

The *Essai*'s three intersecting scenes of writing undermine the knowledge produced by the reading motivated by the desire to locate "the real Diderot." Displacing that object, the *Essai* suggests that it amounts to no more – yet no less – than a safeguard against the realization that the self one wishes to discover in the text, and the self-knowledge it would provide are of one's own invention. To a certain extent, this turning of interpretive desire back upon itself amounts to a negative critique. It reveals the Enlightenment's tendency to contest forms of knowledge that are based on ideal, *a priori* principles by ungrounding such knowledge. Such a critique does not deny or destroy the possibility of knowledge. It is not radical skepticism or nihilism. Enlightenment critique may reject other forms of knowledge, but it produces its own, which it claims is more powerful because it is better able to account self-reflexively for the production of knowledge itself. This critical displacement, and its consequences for the discourse of interpretation, can be further gauged by considering the corresponding scenes of reading implied by these scenes of writing, as well as the interpretive models that derive from them.

In a first scene of reading, Shaftesbury's faithful reader who passively receives the *Essai* in order to reproduce it implies a reception of the text that displays the least insight concerning reading as a productive act. To remain faithful to an original text, this reading must overlook the desire that drives any reading. It must disregard above all one that seeks to cast itself in Diderot's image, to capture his original intent. Shaped by the desire to "fill oneself with the spirit of the other," a form of self-procurement and self-fulfillment, this type of reading attempts to block out the lack that desire always figures. Unlike the Diderot who refuses to read (Shaftesbury) in order to write (his translation and especially his commentary), such a reading refuses to confront the mechanisms and enabling conditions of its own text.

To the second scene of writing as translation corresponds a second type of reading. Unable to avoid the deformation translation must produce, this reading apprehends the *Essai* in all its polyvocal intertextuality, willingly recognizing all texts as translations that rewrite other texts.[13] Ultimately, this type of reading would have to consider whether it too continues Diderot's translation, rewriting the *Essai* in order to "convert" its "metaphysical" story into an "ethical" one by telling its own self-reflexive story about reading. This manner of linking Diderot's text to that of its reading could not transport the former intact and would certainly disfigure it. Yet this kind of translation cannot do otherwise, for what it conveys is the treason – or treachery – of metaphor (*trans-laten*, *meta-pherein*), interpretation being able only to figure its own text and not reproduce faithfully any other. Only by failing or refusing to present the other('s) text can interpretation figure its own. Only thus can interpretation capitalize on this resituation of the knowledge it produces, and only thus, in hopes of avoiding narcissistic, self-referential closure, can it redirect the critical force of interpretation in another direction. This other direction interpretation might take is suggested by a third scene in the *Essai*, and which is staged in the notes that accompany the *Essai*.

Absent from Shaftesbury's *Inquiry*, providing explanations, amplifications, and illustrations, the notes constitute most properly Diderot's own text, however marginal. At one remove from any original, whether English or French, the notes stem from a digressive, centrifugal energy that is the hallmark of Diderot's thought and writing.[14] The notes also stand for a reading involving not the passive reception of an original text, nor even its "translated" reformulation. Instead, the notes foreground reading as the production of (yet) another text, however marginal, dispersed or derivative it may appear, a text characterized above all by the explicitly forceful way it links up with another, as the following note suggests in emblematic fashion.

Why, reflects Diderot at one point, do texts designed to provide persons infinite happiness by enlightening them to supernatural truths often fail to realize their objective? What prevents the truth from being revealed, accepted, and made known? The fault, he replies, lies with either the reader ("la méchanceté du lecteur") or the writer ("l'insuffisance de l'écrivain"). Knowledge of the truth cannot be conveyed to ill-disposed readers by inept writers. This somewhat trivial remark becomes more interesting as Diderot relates the activities of writing and reading to what he calls "les passions." "Le lecteur, pour juger sainement de l'écrivain, devrait lire son ouvrage dans le silence des passions; l'écrivain, pour arriver à la conviction du lecteur, devrait par une entière impartialité, réduire au silence les passions, dont il a plus à redouter que des raisonnements" (I, 303–4). Reflecting the Shaftesburian ideal of reasoned impartiality as the foundation of sound judgment, this denunciation of affect ("les passions") rejoins the quietistic current of English deism, as well as a far larger philosophical tradition. In France, Descartes had affirmed the precondition of rational self-knowledge was distinguishing between mind and body, reason and sense impression, truth and affect. Well before Descartes though, philosophy defines itself by formulating a similar distinction, in terms of two specific arts: logic which involves reasoning, and rhetoric which involves affect. For philosophy, rhetoric must be (no more than) a set of argumentational techniques employed to persuade, an art incapable of revealing truth through logical demonstration and reasoning. If rhetoric refers only to techniques for mobilizing opinion through powerful means of producing appearances, if it works only on affect, then it can have no legitimate place in the pursuit of truth. To define itself, philosophy wages constant assault upon rhetoric and affect, upon the art that sways a body of desires into taking things for what they are not, into viewing *simulacra* as truth. Rhetoric must be guarded against vigilantly, its techniques employed judiciously, scrupulously, in short morally – since for the philosopher, rhetoric is a deceptive, immoral thing – if the discourse of reason can reach the truth. This is the argument the discourse of philosophy repeatedly puts forward, obsessively, as if it could never completely eliminate the art called rhetoric.

The attempt to delimit this art amounts to philosophy's constitutive failure, an essential goal yet unrealizable. Beginning at least with Nietzsche's return to philosophy's historical and discursive origins, readers of the philosophical text have shown that this art cannot successfully be contained by philosophy's own definition of rhetoric.[15] The supremely rational gesture of limiting the rhetorical to a set of techniques, contained in a concept that reason could thus comprehend, classify, and control, can only take place in artful language, in which the play of rhetorical art can be shown to be indistinguishable from the ploy of reason.

The failure to purge the artfulness of language occurs in Diderot's text as well. Immediately following the most classical denial of rhetoric – affect must be silenced to attain disinterested rational quietism – we read that this silencing is necessary to persuade the reader all the more effectively ("arriver à la conviction du lecteur"). This silencing of affect appears as a ploy to convince rather than demonstrate, to persuade rather than reason, insofar as such oppositions remain intact. Far from being excluded from this "démonstration metaphysique," an artful instrumentality invades the discourse of reason to which the *Essai* refers.

With the following advice to writers, Diderot shatters the harmonious calm of deist rationalism.

> Je dirais donc à tous ceux qui se préparent d'entrer en lice contre le vice et l'impiété: Examinez-vous, avant que d'écrire. Si vous vous déterminez à prendre la plume, mettez dans vos écrits le moins de bile et le plus de sens que vous pourrez. Ne craignez point de donner trop d'esprit à votre antagoniste. Faites-le paraître sur le champ de

bataille avec toute la force, toute l'adresse, tout l'art dont il est capable. Si vous voulez qu'il se confesse vaincu, ne l'attaquez point en lâche. Saisissez-le corps à corps: prenez-le par les endroits les plus inaccessibles. Avez-vous de la peine à le terrasser? n'en accusez que vous-même (1, 304).

In a sense consistent with Shaftesburian deism and Christian metaphorics, the "antagonist" here personifies vice and impiety, the baser side of the individual. The war to be waged is thus a spiritual one, part of the writer's search for quietism that must occur prior to writing. Yet the battlefield referred to here is not so spiritual that it can be totally removed from textual matters. In calling for the adversary to be presented with "force, skill, and art," Diderot rewrites deism as a play of rhetorical forces. Through figures of militarism, Diderot not only embraces the art of rhetoric; he conjoins reason and power in a manner that presents the most powerful kind of critical discourse as a fundamentally agonistic one.

The world Shaftesbury describes in the *Inquiry* may be a harmonious place, but the text of Enlightenment critique is not. The figures of militarism that characterize the conflictual tension between text and reader here suggest a discursive model involving a critical agonistics, a discursive play of forces thematized through reference to rhetoric. Diderot ultimately rejects the intellectual model of Shaftesbury's deism and his optimistic yet compromising notion of an ideal, harmonious nature. He does so moreover because deism, as a discursive practice, lacks the critical force necessary to account for real tensions and conflicts within both human and social bodies. Diderot's experimentation with models of writing and reading in the *Essai* resituates critically the knowledge provided not only by deism, but also by present-day interpretive models based on a notion of ideal harmony and unity curiously reminiscent of the Shaftesburian compromise.

Consider for example the following comment by Herbert Dieckmann, whose contribution to Diderot studies remains undisputed.

Diderot est de ceux qui se trouvent dans l'autre et par l'autre; c'est dans la conscience de l'autre que son unité s'établissait, c'est dans la conscience de celui à qui il s'adressait – ami et lecteur – que ses idées s'ordonnaient. Si forte était cette nécessité de communiquer à une personne réelle qu'en son absence Diderot la recréait dans toute la proximité d'un échange vivant.[16]

This explanation of how Diderot's ideas became organized and his "unity" established also exemplifies the interpretive logic employed to discover the unified consciousness referred to, his self-becoming. If, as Dieckmann claims, such unity is established "in the consciousness of the other," an other who is both "friend and reader," the reading Dieckmann proposes reduplicates precisely the phenomenon it wishes to explain. To encounter this unified consciousness, the reader must occupy that other position, functioning as that other consciousness which allows the unity of self-consciousness to be established. Yet this amounts to saying that "Diderot" comes into being as unified (or unifiable) consciousness not through a particular form of "address," a dialogical interpellation of an other, but rather as the product of a specific type of reading. If such an entity is an arbitrary one, produced by (one's) reading rather than by (Diderot's) writing, then we can legitimately refuse to be the "friend and reader" Dieckmann wishes (us) to be.

Roger Kempf has argued that for Diderot, "le lecteur n'est menaçant que s'il s'établit en dehors de l'œuvre, et qu'il la tienne assujettie à son plaisir."[17] Diderot's text constantly counters the threat not of the unsympathetic reader, but of a more powerful reading, one driven by the desire to situate the text so as to avoid being situated by it. Diderot works to neutralize this threat by drawing in the reader, staging scenes of writing and reading that display not so much an essential meaning one could come to know, but rather the constitutive practice – both in and of the text – that makes such knowledge possible. The more Diderot experiments artfully with the critical potential of other models, the more difficult it becomes for his reader to remain outside this experimentation's plays of force.

Jacques le fataliste will recount one version of the struggle to situate oneself and others through the powerful act of telling stories; in the constant dialogue between narrator and fictive reader one finds a fictional avatar of the "antagonist" the *Essai* calls to appear on the textual "battlefield." This struggle is played out in all Diderot's works however, even in his apparently more sincere and intimate writing, such as the most self-revelatory texts addressed to friends (Grimm), a lover (Sophie Volland), and posterity. In the *Essai*, the presence of this sincere self results from a self-presentation that is an integral part of Diderot's attempt to fashion an effectively critical discourse. These instances of self-reference refer above all to a conflictual practice of representation, and Diderot's goal is to display what is most critically powerful in that practice. The power of the *Essai*, and which Diderot's commentators frequently enough are drawn in by, lies in its manner of presenting a subject one thinks one knows: the "real" Diderot. At the same time though, the *Essai* foregrounds that presentation, staging it artfully and theatrically, constantly shifting attention from the subject one thinks one knows to the practice producing such knowledge.

Is it possible not to be enmeshed in this practice? Does there exist a way of writing that can extricate itself from an adversarial reading? Is there a critical discourse that remains untouched by the power of critique, a manner of presenting knowledge that does not risk being re-presented by other manners and thus repositioned and disempowered? Diderot tries his own hand at asking these questions in two other early texts, the *Pensées philosophiques* and the *Promenade du sceptique.*

Allegorizing interpretation: "some fixed point"

The *Pensées philosophiques* begin tersely with the statement "J'écris de Dieu." This inaugural phrase establishes the text's referent and the philosophical position of deism it argues for: "I am writing *about* God." It also seeks to ground deist discourse, affirming that the latter originates *from* the position of God ("*de* Dieu"). Insofar as the discourse of deist faith is at one with God, that transcendental entity is instantiated by the very act of referring to it. No sooner though do these "philosophical thoughts" ground themselves through reference to God than a menacing presence appears, which threatens to destabilize an otherwise firm discursive foundation. "J'écris de Dieu; je compte sur peu de lecteurs, et n'aspire qu'à quelques suffrages. Si ces pensées ne plaisent à personne, elles pourront n'être que mauvaises; mais je les tiens pour détestables si elles plaisent à tout le monde" (I, 127). Despite the reference to an extratextual guarantor, these philosophical thoughts remain subject to an adversarial contingency, thematized here as reading.

A similar reference to the contingency of reading appears in the introduction to the *Essai sur le mérite et la vertu*: "Quiconque n'a pas la force ou le courage de suivre un raisonnement étendu peut se dispenser d'en commencer la lecture [de l'ouvrage], c'est pour d'autres que j'ai travaillé" (I, 300). Valorizing logic over style, philosophical rigor over esthetic pleasure, the demands of rational inquiry over the classical esthetics of well-wrought form, this characterization of the philosophical text expresses Enlightenment's desire to free itself from the constraints and limits of classicism. To realize its potential, Enlightenment critique must first undo the straitjacket of classical style. But can that critique free itself of its reception? Just as classical style reflects the codified attempt to control the contingent, to predetermine the effects of reception, here addressing an ideal reader by delegitimating improper ones anchors the text all the more inextricably in the contingency (of reading) that the deist moral philosopher of the *Pensées* wishes to avoid.

Like any discursive act, writing is a form of address that can never be controlled completely. The contingency of reading, which may produce the most improper responses, is a condition of all texts. The *Pensées philosophiques* recognize this condition, yet in a negative way. In an epigraph attributed to Persius, the *Pensées* pose the question of all texts: *Quis leget haec?* Who reads here? Placing this question in the margins, Diderot stages a marginal scene of reading that displays the paranoid fear of the improper reading. He characterizes this impropriety in terms of the pleasure such a reading produces, as if to suggest a fundamental incompatibility between the stern truths the *Pensées philosophiques* will state and a manner of receiving them marked by the pleasure it gives. Feared most of all is a reading drawn to the language in which such truths are stated, to plays on words and the play of words that gives pleasure to all but the most classically serious and unplayful of readers. Such fears are not totally ungrounded, for if the discourse of truth had to confront itself in its language, its materiality, it would also have to recognize itself as an art, one of contingencies and not absolutes. Later texts will stage this confrontation far differently. But here, in order to begin writing (about God and divine truths), Diderot experiments with a manner of writing that seeks, unsuccessfully, to place itself above and beyond the mediating contingency of its reading.

Ultimately, the *Pensées philosophiques* are about a type of discourse called philosophy. "Il y a, je le répète, des lecteurs dont je ne veux ni ne voudrais jamais; je n'écris que pour ceux avec qui je serais bien aise de m'entretenir. J'adresse mes ouvrages aux philosophes; il n'y a guère d'autres hommes au monde pour moi (1, 414–15). The exclusionary gesture that delegitimates certain readers and readings founds the claim to be a philosopher, which here at least can only be made negatively. Reference to an ideal reader-*philosophe* delegitimates all other kinds of reading, especially those that take this text to be anything other than a philosophical conversation among like-minded men.

Excluded above all is the illegitimate reading that senses in this delimitation of reading the desire to circumscribe philosophy's relation to a certain dialogical alterity. Such a reading counters its exclusion by remarking that the discourse purporting to speak (of) truth always remains vulnerable to the disruptive threat that comes not from outside but from within, lodged in the discursive practice designed to found philosophy legitimately as such. The claim to truth made by the kind of philosopher Diderot's text presents here, who wishes only to dialogue with his peers, is founded on discursive ventriloquism. If the only interlocutors to which such a philosopher seeks to speak are like him, then the sole interlocutor he desires is himself. To become the philosopher you desire, even truth must speak through you, no matter how humbly you claim to be but its conduit. Philosophy must refuse this rejoinder, for it means there can be no way of distinguishing truly between speaking truth and forcing it to speak with a disguised voice. Such truths cannot be those of an extradiscursive entity, an essence that language could reveal. Rather, such truths could only refer to an object presented as knowable through the discursive practice that invents it.[18] The question Diderot's text asks then is whether the philosopher's project of speaking (of) truth must not always go awry, short-circuited by the very acts of language that provide the sole way to guarantee its realization.

Diderot's manner of phrasing this question suggests that to attain truth, philosophy must present itself as the monologue of truth by suppressing the dialogical within itself. Through one of monological discourse's most repressive ruses, this alterity is made to appear as that which is different from truth, outside it or at least able to be separated from it through a process that founds the possibility of critique. In its staging of this exclusionary separation, Diderot's text suggests though that this alterity is in fact the condition for figuring truth, for materializing it and making it "presentable." Alterity, then, is perhaps the name philosophical discourse gives its own artful practice. Yet the more philosophical discourse presents itself as situated above and beyond this practice, unable to be resituated by others' reference to its own artful practice, the more it anchors itself in the discursive situation it seeks to escape or at least control.

Distinct from the inaugural scenes of writing and reading in the *Pensées philosophiques*, Diderot's text stages a series of debates among spokespersons for various philosophical positions such as deism, atheism, and skepticism. Clearly, Diderot wishes to affirm the preeminence of the deist position. Yet his careful elaboration of the skeptic's argument indicates if not sympathy towards it, then at least the possibility that doubt rather than disbelief poses the most serious challenge to deist philosophy. Linking this argument to the staging of philosophical discourse in the text's opening phrases, one might say that the most radical challenge Diderot senses in his encounter with skepticism involves doubting a particular manner of philosophizing.

The exclusionary gesture of delegitimating certain kinds of readings amounts to a negative and ultimately ineffective attempt to contain this doubt, marking all the more a corrosive contingency that can never be controlled absolutely. Gravitating towards a philosophy of materialism, Diderot will skeptically question the premises of deism. Moreover, skepticism concerning the formal, discursive mechanisms of philosophizing will provide the means for resituating the philosophical project and for inventing a different philosophical practice. Experimenting with a way to capitalize on this skepticism, immediately after the *Pensées philosophiques* Diderot writes the *Promenade du sceptique*, in which he experiments far more productively with the practice of critical discourse.

The *Promenade* brings together the characters of pyrrhonist, atheist, skeptic, spinozist, and deist. It marches them through a garden of eighteenth-century philosophy in which nature constitutes a vast "livre allégorique." Unlike the pithy *Pensées philosophiques*, the *Promenade* displays a certain plodding, didactic inelegence. This has led Diderot's commentators to regard the text as the heavy-handed effort of a young writer still seeking the right style, genre or form for his ideas. In this view, allegory represents Diderot's unengaging and unsuccessful experimentation with a genre to which eighteenth-century writers and readers (as well as modern ones) are generally ill-disposed.

The *Promenade*'s central allegory invites one to understand the term "skepticism" as a philosopheme, signifying a specific philosophical idea or concept. Yet the manner in which Diderot's text stages that concept suggests that this understanding of skepticism is a limited, restrictive one. For in addition to its central allegory, the *Promenade* also contains a brief introductory dialogue or fictional frame that sets the stage for the apparently more philosophical discussion that follows. It is here, on the fictional, literary borders of the philosophical text proper, that a skeptical act takes place, one more radical than any conceptual statement of skepticism. This act opens a breach in the garden of philosophy, and through this opening it signifies Diderot's working out of a different kind of critical practice.

The *Promenade*'s introductory dialogue joins Cléobule, a *philosophe* who has retreated from society to the calm and security of the country, and the *militaire philosophe* Ariste, his youthful, impetuous, and more worldly admirer. The subject of their dialogue – and their disagreement – concerns philosophy's social and ethical ends. Ariste wishes to have Cléobule's philosophical reflections published so that more than their small circle of friends may benefit from his wisdom. Refusing to consent to this venture, Cléobule points out its dangers.

> Vous n'avez pas seulement affaire à des gens qui ne savent rien, mais à des gens qui ne veulent rien savoir. On peut détromper celui dont l'erreur est involontaire; mais par quel endroit attaquer celui qui est en garde contre le sens commun. Ne vous attendez donc pas que votre ouvrage serve beaucoup aux autres; mais craignez qu'il ne vous nuise infiniment à vous-même (I, 181).

Undaunted by the threat of potential adversaries, Ariste remains determined to produce a work of merit and to avoid persecution. To do so, he concludes he must find a powerful benefactor, behind whose name he can shield himself.

This short introduction frames the *Promenade*'s central section, which according to this fiction Ariste finally publishes. Through its form (dialogue) and thematic oppositions (age/youth, private/public, wisdom/impetuousness, meditation/activity, speech/writing, country/town, and knowledge/error), the introductory section inscribes the *Promenade* in the traditional genre of the philosophical dialogue. This framing fiction is thus more than a simple stylistic embellishment, for it establishes the conditions and circumstances in which philosophizing will take place. The more literary elements here, such as fictive characters, places, and events, are not just props on a stage set for philosophy though. Rather, they signify the manner in which the literary provides the necessary material for presenting philosophy. Distinct from the philosophical *énoncé* or conceptual statement, this fiction foregrounds philosophical *énonciation*, the discursive apparatus in and through which the statement is produced, the art and techniques through which philosophy is performed.[19] If, as Diderot writes in the *Commentaire sur Hemsterhuis*, "le philosophe veut être vrai," the *Promenade* shows that more important than the philosopher's desire for truth (or, for that matter, any judgment we might make concerning the *sincerity* of an author's desire) is the discursive, literary, artistic framework that refers to truth, a framework that simultaneously marks the limiting conditions of such reference. The *Promenade*'s more radical skepticism, then, is of a self-reflexive nature, a manner of questioning the means whereby the philosophical desire for truth takes form.

In the case of Cléobule, this desire leads him to withdraw from public space and retreat to the private space of the philosophical garden. Representing a common pre-Enlightenment solution to the tension between public and private, this retreat defines both the philosopher and a certain type of philosophizing.[20] Through Cléobule's retreat to the philosophical garden a symbolic space is invented, in which philosophy can situate itself in relation to what is figured as outside it. In this exteriority, philosophy situates certain institutions, powers, and tensions, presenting them as absent from the philosophical garden, set apart by the act of personal will that is the philosopher's retreat. The real retreat lies in philosophy's refusal to confront the possibility that this exteriority is a fabrication, a paradoxical *hors-texte* that the text of philosophy itself invents, thereby reaffirming the disruptive power of all that it would retreat from.

This is precisely the situation Diderot stages in the *Promenade* and reworks through the character Ariste. A *militaire philosophe*, Ariste moves between two spaces, which explains why the distinction between private and public is both more difficult for him to maintain and less desirable than for Cléobule. To be sure, Ariste still presents things as if this separation were simply a matter of individual choice, as if the philosopher (and philosophy) were free to invent their own domain, distinct from that of the public. Yet what he chooses is to refuse Cléobule's retreat, undertaking to publish and thus make philosophy public. Characteristic of the Enlightenment's repositioning of its own place and its reworking of a critical practice, Ariste's decision to disseminate Cléobule's meditations inscribes philosophy within a public, social, and political arena. Indeed, Diderot's invention of the character Ariste suggests a philosophical practice that recognizes it has always been located in that public arena. The notion of the private space of philosophy "proper" is but an ideal fiction designed to camouflage the imbrication of philosophical discourse within what it claims to be above or different from.

In the dialogue between Cléobule and Ariste, the *Promenade* stages once again the relation between philosophy and what it takes as its other, between a conceptual discourse concerned with the question of truth, and discursive, textual self-reflexivity. Furthermore, by staging this relation as a conflictual one, Diderot seeks to establish a critical position with respect to the discourse that claims knowledge of truth. In the dialogue between Cléobule and Ariste a conflictual encounter occurs between a *clio-bulla*, a sealed history or story that cannot or should not be told, and the *aristos*, the story's best judge, pupil or listener. Yet the best is not good enough, or not strong enough, since Ariste/*aristos* must ally himself with force, *cratia*, that of an aristocratic protector, in order to publish Cléobule's philosophical writings. As his name suggests, Ariste must become an artist, an artful philosopher.[21] Described as a *philosophe militaire*, Ariste engages himself (and philosophy) in the play of forces that philosphy can neither retreat from nor dispense with.

The *Promenade* represents at least one strand in the tangled skein of the Enlightenment's relation to power. When defined in sociopolitical terms, power is commonly seen as vested in individuals, groups, and institutions. Yet it materializes in other ways, which such a definition tends to idealize. One such materialization takes place in the *Promenade*, although not in a simply referential sense. Diderot's text does more than thematize the Enlightenment's strategic complicity with power, for it also presents the attempt to empower critical discourse, and in a way that forces a confrontation within philosophy itself. As writer, Ariste seeks to invert or circumvent the interlocutor's power and the threat of violence awaiting the writer *beyond* discourse; he does so by capitalizing on force *through* and *within* discourse. Ariste figures a critical discourse that no longer forecloses the issue of its reception and the question of its own artful status. Whereas Cléobule understands power as being vested in the outsider to the philosophical garden, Ariste conceives of power differently. Refusing to treat power as unbefitting philosophy, the artful Ariste figures an empowerment of critical discourse achieved only by capitalizing on the undeniable link between the twin practices of philosophy and power.

In writing, Ariste will attempt to find "dans les airs quelque point fixe hors de la portée [des] traits [des adversaires], d'où l'on puisse leur annoncer la vérité" (I, 181). This "point fixe" where truth can powerfully and effectively be presented is none other than the artful text. Thus, the most far-reaching skepticism in the *Promenade* consists of the literary, theatrical manner in which philosophical discourse is produced here. Foregrounding that production, Diderot's text questions whether philosophical discourse can ever realize its critical potential without embracing its artful, technical side. Can reference to what Ariste (and Diderot) call truth be effectively empowered without embracing the means that make such reference possible? This is the question posed by the *Promenade*'s introductory dialogue, which stages the text's most interesting allegory by far as a self-reflexive story about the enabling conditions of critical discourse. In calling Diderot's art of philosophizing allegorical, I do not mean it presents an enigma – the text – that must be deciphered in exegetical fashion. At issue in this art is less the establishing of meaning than those acts making meanings possible – in both Diderot's text and his reader's – whatever these meanings might be. These are self-reflexive acts, but in a technical, discursive sense rather than in a psychological or ontological one, as is highlighted in the following passage from the *Discours préliminaire* to the *Promenade*.

"Les prétendus connaisseurs en fait de style chercheront vainement à me déchiffrer." In this passage boasting of stylistic skills, Diderot takes a jibe at his censor, who in fact failed to realize the *Promenade* had been written by the author of the *Pensées philosophiques*, which was publicly condemned by Parlement. The passage refers to another form of censorship, however, less egregiously partisan perhaps, yet still a policing performed by those readers seeking to "decipher" the text in their search for the subject that produces it.[22] These "prétendus connaisseurs en fait de style" base their reading on the claim to know how language works, especially how it reveals the writer, that instance of subjectivity behind or beyond language. Yet Diderot's text thwarts this kind of reading, claiming its search to be "in vain." Resisting the attempt to "decipher" it, Diderot's text marks the limits of the kind of knowledge that chooses to ignore or fails to account for the way knowledge is produced. That is, it contests the way of phrasing things that includes no reference to the art of phrasing, to the technical, performative aspect of language through which the presentation of knowledge occurs.

In this resistance lies the critical potential of the art of philosophizing with which Diderot experiments. Marking this self-reflexive turn in various ways, he seeks to invent a way of presenting knowledge that is better able to resist, counter, and situate other claims of knowledge, made in his own texts and his readers'. So far we have encountered this self reflexive turn primarily in the margins of the early texts, in a translator's preface and notes, in first lines and an epigraph, and in an introductory dialogue. This self-reflexive turn will become a far more central concern, as Diderot seeks to capitalize on its potential for the critical practice of knowledge.

Naturalizing interpretation: nature writing

Diderot's involvement with the *Encyclopédie* project brought him into direct contact with the most contemporary of developments in the eighteenth-century sciences. As a result, he questions the idea of a nature whose well-structured order reveals a divine imprint, a natural rationality that faith alone makes believable. Stemming from this encounter with contemporary scientific thought, *De l'interprétation de la nature* reflects

Diderot's keen interest in emerging areas of scientific experimentation such as obstetrics, electricity, magnetism, and metallurgy. This text also formulates a new and experimental methodology designed to improve research and accelerate scientific progress.[23] More important is the way Diderot phrases this methodology, making *De l'interprétation* as much an experimental text as one about scientific experimentation. It formulates not only a properly scientific method for interpreting nature, but also a manner of philosophizing more in touch with the "new" nature contemporary science makes knowable.

"Nous touchons au moment d'une grande révolution dans les sciences," Diderot writes, referring to the break Enlightenment science makes with past forms of knowledge and the emergence of new fields of knowledge such as chemistry, natural history, and biology. The appearance of these fields betokens a shift towards apparently more objective, more scientific, in short more modern forms of knowledge. Diderot marks this shift by opposing two types of philosophy. The first, "rational philosophy," valorizes absolute judgments over hypotheses, abstract speculation instead of empirical experimentation, explanations of phenomena based on *a priori* notions of final causes instead of direct observation and intuition ("génie"). In place of "rational philosophy," Diderot proposes a second practice of knowledge, termed "experimental philosophy." The latter holds the potential to reveal the workings of a nature unknowable to "rational philosophy." For Diderot, this scientific revolution results above all from a different way of practicing science, indeed from an understanding of science *as practice*, a discursive procedure designed to make things knowable. If knowledge practices of the past must be discarded, it is not because they produce erroneous knowledge, but rather because they are less operative, less effective ways of producing the knowledge Diderot (and the Enlightenment) wish. All science involves a particular representational practice, all forms of knowledge result from techniques of presenting the subject and object of knowledge. The most critical shift *De l'interprétation* testifies to involves epistemology and not science exclusively, for it concerns knowledge of the practice that makes representing scientific knowledge possible.

Diderot lays out the critical consequences of this insight in his discussion of mathematics. Countering the centuries-old belief in geometry as the abstracted reflection of the divinely created and perfect order of the universe, he defines geometry's truths as resulting from an arbitrary, human practice, from invention rather than from revelatory discovery. Mathematics, he claims, resembles a game ("un jeu"); it is "une affaire de conventions." Consequently, the practitioner of knowledge can freely change the rules of the game, inventing new practices and reshaping the playing field (of knowledge). As a result, other practices such as mathematics are revealed to be limited and nonpertinent. "La région des mathématiciens est un monde intellectuel, où ce que l'on prend pour des vérités rigoureuses perd absolument cet avantage quand on l'apporte sur notre terre" (IX, 28). Mathematics cannot account for the phenomenon of nature as the Enlightenment sciences were coming to perceive it. A pre-Enlightenment mechanistic science of bodies in space fails to explain the dynamic transformation of living beings over time. The world Descartes lays out in *Le Monde* and that Cartesian science represents may result from "rigorous truths," yet that world remains an "intellectual" one, a pure ideality. "La *chose* du mathématicien n'a pas plus d'existence dans la nature que celle du joueur" (IX, 29).

Does the "thing" Enlightenment science makes knowable actually exist in nature, whereas prior scientific practices present only ideal, speculative abstractions? Does Enlightenment science take us a step closer to knowledge of objective reality, in all its concrete materiality? Diderot (and perhaps we too) might wish to believe so. And yet his critique of mathematics suggests that all science is an "affaire de conventions," that is, a representational practice. Thus, the objects such practices produce, knowledge of any kind, could never exist in nature. Enlightenment science does provide knowledge of the real, yet a constructed one whose reality stems from the material practice producing it. Such a reality can be known, but only in relation to the discourse in which it has its place as representation.

By resituating the productive instance of knowledge, Diderot gains critical distance from the epistemological paradigm of mathematics, which he criticizes as "une métaphysique générale, où les corps sont dépouillés de leurs qualités individuelles" (IX, 29). Moreover, he freely imagines other paradigms, other discursive models such as "experimental philosophy," this new scientific method that enables nature to be presented otherwise. In this text and throughout his writing Diderot attempts to find a means of restoring these qualities to "les corps," to the natural body and the body of nature. His search occurs moreover through an experimental practice, a representational technique, located in the text rather than the laboratory. This is why in order to formulate and exemplify the new practice of knowledge Diderot imagines, he must take up the question of language.

What kind of language can explain the new nature the Enlightenment life sciences refer to? Can such an object even be represented and made knowable? "Si les phénomènes ne sont pas enchaînés les uns aux autres, il n'y a point de philosophie. Les phénomènes seraient tous echaînés, que l'état de chacun d'eux pourrait être sans permanence. Mais si l'état des êtres est dans une vicissitude perpétuelle; si la nature est encore à l'ouvrage; malgré la chaîne qui lie les phénomènes, il n'y a point de philosophie. Toute notre science naturelle devient aussi transitoire que les mots" (IX, 94). If there exists no causal link joining natural phenomena, no structuring order to things, the philosopher is out of business. Nor can philosophy exist if the structuring linkage of things is constantly changing, if nature is a process rather than an object. Threatening the discourse of knowledge is the possibility that a dynamic nature simply cannot be known. In attempting to explain not being but becoming, the discourse of knowledge risks losing any solid ground, becoming as fleeting and transitory as language itself.

In raising this issue in 1753, Diderot is perhaps a step behind the Enlightenment life sciences. Experimental scientists already conceived of nature as existing in a state of dynamic flux, "une vicissitude perpétuelle." "Tout change, tout passe, il n'y a que le tout qui reste," exclaims the dreaming D'Alembert in *Le Rêve de D'Alembert*, expressing geometry's worst nightmare. This "ever-changing all" is simply a fact of life for Dr Bordeu though, the spokesman in *Le Rêve* for the leading edge of knowledge in the natural sciences. Yet the manner in which Diderot poses the problem of representing this kind of nature, in *Le Rêve* and elsewhere, situates him not so much behind the life sciences of his time as at one remove from them. His constant linking of epistemology and language suggests the real issue involved in any interpretation of nature is not so much scientific as discursive.

An inaugural text, *De l'interprétation* has been called an Enlightenment discourse on method.[24] Diderot's text resembles Descartes' above all in the self-reflexive way it links knowledge and discourse. Descartes founds the truth of the *cogito* in the discursive performance of its being, of its being presented in the autobiographical text.[25] Similarly, Diderot proposes that the real power of the life sciences and epistemological discourse in general lies in their capacity to invent a new way to represent nature, by means of a discursive method whose very performativity makes nature knowable. The scientific, epistemological, and philosophical problem of knowing nature converges with the discursive problem of presenting it. The most pertinent question Diderot raises here thus concerns not what nature is, but rather the manner in which reference to that object is made. Consequently, it is not entirely correct to say that *De l'interprétation* replaces one form of knowledge with another, "old" science with "new." It critically displaces science in general by presenting another way of understanding the production of (scientific) knowledge.

This chapter began by considering how Diderot destabilizes the hierarchical relation between science and art by suggesting instead that they may be linked in a single representational practice of knowledge. This linkage produces various displacement effects, one of which is to reveal the limits of the kind of knowledge practice that ignores its own performativity, suppressing or attempting to eliminate the means whereby reference to that practice can be made. In the manner whereby Diderot stages scenes of writing and reading, the effects of this displacement are not limited to or contained within his text proper, for they occur in other texts as well, resulting from those interpretive acts Diderot's readers also perform. As Diderot's text shows, the critical power of such acts can be judged by the extent to which they capitalize on their own performative potential to mark the limits of knowledge, be it that produced by other practices of knowledge or by their own.

Let us consider a final question that *De l'interprétation* raises, and which is the limit question of Enlightenment. How is one to define this marking of the limits of knowledge? What sort of understanding can grasp it? If, in reading (Diderot), we sense something at work that marks the limits of knowledge, how can this sensation be phrased, without inevitably presenting it in recognizable fashion, as an object of cognition, in short as yet another instance of knowledge that in its affirmation must ignore its own understanding of (its) limits?

We can begin to play out this question by suggesting that this critical marking of limits cannot truly be defined, that is, phrased in terms of truth. A definition is a performative statement, a particular variety of speech act to which the criterion of truth does not pertain. What one knows through definitions is perhaps only that a speech act is being performed, if indeed this is still knowing in a strict sense. What *happens* though as Diderot defines nature in *De l'interprétation* is that a shift occurs from a declarative mode to a performative one, a turn from knowledge presented to the discursive act of its presentation. In the (re)turn to discourse, this *vicis* (turn, change) involving a displacement of knowledge that positions it squarely in the "vicissitudes" of its discursive situation, *De l'interprétation* presents a knowledge of nature – and the nature of knowledge – that has become "aussi transitoire que les mots."

In this text situated on the limits of the discourse of scientific knowledge, Diderot marks the limit of epistemological discourse in general, the impossibility of presenting knowledge in declarative fashion, as if it involved a purely cognitive, nondiscursive activity. Furthermore, he reaches this limit through a manner that may be the very condition for the "new" science *De l'interprétation* refers to, through another way of phrasing knowledge. "C'est de la nature que je vais écrire. Je laisserai les pensées se succéder sous ma plume, dans l'ordre même selon lequel les objets se sont offerts à ma réflexion, parce qu'elles n'en représenteront que mieux les mouvements et la marche de mon esprit" (IX, 27). Read all too frequently from either a narrow stylistic perspective or a broad psychological one,[26] this reference to the manner in which Diderot writes about nature frames the knowledge *De l'interprétation* provides. This framing brings about a shift from the conceptual knowledge interpretation produces to the discursive practice producing that knowledge. More important still, by doubling reference to the object of knowledge ("nature") with reference to the practice in which the presentation of that knowledge takes place, *De l'interprétation* effectively reworks the field of knowledge. In order to write "de la nature," Diderot cannot just write "about" it, that is, as if he were outside it, as if the subject of knowledge occupied some transcendental position from which to survey, master, and comprehend nature. Rather, Diderot will write "de la nature," from *within* it, so to speak, thereby marking the link between knowledge and its object. Diderot's insight here is to refuse the kind of knowledge that claims to know nature *as such*, and he does so in the name of another kind of knowledge, that of nature as representation.

This explains his insistence on the need to write a text displaying what he calls "ma réflexion" and "les mouvements et la marche de mon esprit." Terms such as "réflexion," "pensées," and "esprit" do not refer to a mental operation that can be understood independently from what Diderot calls writing. Both are instances of a representational practice. We may take the products of this practice to be ideal, essential entities (thought, self-consciousness, knowledge). Yet what Diderot's text shows is how such entities are but inevitably limited ways of phrasing a linkage to what is called "nature." Consequently, the most productive manner of intellectual speculation can occur only in the specular text, which seeks to perform the dynamic working of "thought." For this is the kind of practice that can "know" a nature in constant flux, that can join with it and become "of" nature and part of its presentation.

The limit question we as readers of Diderot's text can pose concerns how to phrase what can be sensed to be at work in this attempt to be "of nature." The question moreover is Diderot's own. As he turns from deism and idealism towards sensationalism and materialism, he too will seek to find a way to "phrase sensation." To limit this search to his attempt to formulate a coherent *theory* of materialism, as one would say in the intellectual historical idiom, is to fail to grasp a far more significant materialism, palpably at work in the workings of his texts and which resists the attempt to contain it. The story of the passage from the idealism of seventeenth-century Cartesianism to the more materially oriented empiricism and sensationalism of the eighteenth-century Enlightenment makes sense in terms of a grand, progressive, teleological history. Yet it is far less effective at articulating the enabling conditions of such a history, be it produced by the Enlightenment or by its heirs. By telling such a story one misapprehends the relation between Diderot's experimentations and the production of critical knowledge, not only as it takes place in his texts but also as it bears upon that of interpretation.

Diderot's early texts mark as many attempts to invent a "style" or "genre." Yet they signal more than formal experimentation and thus cannot be treated adequately in terms of an esthetics of form. In these early texts as in all his writing, Diderot seeks to empower knowledge by displaying its art, by reflecting (upon) its practice, by staging it as an artful practice. In other words these endeavors to empower knowledge lead to the limits of knowledge, to the point where only another more artful manner of presenting things can account most forcefully for what Diderot *senses*. This other manner can be elaborated only once Diderot addresses the question of interpreting nature, raising it both conceptually (what is nature?) and practically (how can I write of nature?). Furthermore, the consequences of this turn towards nature, and which also bears on the practice of interpreting it, involve the epistemology of a natural science as well as an ethics and an esthetics. *De l'interprétation* breaks with the moral philosophy of the texts preceding it, at the same time resituating the question of moral philosophy in general. For Diderot, any moral philosophy will be groundless so long as it remains uncoupled from the question of that practice whereby knowledge of the material world is produced.

De l'interprétation is thus a watershed text, and in several senses. Marking a turn towards natural science, it signals the beginning of Diderot's lifelong testing of "the materialist thesis." More important, the statement "c'est de la nature que je vais écrire" announces the topic of all his future writing. From this text onwards, he will not cease to experiment with ways of linking nature and writing, that is, on the one hand the object of knowledge grasped, if not known, in its material phenomenality, and on the other its presentation, which takes place in an experimental, artful practice. With increasing intensity Diderot senses that in the absence of such linkage, knowledge knows little, so to speak, and that the cognitive claims made in its name rest on shaky ground. It is premature to say whether he succeeds in grounding questions of moral philosophy raised in the early texts – and throughout his writing – on the way he chose to interpret nature, and which goes by the shorthand name of materialism. It is equally premature to say whether the manner in which he experiments with a more materialist presentation of things in fact "ungrounds" moral philosophy. Let us say rather, anticipating the following chapter, that this experimentation marks a redirected attempt to empower knowledge by linking it more materially to mechanisms of the body and the text, mechanisms that function to make the object of knowledge graspable.

CHAPTER 3

The matter of judgment and the art of phrasing sensation

> If the body had been easier to understand, nobody would have thought that we had a mind.
>
> Richard Rorty, *Philosophy and the Mirror of Nature*

> The body is to be compared, not to a physical object, but to a work of art.
>
> Maurice Merleau-Ponty

The humanist idealism Diderot and his contemporaries inherited attributed to the mind the regal privilege of making visible the rational order of things. Tirelessly constructing elaborate systems, Cartesian science and philosophy sought to comprehend nature by representing it as an object of vision. The work of reason and the act of revelation thus were not incompatible, since the Cartesian mind viewed matter as passive and inert, as bearing the unchanging imprint of an eternal, divinely created order that the mind could demonstrate and thus reflect. Enlightenment philosophy and science increasingly questioned such an ideal order, as well as the preeminent place accorded to the Cartesian notion of mind. Seeking to grasp an active, dynamic nature, the Enlightenment discourse of knowledge formulated other manners of presenting the relation between the human subject and the material world.

This experimentation occurs already in Diderot's earliest writings on nature. In the *Encyclopédie* article "*Animal*," for instance, he proposes that nature is essentially continuous, distinctions between animate and inanimate, animal and human, marking only a different degree of natural organization. The *Lettre sur les aveugles* also presents the human subject as part of one great whole and possessing no guarantee of a preestablished order to things grounded on some divine entity or transcendental principle. Lacking faith in such an order, Diderot turns to sensationalism, according to which all knowledge is derived from the interaction between the senses and the material world. Ultimately, he seeks to expand sensationalism into a more encompassing materialism that attributes an active, organizing, and meaning-giving causality to matter itself.

The material determination of both being and knowledge is a question Diderot grapples with constantly. It appears explicitly in *Le Rêve de D'Alembert*, the *Eléments de physiologie*, the *Réfutation d'Helvétius*, the *Commentaire sur Hemsterhuis*, and less directly in countless other texts, such as the *Lettres à Sophie Volland*, the *Paradoxe sur le comédien*, and *Le Neveu de Rameau*. Interestingly enough, none of these texts were published during Diderot's lifetime, the *Eléments* appearing a century after his death, for example, and the *Commentaire* only in 1964. This publishing history, comprising delays and discoveries, misrepresentations and vitriolic hostility, explains (yet only partially) why earlier readers had to misapprehend a "materialist" Diderot that for them remained unknowable. That Diderot now exists. To grasp his materialism in all its intensity, however, present-day readers must first pose the question of how to read these so-called materialist texts.

Above all, Diderot's manner must be considered, the way he engages in a "questionnement continu sur le réel à interpréter."[1] As the *Réfutation* of Helvétius' *De l'homme* reveals, Diderot was more skeptical than many of his philosophical fellow travelers regarding any consolidated, overarching theory of materialism. And he was far more hesitant than Helvétius to draw certain ethical and political consequences from such a theory. For Helvétius, to sense is to judge. Consequently, by modifying the type of sensations an individual receives one can modify the individual. Things are not so simple for Diderot. "Si, partant du seul phénomène de la sensibilité physique, propriété générale de la matière ou résultat de l'organisation, [Helvétius] en eût déduit avec clarté toutes les opérations de l'entendement, il eût fait une chose neuve, difficile et belle."[2]

Given Helvétius' rigidly mechanistic, behaviorist explanation of human thought and action, he will claim that personal happiness and social harmony can best be achieved under a political system of enlightened despotism. In response, Diderot repeatedly invokes the complex particularity of human thoughts, experiences, and emotions. Paul Vernière correctly notes that Diderot found no adequate explanation for such particularities in the Enlightenment sciences, and thus could not accept them as the basis for the ethical and political conclusions Helvétius draws from the sensationalist premise. Yet Diderot's sense of the limits of scientific knowledge also involves the manner in which such knowledge is presented. Vernière is thus incorrect (or too unnuanced) when he claims that "Diderot veut une explication totale de l'homme."[3] What Diderot's writings on nature suggest is not that more knowledge is required to explain the complexity of the human subject, but rather knowledge of a different sort, phrased in other manners.

This is why Diderot's refutation of Helvétius extends to the very genre and idiom adopted. Helvétius' work, he notes,

> est très méthodique, et c'est un de ses défauts principaux; premièrement, parce que la méthode, quand elle est d'appareil, refroidit, appesantit, et ralentit. Secondement, parce qu'elle ôte à tout l'air de liberté et de génie ... Un auteur paradoxal ne doit jamais dire son mot, mais toujours ses preuves: il doit entrer furtivement dans l'âme de son lecteur, et non de vive force. C'est le grand art de Montaigne qui ne veut jamais prouver, et qui va toujours prouvant, et me ballotant du blanc au noir, et du noir au blanc (IX, 310).

Knowledge must be experimented with as an "art," through trials or *essais* as Montaigne calls them. Only thus can the "artist" of knowledge paradoxically prove things most effectively by refusing to prove in proper methodical fashion. Diderot's art is not that of methodical demonstration. Just as he contests the political regime of despotism, so too his art contests the discursive regime of despotic method. More "furtive," more "paradoxical," it "shakes up" the very place where demonstrations of method are founded by shifting attention towards other ways of phrasing knowledge. Consequently, Diderot is not only more skeptical than other proponents of the sensationalist thesis, he is also more audacious. Unlike Helvétius, La Mettrie, d'Holbach or Condillac, he shows little interest in trying his hand at philosophy's noble genre, the systematic treatise. He turns instead to marginal genres, such as letters, dialogues, tales, and commentaries, to experiment with other manners of posing the question of the material.

One consequence of this experimentation is that an art of philosophizing about the material is present not only in texts referring explicitly to a theory of materialism. In the *Salons*, for instance, the treatment of art – as topic but also as material substance – involves an esthetics of the material as important for grasping Diderot's materialism as anything written in the *Eléments de physiologie* or the *Commentaire*. Similarly, in *Le Rêve de D'Alembert* Diderot stages in the most theatrical of fashions the intractable problem of sensationalism: how to make sense of the sensing, sensuous body. From the *Lettre sur les aveugles* to *Jacques le fataliste*, from the dry descriptions of the *Eléments de physiologie* to the juicier fictions of *Le Supplément au voyage de Bougainville*, *La Religieuse* and *Le Neveu de Rameau*, the question of the material repeatedly returns, as Diderot artfully experiments with ways of phrasing sensation.

Lacking a systematic exposition of Diderot's materialist theory, interpreters initially turned to the more literary, fictional, and poetic aspects of his texts, rephrasing them in a more expository and theoretical idiom. In their rush to synthesis, interpreters displayed a haste uncharacteristic of Diderot, whose eponymous character in *Le Rêve* states, "notre véritable sentiment n'est pas celui dans lequel nous n'avons jamais vacillé, mais celui auquel nous sommes le plus habituellement revenus" (XVII, 113). More seriously, they tended to misapprehend the "vicissitudes" of Diderot's writing, its idiomatic and constantly experimental marginality with respect to the theoretical genre. Diderot's theory of materialism has been extracted from *Le Rêve*, for instance, but often enough at the price of failing to understand the text's hybrid genre, the manner in which it stages the matter it treats, the human body. This situation may be changing. Most readers of *Le Rêve* would now no longer classify it as "lyric philosophy, with all its poetic excess."[4] No longer cordoning off "the poetic" in Diderot's texts to read him as a philosopher in his own right, interpreters have realized the impossibility of such an exclusion.[5] "The poetic" in Diderot's writing cannot be put aside as "excessive" with respect to his materialism, for it signals the latter's most challenging aspect.

It should be stressed that Diderot's materialism is not the same as his theory of materialism. His texts contain statements that seem to spring from the desire to theorize, to account for particularities through conceptual formulations, to provide an explanatory master discourse concerning particular objects, individuals, and events, finally to present a way of judging things in cognitive fashion. Yet the most bracing aspect of Diderot's materialism cannot be understood by assuming that his texts stem from a desire to theorize. Diderot's materialism involves above all the artful, material practice of engaging the material in a way that does not and cannot seek to transcend it. Any theory of materialism ascribed to Diderot can at best point to that practice, but by rephrasing it and thereby mistaking it for something else, such as Diderot's thought, his idea or concept of the material.

More seriously, reading Diderot as a theorist of materialism recontains the manner in which he engages the material, as if it were necessary to neutralize the consequences of that engagement for the practice of interpretation. Thus, statements referring to Diderot's theory of materialism reflect in all likelihood the theoretical desire of whoever makes them, and not any essential desire to theorize on Diderot's part. Desirous of theory, Diderot's reader will misapprehend his art of philosophizing and the importance of its marginality with respect to the theoretical idiom. As Diderot seeks not to lose touch with the manner in which the material can be presented, his experimentations at times resemble the idiom of theory. In the most gripping of cases, however, they also contest it and make tangible its limits. These limits take shape in matter(s) that cannot be theorized, at least not without translating them into another idiom, conceptualizing them according to the rules of another genre. By attending to Diderot's own idiom, through which he seeks to invent a way to take a critical distance from the theoretical idiom, the force of his materialism can best be gauged, a materialism that is not so much a concept of philosophy as a manner of being.

A traditional understanding of the relation between form and content is of little help in formulating this manner. According to Jacques Proust one must

> cesser de penser à part le noyau philosophique que ses œuvres peuvent contenir et l'enveloppe littéraire – ou poétique–, qu'il aurait donné à ce noyau, pour en considérer au contraire *l'équivalence* ontologique. Car le rapport du "poétique" au "philosophique" n'est pas chez Diderot celui qu'un contenant entretient avec son contenu. Ce n'est pas non plus – ou plutôt ce n'est pas seulement – une opposition entre deux manières de formuler, d'exprimer les choses. C'est aussi, c'est d'abord une différence entre deux manières de les *concevoir* . . .[6]

For Proust, Diderot is an "authentic philosopher" because of the way he reworks the hierarchical relation between "the philosophical" and "the poetic," presenting them instead as indissociably entwined. The philosophical desire for the truth of things cannot be severed from, nor can it ever get beyond, the richly inventive act and art of (re)presenting them, of giving them (another) material form in language.

Diderot's language is as inventive, as creative, and thus as poetic as the material nature he sensed at work and sought to work with in his art. This poetic inventiveness, this creative dynamics, is what defines Diderot's "philosophical language," which, as Georges Benrekassa suggestively maintains, "reste sans cesse à inventer, et, chaque fois, à côté de tous les usages recensés du langage."[7] What matters for Diderot is not so much a theory of materialism *in* the text as the material *of* the text. Turning to the *Lettre sur les aveugles* and the *Lettre sur les sourds et muets*, two of many experiments in posing the problem of the material, we encounter the beginnings of Diderot's "materialist thought" and the materiality of (his) thinking, in the art and manner in which what matters is phrased.

The body of the letter (I)

The *Lettre sur les aveugles* is Diderot's earliest sustained exploration of the sensationalist hypothesis which by 1749 had become common currency among French materialist philosophers. Roughly a century earlier, Descartes had already been criticized for according such primacy to mind that his explanation of understanding could be maintained only by appealing to divine intervention in the form of innate ideas existing prior to all experience. Numerous philosophers refused that primacy, arguing instead that knowledge derives from sense impressions and not from an ideal, divine causality. (Diderot too rejects Cartesian idealism, claiming that in invoking the notion of the soul to explain understanding, Descartes employs "un mot vide de sens.") A hypothetical test case for the sensationalist argument was the celebrated Molyneux question posed by Locke in his *Essay on Human Understanding*, which had considerable impact on French materialist thought. Having learned to distinguish by touch between a cube and a sphere, the English philosopher asked, could a blind man still tell them apart if he regained the use of his eyes? Locke the sensationalist held he could not. Berkeley, Voltaire, La Mettrie, Condillac, Buffon, and numerous others took up the same question. Diderot too tries his hand at it in the *Lettre*, but in a manner more empirical, materialist, and artistic than that of his fellow philosophers.

After some framing remarks, to which I shall return, the *Lettre* begins by describing Diderot's visit to a blind man outside Paris. One of the text's many *écarts*, Diderot's displacing himself from the City of Lights to the darkness of Puiseaux signals the displacement of the idealist philosophical position the *Lettre* will perform. The eye no longer reigns sovereign among the senses, as in Descartes, for whom vision provided the master metaphor for thought, the way to represent things spatially and to theatricalize extratheatrically.[8] The blind man represents an exception to the rule of sight, an *écart de la nature*, one of the many "ex-centrics" and monsters populating Diderot's texts.

Initially, Diderot observes this difference from a distance, apparently certain of the difference between "us" and "them," between the mental operations of the sighted and those of the blind.

Nous combinons des points colorés; il ne combine lui que des points palpables, ou, pour parler plus exactement, que des sensations du toucher dont il a mémoire. Il ne se passe rien dans sa tête d'analogue à ce qui se passe dans la nôtre: il n'imagine point; car pour imaginer, il faut colorer un fond, et détacher de ce fond des points, en leur supposant une couleur différente de celle du fond . . . du moins, c'est ainsi que les choses s'exécutent dans mon imagination (IV, 95).

Relying on a familiar pictorial model, this description of thought characterizes it as mimetic reduplication. Yet as he presents this model of thought, Diderot effectively breaks up the mental pictures of epistemological theory by considering them in their materiality as a set of points and colored backgrounds. Similarly, in referring to his own way of thinking, and especially to his particular way of imagining things, he points to a mode of perception characterized not by identity but by difference. From the outset, then, the *Lettre* is marked by an *écart* or shift that displaces any general theoretical model for thought and presents other ways of thinking, notably, by imagining different points or points of difference.

The blind man of Puiseaux conceives of vision as a kind of touch, thus misapprehending this sense by conceptualizing it as lacking. For Diderot, however, blindness may not be an exception, a lack to be compensated for, but rather a way to present another means for grasping thought. Hence he introduces a second blind man, the English geometer Saunderson, whom he imagines as possessing a kind of vision, figuratively speaking. "Saunderson voyait donc par sa peau" (IV, 117). What intrigues Diderot most about Saunderson's philosophical "views" is how this knowledge is produced without the intervention of literal vision. Through Saunderson, Diderot takes up the question of blindness in a different and more imaginative manner.

Comme je n'ai jamais douté que l'état de nos organes et de nos sens n'ait beaucoup d'influence sur notre métaphysique et sur notre morale, et que nos idées les plus purement intellectuelles, si je puis parler ainsi, ne tiennent de fort près à la conformation de notre corps, je me mis à questionner notre aveugle sur les vices et sur les vertus (IV, 26).

What Diderot hears here is that the ethical sense of the blind differs from that of the sighted, and that their respective "metaphysics" are irreconcilable. The ethical or metaphysical ideas of the sighted and the blind are relative, determined by each individual's particular sensual apprehension. Saunderson amply demonstrates this determinism, leading Diderot to remark, "le grand raisonnement qu'on tire des merveilles de la nature, est bien faible pour des aveugles." Not only does Saunderson literally embody the sensationalist hypothesis, which alone explains his admirable knowledge of geometry; as philosopher he carries the hypothesis of sensationalism to its logical conclusion, refuting the existence of any divine or otherwise comprehensible causality determining natural order. In Saunderson's melodramatic deathbed soliloquy, he describes nature as a continual process of combining matter, of destruction and reconstruction, during which there occasionally appear certain "combinaisons vicieuses" and "productions monstrueuses," such as the blind man himself. Far from reflecting any divine harmony or rational order, the world Saunderson presents is a transitory, momentary arrangement, whose organizing principle he quite simply cannot see.

Through Saunderson, Diderot presents the experience of blindness *en philosophe*, shifting the question of vision from a literal to a metaphorical level. Seeing refers figuratively to understanding, an operation the blind philosopher can perform just as well as the sighted one. Such a shift was already announced in the text's full title, *Lettre sur les aveugles, à l'usage de ceux qui voient*. For the *Lettre* to be used philosophically, as a way to see things or to grasp them, it must be read *en écart*, by marking the shift that transforms the blind man from an aberrant exception into an exemplary model. No longer disqualified from insightful thought because of the sense he lacks, the blind man constitutes a model that foregrounds – for the insightful – how metaphysical and ethical ideas come into being in the blind and the sighted alike. Thus, through these exemplary bodies Diderot provides models for a different way of grasping the determinate role the body plays both conceptually, in terms of metaphysical-ethical theory, and textually, in terms of the way ideas are presented. Bodies provide the object of philosophical speculation in the *Lettre*; they also furnish the material for Diderot's art of philosophizing, an experimental art performed on the body of the blind, as the opening lines of the *Lettre* suggest.

The text begins by setting up a fictional frame surrounding the body of the *Lettre* proper and the theoretical remarks concerning sensationalism it contains. Here as elsewhere, Diderot foregrounds the discursive act or event, entitling the text a letter, addressed to "Madame." This philosophical enterprise is marked as involving two activities, writing and reading, and two minds, It also involves two bodies, since the letter form here, with its female addressee, genders as well as engenders the text. The act of foregrounding *énonciation* never occurs gratuitously in Diderot, and here it serves to explain why this letter came to be, as well as how this text can be used. Moreover this foregrounding destabilizes oppositional classifications such as fiction and theory, frame and contents, and even the body "proper" that seemed initially to provide one way to discuss this text.

Diderot begins the *Lettre* by apologizing to his interlocutor for being unable to provide her with the promised account of an event representing the cutting edge of eighteenth-century eye surgery, Ferchault de Réaumur's removal of a blind girl's cataracts. Réaumur it seems had refused to allow Diderot and other *philosophes* to witness the experiment. But this missed opportunity turns out to be of little consequence, for the real philosophical experiment occurs elsewhere.

> Forcé de me passer d'une expérience, où je ne voyais guère à gagner pour mon instruction ni pour la vôtre . . . je me suis mis à philosopher avec mes amis, sur la matière importante qu'elle a pour objet. Que je serais heureux, si le récit d'un de nos entretiens pouvait me tenir lieu auprès de vous du spectacle que je vous avais trop légèrement promis! (IV, 17–18).

Excluded as eyewitness from the medical experiment, Diderot conducts his own by recounting (or inventing) what his interlocutor will read, his encounter with the blind man of Puiseaux and with a book about Saunderson. More than a literary embellishment or example of Diderot's conversational style, these framing remarks determine the kind of philosophizing occurring in the *Lettre*. They situate the text at one remove from the type of analysis that depends on witnessing an event, as well as from the idealist speculation that requires no event at all. Diderot can remain blind to what actually occurred during Réaumur's surgery and still philosophize, in the dark so to speak, yet far more productively. Neither a passive witness, simply recording an experience, nor an abstract theorist, speculating out of touch with any possible event, he presents himself as writer-philosopher, participating in an invented event upon which he comments, after the fact, at the moment of another event constituted by the writing and reading of the *Lettre*.

If for Locke and all the others who took up the Molyneux question, the *idea* of a blind person acquiring sight provides sufficient material for philosophizing, for Diderot it does not. He requires an event, an experience. Putting this somewhat differently, one could say that the idea for Diderot is always an event, something that happens. Thinking is an act in the most theatrical of senses, for ideas in Diderot are always staged, played out, performed. Diderot's theory of knowledge is a theatrical one, in which the representation of ideas is also their performance (*représentation*). Consequently, he need not have witnessed the supposedly real event, "[le] spectacle que j'[avais] . . . promis," for having missed one such spectacle he easily fabricates another, passing from one stage to another. The most spectacular *expérience*, perhaps far more philosophical than anything Réaumur could have done, said or heard, takes place then in the way Diderot presents not only the encounter the *Lettre* relates, but also the encounter that the *Lettre* is. In expressing the hopes his letter will take the place of viewing Réaumur's medial experiment, Diderot wagers on producing a text in which the real philosophical matter involves not only the event recounted but also its recounting, not only the idea of blindness but also its presentation. The most telling *expérience* in the *Lettre* thus concerns the type of experimental philosophizing, or philosophical performance, that this text stages. To treat the idea of sensationalism philosophically, the *Lettre* questions philosophy's genre through reference to generic terms such as letter, story, and spectacle, thereby shifting the question from the real event to language, from apprehending to phrasing (as if the question were not already there in the first place).

This self-reflexive reference to the *Lettre*'s own genre materializes the question of philosophizing about the material. Epistemological issues conjoin with linguistic ones here, and not only on a theoretical, conceptual level but also on a performative, textual one. In the fiction whereby Diderot presents sensationalist epistemology, the first question he asks the blind man concerns his use of language. "Je lui demandai ce qu'il entendait par un miroir . . . Et qu'est-ce à votre avis que des yeux?" (IV, 20–21). Elsewhere he explains what words such as "beauty," "vice" or "virtue" must mean to the blind man.[9] Reflecting the attempt to grasp and present the experience of blindness, these questions and statements also concern the relation between word and idea, signifier and signified. This turn towards language, which for Enlightenment epistemology was the materialization of thought, occurs repeatedly in Diderot's texts, without however reducing this materiality to a transparent representation of the idea. Such a reduction would amount to the linguistic equivalent of philosophical idealism, which is the real target in the *Lettre*.

Diderot finds the most extreme form of such idealism in George Berkeley's claim that only sense impressions can be known and not any form of exterior reality. According to Berkeley, "nous ne sortons jamais de nous-mêmes, et ce n'est que notre pensée que nous apercevons" (IV, 44–45). Defining the individual as cut off perceptually from everything exterior, this solipcistic idealism assumes that specular self-reflection, the condition of thought, is pregiven. For Diderot, Berkeley's system is "extravagant," "le plus difficile à combattre, quoique le plus absurde de tous." Elsewhere he professes his inability to comprehend how he thinks, to "prendre mon esprit sur le fait," adding that it would take some form of two-headed monster to understand such self-reflection. But even if the mind cannot be caught "in the act," even if one cannot think the act of thinking, that act can be performed. One can stage or phrase it through language, and thus (re)present that act. The image of a two-headed monster or the *clavecin sensible* are two such attempts to figure thinking.

In the *Lettre* also, language provides Diderot with a means of self-exteriorization and self-reflection that Berkeley's idealism does not. In theory at least, language is instrumental in organizing individual sense impressions, providing a way to judge individual perceptions of things and to communicate that judgment to others.[10] This explains why Diderot argues that the ethical and esthetic judgments the blind perform are different from those of the sighted, and that these judgments can be communicated to – or elicited by – the sighted person, at least the one intuitive enough to ask the right questions. Language would provide the way out of solipcistic thought, insofar as it represents sense impressions, both to oneself and others. The real model for thought the *Lettre* puts forward, then, is not the blind man or even the sighted, but language, whose workings would reflect the order of thought. This at least is how Diderot's argument can be rephrased in the theoretical terms of eighteenth-century linguistics and epistemology.

Theoretically, Diderot's turn to language refutes the "système extravagant" of Berkeleyan idealism. Or does it? If language does no more, although no less, than represent thought, only the latter is apprehended and not an exterior reality. Yet if language represents thought, this means that thought is literally unpresentable, except at one remove. In seeking to break out of Berkeley's solipcistic idealism, has Diderot lost touch with thought altogether? Perhaps he was right in calling Berkeley's extravagant system the most difficult to combat. Putting this difficulty somewhat differently, I would suggest that the most serious and successful refutation of solipcistic idealism does not occur on a theoretical level, in either this text or any other. In fact the *Lettre* reaches the limit of the theoretical refutation of idealism, the point beyond which refutation *in theory* cannot proceed. All that can be done is to *displace* the question, to situate philosophy at one remove from the theoretical. This does not mean rejecting one theory (idealism) in favor of another (materialism), but rather displacing the theoretical through a thoroughgoing practice, by working upon the material of philosophy, its language. Diderot presents language as situated at one remove from thought, and it is at this remove, this distance from (Diderot's) thought or theory, that the *Lettre* must be read. The real "expérience" in the *Lettre* involves language, an experiment/experience that presents Diderot's way of phrasing thought, not only theoretically as a philosophical problem, but also artfully, involving the practice of philosophy. Foregrounding a philosophical-artistic practice, the *Lettre* produces displacements, discursive *écarts*, from theory towards art, towards the artistic manner in which the problem of sensation is treated.

Framing the account of the meeting with the blind man and the description of Saunderson, these frequent interjections establish a dialogue between narrator/writer and reader. Highlighting the text's enunciative structure, these interjections also foreground its genre, distinguishing it from that of the treatise. "Et toujours des écarts, me direz-vous: Oui, Madame, c'est la condition de notre traiteé" (IV, 66). The term "écart" refers to the loose, conversational style of the *Lettre*. More interestingly though, Diderot's comment also suggests that the very condition of possibility for treating the question of the blind and sensationalist epistemology in general must be conceived in terms of an *écart*. The *Lettre* displaces the philosophical genre, and with it the theory of sensationalism worked out by other philosophers who adopted the philosophical genre to do so. Diderot incorporates into his treatment of sensationalism a dialogue between himself and a blind man, Saunderson's direct discourse, as well as frequent interjections addressed to a fictional reader. This "literary" use of language operates precisely the kind of exteriorization from self through language that Berkeley's solipcistic idealism does not provide for. Diderot's understanding of the blind man's world does not derive from a visual experiment – Réamur's operation which he did not witness – but from a linguistic one, his questioning the blind man, his reading about Saunderson's life. And if Diderot is situated at one remove from direct apprehension, he situates his reader at two, presenting a text that recounts an experience, that includes another text (Saunderson's biography) and that urges the reader to read still more ("Madame, ouvrez la *Dioptrique* de Descartes").

This linkage between the text's particular genre and the philosophical genre becomes clearer in a second occurrence of the term *écart*. Diderot remarks on the "felicitous expressions" found in Saunderson's speech, turns of phrase that are literal in relation to one sense and figurative in relation to another. Diderot adds though that the "accidental" production of metaphor characterizes not only the blind, but idiots and the most witty of speakers as well. Once again the model of the blind man undergoes slippage, a displacement towards language, and that of imagination in particular.

> Mais toute langue en général étant pauvre de mots propres pour les écrivains qui ont l'imagination vive, ils sont dans le même cas que les étrangers qui ont beaucoup d'esprit, les situations qu'ils inventent, les nuances délicates qu'ils aperçoivent dans les caractères, la naïveté des peintures qu'ils ont à faire, les *écartent* à tout moment des façons de parler ordinaires, et leur font adopter des tours de phrases qui sont admirables toutes les fois qu'ils ne sont ni précieux ni obscurs (IV, 42, my emphasis).

With its "disette de mots," language is a sorry tool for expressing the delicate nuances characterizing a vivid imagination. The language of imagination, which Diderot finds in both imaginative writers and witty foreigners, possesses a kind of poetic foreignness (or a foreign poeticness) with respect to "ordinary," impoverished language. What Diderot calls imagination produces a displacement, an *écart*, from the ordinary and familiar towards the metaphorical and poetic. This displacement results in turns that produce the feeling of either admiration or incomprehension in poetic texts (or artworks) whose incalculable, uncontrollable effects either succeed or misfire.

Diderot's art of philosophizing can be gauged, then, by the displacement or *écart* it effectuates with regard to a more familiar yet impoverished way of phrasing things. Diderot can treat the question of knowledge only on the condition of displacing it, by foregrounding the philosophical art that must be involved in imagining it. "Nous voilà bien loin de nos aveugles, direz-vous," he remarks at one point. We are far indeed from the blind man as epistemological model and from any theoretical discourse that relies on abstract, speculative models. Yet we are far closer to grasping how philosophical discourse makes use of the body as model in order to incorporate its truth. The real embodiment in the *Lettre* concerns much more than a simple thematics of the physical body could show, for at stake is the artistic practice whereby the truths of Diderot's philosophy of the material are phrased in the body of the text. We must turn to a second text on monstrous bodies, examining how it entwines the questions of epistemology and esthetics.

The body of the letter (II)

Written in 1751, two years after the *Lettre sur les aveugles*, the *Lettre sur les sourds et muets* pursues the sensationalist hypothesis concerning the determinate role the senses play in the generation of ideas. Like the blind man, the deaf-mute constitutes a limit case or test fiction, another monstrous abnormality that the philosopher of sensationalism sets up as a model for understanding the normal generation of ideas. Yet the *Lettre sur les sourds et muets* proves to be less a continuation of the previous *Lettre* than yet another *écart* or displacement. The first *Lettre* presented language as the manifestation of mind. Insofar as linguistic order duplicates mental order, the question of knowledge can be treated separately from that of language. The second *Lettre* engages the question of language differently, however, reworking the very basis of epistemological theory. Here Diderot considers the possibility of an irreducible difference between thought and language, especially in the experiencing of the esthetic object. Through examples drawn from poetry, painting, music, and theater, the *Lettre* delineates a conceptual domain, an artistic practice, and a way of sensing that sensationalist epistemology cannot account for, at least not without revealing its own limits and perhaps those of epistemological theory in general.

Diderot approaches the relation between thought and language through a discussion of syntactical inversions. Already an old chestnut by the mid-eighteenth century, the inversion question attracted both grammarians and philosophers as a way to analyze the structuring principle at work in both the mind and language. As Diderot puts it, "nous disons les choses en français comme l'esprit est forcé de les considérer en quelque langue qu'on écrive. Cicéron a pour ainsi dire suivi la syntaxe française, avant que d'obéir à la syntaxe latine" (IV, 164). With the notion of inversion, grammarians sought to reconcile the obvious differences in various languages' syntactical structure with their fundamental claim that linguistic order mirrors mental order.[11] Mimetically displaying the operations of mind, albeit perhaps in inverted fashion, language still provided the grammarian-philosophers with a royal road to the most ideal of orders, thought. For even in an "inverted" language such as Latin, they found a seamless passage between mind and its material manifestation.

Diderot, with his own brand of sensationalist epistemology, sets off too on such a path. The idealism of general grammar need only be rewritten in a more sensationalist key, as he appears to suggest in the following example of inversion. Whereas in conventional French "un corps" would be defined as "une substance étendue, impénétrable, figurée, colorée et mobile," the "natural order" of this definition would be "colorée, figurée, étendue, impénétrable, mobile, substance." The latter order is natural, not inverted, because it reflects the order in which a person seeing a body for the first time would be affected. "L'œil serait frappé d'abord de la figure, de la couleur et de l'étendue; le toucher s'approchant ensuite du corps, en découvrirait l'impénétrabilité; et la vue et le toucher s'assureraient de la mobilité. Il n'y aurait donc point d'inversion dans cette définition" (IV, 137). This way of defining natural order raises more problems than it solves though.

Individual variations of speech cannot easily be explained by the model of a normative, universal linguistic subject this definition presupposes. Nor does such a model allow individual linguistic acts to be analyzed over time, in a diachronic, historical manner. Consequently, Diderot leaves behind this idealizing definition, remarking that this kind of natural order pertains only to a primitive or primary order of language with its "conventional" or "scientific" order.

In Diderot's comments on language, nature and the natural are presented as primitive, primary, and original. The most frequently invoked explanatory paradigm in Enlightenment discourse, the concept of "nature" was constantly invoked to judge all facets of human experience, all institutions and orders. One should however be cautious of making any ultimate judgment concerning the Enlightenment's idea of nature, for it is not at all certain one can assume in advance any knowledge of just what the term "nature" might refer to in a given Enlightenment text, and clearly not prior to reading it. Even the discourse of Enlightenment science, whose understanding of physical phenomena seems to announce a more modern type of scientific thought, cannot be evaluated in terms of a positivistic, "objective" understanding of nature, which is but another explanatory paradigm, however familiar. The prime interpretive difficulty encountered in reading the Enlightenment reference to nature is that the term can refer to particular sets or concepts, but it can also function as a metaphor, signifying a local textual or discursive logic. The Enlightenment discourse on nature often appears to be marked by tensions and instability, which makes it seem embryonic or prescientific with respect to a more present-day view of things. These tensions testify to the increasingly symbolic role the term "nature" was pressed into playing in order to ground, make comprehensible, and legitimate various orders and institutions, whether linguistic and epistemological, or social and political. The more the term "nature" took on a symbolic and ideological function, the more it became subject to the most unforeseeable slippages and displacements.[12]

This process marks the *Lettre* as well. In the passage

previously quoted, precisely when Diderot attempts to distinguish between a natural linguistic order and an inverted one, orders suddenly proliferate: *ordre naturel, ordre d'institution, ordre scientifique.* As if to provide at least some kind of order, Diderot proposes an analytical equivalent of natural linguistic order in the person of a "muet de convention," whose answers to questions would reveal "quel est l'ordre d'idées qui aurait paru le meilleur aux premiers hommes pour se communiquer leurs pensées par gestes" (IV, 139). As in the case of Rousseau, Condillac, Montesquieu, and even Sade, Diderot's invention of the fictional "muet de convention" represents a common Enlightenment strategy of presenting and interrogating a figure standing for a supposedly natural or original order so as to establish a critical perspective onto various institutional orders, be they linguistic or social. The effective strength of these critical perspectives depends, moreover, on the extent to which the text that sets them up explicitly presents the linguistic, discursive determinations of natural or original order. The more the Enlightenment text foregrounds these determinations, the more the natural turns out to be accessible only by analogy, through a fictional, constructed analogue, in short through metaphor, which signifies the natural without ever being identical to it. Thus, Diderot's invention of a "conventional" mute person complicates the problem of knowing objectively what any "natural order of ideas" might be. Like any figure, that of nature can stand for whatever Enlightenment wants it to (and sometimes what it doesn't, since no discourse of knowledge can hope to control its own metaphorics). This arbitrariness and constructedness do not invalidate the figure as a means of knowledge however, although they do place limits and conditions on knowledge by foregrounding what makes it possible. It is in terms of the limits of knowledge – and of epistemological theory – that we can grasp why Diderot presents a model for understanding natural linguistic order only to digress from it.

The formal model of the "muet de convention" is quickly discarded as a possible analogue for the original language of "les premiers hommes." Diderot experiments with another figure representing a different nature, this time a deaf-mute who will be asked to translate discourse into gestures. Since the deaf-mute has no preconceived ideas concerning the proper or conventional way to communicate, or so Diderot claims, any inversions appearing in his gestural language would be natural ones. However analytically appealing this model might be, Diderot remains less interested than a Condillac or a Rousseau in the possibility of a "return" to nature through some putative natural form of expression. No sooner does he set up a theoretical model and experimental method designed to detect the natural, primary order of thought than a hesitation arises, which in turn generates a series of apparent digressions from the topic of inversion.

How can this experiment in translating language into gesture reveal a natural order, Diderot asks, given that the language of gesture does not correspond to that of words? Certain gestures simply cannot be translated: "il y a des gestes sublimes que toute l'éloquence oratoire ne rendra jamais" (IV, 142). Three examples of such sublime gestural language follow: Lady Macbeth's sleepwalking scene, and scenes from Corneille's *Héraclius* and *Rodogune*. In each, "le geste triomphe du discours." Concerning Lady Macbeth, for example, Diderot writes, "Je ne sais rien de si pathétique en discours que le silence et le mouvement des mains de cette femme. Quelle image du remords" (IV, 143). Not only is gesture more expressive, powerful, and moving than language, gesture at its most sublime belongs to an order different from that of thought. This is highlighted in a remark following the description of another scene. "On oublie la pensée la plus sublime; mais ces traits ne s'effacent point. Que de réflexions ne pourrais-je pas faire ici . . . sur le sublime de situation, si elles ne me jetaient pas trop hors de mon sujet" (IV, 143).[13]

These comments concerning theater seem to digress from the linguistic and epistemological question the *Lettre* engages. In fact, however, reference to the theatrical sublime pushes that question to its limit. The experience of "le sublime de situation" the theatrical gesture produces amounts to nothing less than another natural order, an experience far more intense than sensing "un corps." Concerning Timogène's words and gesture in a scene from *Rodogune*, Diderot exclaims, "Quelle foule d'idées et de sentiments ce geste et ce mot ne font-ils pas éprouver à la fois! Mais je m'écarte toujours" (IV, 144). These sublime theatrical moments, these experiences of actors' bodies in an illusionary time and space, unleash more energy and more signification than language can account for. One may attempt to express in language the "hoard of ideas and feelings" to which a particular gesture gives rise, to make the theatrical sign comprehensible as an object of cognition. In doing so, however, the sign will inevitably be impoverished, as its intrinsic energy is reduced, along with its disruptive potential to produce *écarts*.

Diderot's effusively enthusiastic responses to plays and paintings are symptomatic of a more general shift occurring in the esthetic theory of the classical age, which increasingly invoked sensation rather than reason to explain esthetic judgment. Seen not said, perhaps unphrasable because it can only be felt, the theatrical sublime as Diderot presents it recalls the esthetic theory of Boileau, Bouhours, and Rapin, for whom the term "sublime" refers to an ungraspable trait in the work of art, something the critic can define only by pointing to the effects (and affects) it produces. As Louis Marin puts it, commenting on Boileau and Pascal, "[the sublime] is definable primarily through its effects – but these effects in turn are definable only through reference to the defining proposition: the sublime is what produces the feeling of the sublime, the sublime as pathos. The presentation of the sublime is thus itself sublime insofar as it performs an 'affect-effect' with no objectively identifiable distinctive feature: it is not a single passion, but the pathos of all the passions; it is not one emotion, but the motion of all emotions."[14] As such, the sublime constitutes a disruptive, dispossessive force, overwhelming the subject of the artwork, its creator as well as its reader, spectator or listener, through the intense emotions it elicits. The sublime disrupts the theoretical subject as well, the critic-theorist who attempts to comprehend the work of art and present it as something knowable. As Marin continues, "the sublime is thus the elusive *je ne sais quoi* not only of the rhetoric and poetics of genres and styles, of their rules and figures, but also of all aesthetic response, of value judgment based on taste, of art theory in general. So construed, the sublime indicates a gap within the theory itself. What the theory approaches but cannot grasp, it positions as the "end" of art – both its ultimate goal and its cessation... [The sublime] paradoxically both completes and supplements: it lies on the borderline of the beautiful form, at the threshold of the undefinable aspect of beauty; yet this threshold of indefinition is also the place where the form encounters the limit that makes it a beautiful form" (p. 342). In response to the sublime end of art, the esthetic theorists of classicism could do no more than characterize the sublime by its *je ne sais quoi*, a term that integrates the sublime within a theory of classical representation by naming and conceptualizing it, and at the same time marks its disruptive, negating power.

Marin's remarks concerning the sublime are helpful in understanding Diderot's discussion as it moves from the esthetic sublime (his theatrical experiences) to what might be called the sensationalist sublime. The disparity between language and certain untranslatable gestures on the stage turns out to be but one instance of an incommensurability between language and sensation in general. In a sense, the cause of this nonequivalence is merely structural. "La sensation n'a point dans l'âme ce développement successif du discours... Notre âme est un tableau mouvant d'après lequel nous peignons sans cesse: nous employons bien du temps à le rendre avec fidélité: mais il existe en entier et tout à la fois" (IV, 161). Whereas sensations occur simultaneously, language can analyze them only by distributing their elements syntactically over time according to a grammatical logic. Diderot posits the relation between thought and language as one of disparity and not of identity, thereby opening a breach between mental and linguistic order, or, as he puts it more suggestively, betwen the feeling of the soul and any anlytical account of it. "Autre chose est l'état de notre âme; autre chose le compte que nous en rendons soit à nous-mêmes, soit aux autres: autre chose la sensation totale et instantanée de cet état; autre chose l'attention successive et détaillée que nous sommes forcés d'y donner pour l'analyser, la manifester et nous faire entendre" (IV, 161).[15]

Significantly, Diderot does not use the term "idea" but rather "sensation" in referring to that which cannot be presented in language. Sensation does not belong to an anterior, primary order that language reveals and represents in material fashion. It is not a structure and thus cannot be copied and represented. "L'âme éprouve une foule de perceptions, sinon à la fois, du moins avec une rapidité si tumultueuse, qu'il n'est guère possible d'en découvrir la loi" (IV, 159). Interestingly enough, sensation comes to resemble the sublime as Diderot characterizes it. The sublime theatrical gestures he describes are exactly analogous to sensation in general, which is to say that the notion of the esthetic sublime undergoes a certain displacement as it comes to refer more generally to a kind of sensation that cannot be translated into another idiom. To be sure, language may analyze sensation, creating an analytical order that attempts to make it comprehensible. Condillac may write a treatise on sensations, but this work, written in the idiom of philosophical, analytic discourse, unavoidably fails to present sensation adequately. Language is not a mirror, but a structuring mechanism, creating a grammatical, analytical, even philosophical order. Required for understanding sensation, this order is situated at one remove from sensation itself and thus impoverishes it as well.[16] The *Lettre sur les sourds et muets* marks the limits of classical age epistemology, questioning the very possibility of phrasing the relation between language and sensation in terms of mimetic representation. Moreover, if the idea as sensation, however analyzable, remains unrepresentable, the *Lettre* shows how even the language of analysis comes up short. Whether that language is called the discourse of reason or the discourse of theory, the *Lettre* raises the possibility that analytical language only presents something that was never originally there. It cannot copy or translate what cannot be presented as such.

For Diderot, syntactical inversions exemplify language at its most empirical. They bear witness to a materiality of language that challenges the claim to universality made by the classical age's idealist theory of language and knowledge. Once having opened a breach in linguistic and epistemological theory though, the materiality of the empirical risks becoming an autonomous domain, ungovernable even by sensationalist theory. The *Lettre* bears witness to this possibility. Intrigued by the materiality of language, at times carried away by its powerful capacity to produce uncontrolled and undeterminable effects, Diderot presents any number of experiences and examples that point to the stresses and strains in the classical age's theory of language and thought, and which, in its breaking up, could no longer be controlled. Indeed, this text's much commented upon disorder, which Diderot himself remarks upon, can best be explained not in psycho-stylistic terms but as the formal consequence of a fragmenting theoretical field.

In his own attempt to formulate a sensationalist epistemology, Condillac too breaks with the idealism of general grammar.[17] Diderot is not Condillac though. However strong the personal and intellectual affinity between the two *philosophes*, the *Lettre sur les sourds et muets* does not simply rewrite the *Traité des sensations* or the *Essai sur l'origine des connaissances humaines*. An artist-philosopher, Diderot is far more attuned to the materiality of language than Condillac, much more in touch with a practice that epistemological theory can only generalize and idealize.[18] It is as if, having reached the limits of epistemological theory, even a sensationalist one, in the limit case of esthetic experience, Diderot senses that the relation between sensation and language, esthetics and epistemology, cannot be phrased in terms of a theoretical model based on identity, analogy, representation. Required instead is a manner that displaces such a model by refusing to be determined by the theoretical imperative of elaborating a systematic epistemological theory of sensationalism. Read from this other perspective, the most challenging aspects of the *Lettre* concern the manner in which Diderot poses the question of phrasing sensation by considering the relation between knowledge and art. Here as throughout his writing, he characterizes the artwork not only as an object but also as a practice giving rise to an event. This event involves a subject whose link to the artwork is both cognitive and affective, occurring through sensation (*sentir*) and feelings (*sentiments*). Esthetic events occur in the *Lettre* as well, resulting from its own artistic practice, and in a way that suggests the relation between knowledge and art cannot be accounted for in terms of an epistemology concerned exclusively with questions of cognition.

If the *Lettre* marks the limits of (sensationalist) epistemology in the way it raises the question of art, it also points to those of esthetic theory. Addressed to Charles Batteux as a rejoinder to his treatise, *Les Beaux-arts réduits au même principe*, the *Lettre* contains what commentators have taken as Diderot's theory of gesture, poetry, the sublime, and art in general. However strong the theoretical imperative at work in Diderot's texts may seem though, it is countered in his manner. In the *Lettre*, the manner whereby esthetic theory is related to knowledge raises significant doubt as to the appropriateness of the theoretical genre for phrasing sensation in general and esthetic sensation in particular. We should take seriously Diderot's claim that Batteux's text was the first to come to mind and that the *Lettre* thus grows out of a fortuitous encounter (IV, 134). Implying far more than the psychological openness or *disponibilité* of a centrifugal mind spinning out towards others, the staging of this chance encounter presents Diderot's own way of phrasing how things "come to mind." The distance taken from Batteux, and which involves not simply a refutation or revision of the latter's esthetic theory, displaces Batteux's cognitive theory of art towards a more artful phrasing of the relation between the cognitive and the esthetic, between reason and sensation. Before considering how this displacement occurs, we must consider what Batteux's "coming to mind" might mean.

The *Beaux-arts réduits au même principe* reflects the attempt to graft esthetic theory onto sensationalist epistemology. Wishing to found esthetic judgment on something more substantial than what Du Bos called a sixth sense located in "the secret workings of the soul," Batteux is convinced that the function and essence of the fine arts can be made comprehensible through rational analysis. Rejecting an idealist esthetics that posits the idea of beauty as innate and pregiven, Batteux situates in the senses the origin of all available knowledge, including that of the fine arts. However much he wishes to formulate a more rational explanation of the artwork by anchoring knowledge of it in perception though, he does not avoid the pitfall of the more subjective, idealist esthetic theories he rejects. For in taking over the sensationalist explanation of the origin of knowledge, Batteux replaces one idealism with another. The enabling condition of his esthetic theory is an epistemology according to which the subject of knowledge is both universal and pregiven, possessing the *a priori* capacity to comprehend the fine arts and explain their effects. Even when *Les Beaux-arts* analyzes the most intrinsically formal of artworks' properties, Batteux's remarks derive from the model of the subject he invokes. He claims, for example, that the common principle of the fine arts resides in their capacity to imitate *la belle nature*. This definition of the artwork's function implies that a subjective act of judgment must occur on the part of both the artist, who decides how to imitate nature, and the spectator-reader-listener, who decides whether the artwork succeeds in such imitation. Furthermore, Batteux bases the faculty of esthetic judgment itself upon an equally presupposed relation of ultimate identity, not only between the real and its artistic rendering, but also between thought and language, that is, between my idea or judgment of the artwork and the words in which I express it.

Accepting the sensationalist premise of Batteux's esthetic theory, Diderot remains far more skeptical, or scrupulous, concerning the universal epistemological subject of sensationalism relied on to explain esthetic judgment. This skepticism remains a constant, from the *Lettre* to the *Réfutation d'Helvétius*, despite Diderot's affinity for the sensationalist hypothesis and for the critique of idealism it enables. This doubt concerning the sensationalist theory of others may reflect Diderot's constitutional inability to formulate his own rigorously systematic explanation of the human subject. In a more interesting sense though, it stems from a deeply rooted antipathy towards the theoretical genre in which sensationalism, to say nothing of any theory, could be phrased.

In the following passage, addressed to Batteux, Diderot questions in his own curious manner whether indeed the sensationalist explanation of the faculty of judgment can be applied to esthetics.

> Cette réflexion, Monsieur, me conduit à une autre. Elle est un peu éloignée de la matière que je traite; mais dans une lettre les écarts sont permis, surtout lorsqu'ils peuvent conduire à des vues utiles. Mon idée serait donc de décomposer pour ainsi dire un homme, et de considérer ce qu'il tient de chacun des sens qu'il possède. Je me souviens d'avoir été quelquefois occupé de cette espèce d'anatomie métaphysique, et je trouvais que de tous les sens l'œil était le plus superficiel, l'oreille le plus orgueilleux, l'odorat le plus voluptueux, le goût le plus superstitueux et le plus inconstant, le toucher le plus profond et le plus philosophe (IV, 139–40).

Analogous to other fictional experiments, this curious lesson in "metaphysical anatomy" constructs a model for the subject in order to analyze the relation between sense perception and the generation of ideas. Whereas Diderot previously imagined interrogating a subject lacking one sense, here he mounts a more complicated anatomical experiment involving the specific attributes of all the senses. Not surprisingly, vision is characterized as the most superficial of the senses. No longer is it the privileged mode of perception, as for Descartes, author of not only a dioptrics but also the *Discours de la méthode*, that story about an "I"/eye in search of dazzlingly clear ideas. Senstionalism requres a far more tangible explanation of things, and vision yields to touch (*le toucher*), characterized as the most philosophical way of receiving sensory impressions, the privileged mode of judgment.

Rejecting the idealism of Cartesian optics and ontology, Diderot's hierarchy of the senses also shifts epistemological questions towards esthetic ones. Touch, this "most philosophical of senses," involves the esthetic experience, the moment when certain works manage to "touch" their beholder, listener or reader, producing an intense sensation or sentiment.[19] Here and in all his writings on art, Diderot seeks to comprehend how such a response comes about. More significantly, he also questions whether this understanding is possible as such. Just as in the case of the theatrical sublime, which can only be analyzed, not translated or reproduced, Diderot constructs a model figuring the subject of sensationalist epistemology, only to mark its limits. He continues:

Ce serait, à mon avis, une société plaisante, que celle de cinq personnes dont chacune n'aurait qu'un sens; il n'y a pas de doute que ces gens-là ne se traitassent tous d'insensés, et je vous laisse à penser avec quel fondement. C'est là pourtant une image de ce qui arrive à tout moment dans le monde; on n'a qu'un sens et l'on juge de tout. Au reste il y a une observation singulière à faire sur cette société de cinq personnes dont chacune ne jouirait que d'un sens; c'est que par la faculté qu'elles auraient d'abstraire, elles pourraient toutes être géomètres, s'entendre à merveille, et ne s'entendre qu'en géométrie. Mais je reviens à nos muets de convention, et aux questions dont on leur demanderait la réponse (IV, 140).

Five individuals, each possessing but one sense, might succeed in making themselves mutually understood, but only as geometers. An understanding of things is possible, but only so long as one engages in reasoning by abstraction, phrasing things in a way far removed from the concrete, the material, from things themselves. Once one speaks of other things, such as art, or presents things otherwise, perhaps in an artful way, understanding can no longer be guaranteed. Moreover, if all language is idiomatic, as Diderot suggests elsewhere, it is because sensation determines the particularity of each speaker's language. As this passage suggests, this particularity can be analyzed and theorized, but only at the risk of losing touch with what is most intensely significant in each particular discursive event.

This lesson in experimental anatomy suggests that Batteux's sensationalism cannot account for the particularity of the esthetic sensation, nor for the particularity of sensation *tout court*. In a sense, he is not enough of a sensationalist, remaining instead a classical theorist who presents esthetic judgment as an exclusively rational, cognitive operation, as if *sentir* were ultimately identical with *penser*. In any event, the idiom of esthetic theory in *Les Beaux-arts* remains a classic one, for it presents esthetic judgment *in general* and abstracts a stable and ideal unity from a set of potentially heterogeneous particularities. In taking his distance from Batteux, Diderot pushes sensationalism to further limits, towards a far more empirical and even material way of grasping things. He is much more aware than Batteux that when esthetic questions are couched in the terms of sensationalist epistemology, the relation to the artwork cannot be defined in exclusively cognitive terms. This is because the key term of sensationalism, *sentir*, refers to two potentially distinct processes, sensing and feeling, the cognitive and the esthetic. For Diderot, the kind of sensationalism he imagines would enable him to break with idealist epistemology, and to grasp what is at stake in the act of esthetic judgment, in this particular experience of intense sensation. Moreover, a thoroughgoing sensationalism would reflect upon its own idiom, questioning whether the theoretical genre could adequately present this manner of sensing things. To sense this questioning and its critical effects, let us return to the passage just quoted, paying particular attention to Diderot's own manner of treating esthetic sensation.

Instead of treating sensation in conceptual, theoretical terms, Diderot adopts another mode. He characterizes the passage as an *écart*, marking its difference from what precedes it ("cette réflexion . . . est un peu éloignée de la matière que je traite") and what follows it ("je reviens à nos muets de convention, et aux questions dont on leur demanderait la réponse"). Not just another example of a digressive, conversational style of writing or thinking, the *écart* remarked here distinguishes the passage from an analytic treatment of sensation. A shift occurs to a different mode of reasoning or rather of presentation, in which the role of the senses cannot be understood primarily (or perhaps at all) in terms of cognitive judgment. This shift also entails a reworking of the way the subject of sensation can be presented, a complete reforming of the stage on which sensing occurs. This stage may be a literal one, the eighteenth-century theatrical stage that the author of *Entretiens sur le fils naturel* sought to reform. It may also be a more figurative one, such as the mind, which Diderot refigures with more material metaphors. In either case, this *écart* signals a more general reformulation by means of a more literary, theatrical mode of presentation.

In this other mode or manner, it is possible to engage in paradoxical enterprises such as "metaphysical anatomy," for example, artistic experiments inappropriate with respect to the rules of other genres. Within the bounds of this *écart*, imagination produces ideas whose validity and effect are as critically powerful as those resulting from any original perception of the real. Thus, one can indeed imagine splitting up a person ("mon idée serait de décomposer un homme") to fashion the strangest of creatures, such as the one of the metaphysical anatomy experiment. In characterizing the eye as superficial, the ear as prideful, smell as voluptuous, taste as superstitious, and touch as profound and philosophical, Diderot appears to employ the trope of personification to construct what could be taken as a theoretical model for the epistemological subject, resembling, say, Condillac's statue. But the passage can also be read as exemplifying a quite different critical idiom than that of theory, one that displays far more openly its fiction-making, artistic practice.

It is tempting to suggest that many of Diderot's flights of fiction are part of the larger enterprise of reworking the theoretical idiom. The *homme décomposé* and the deaf-mute of the *Lettre*, the blind man of Puiseaux and Saunderson, numerous instances of physical abnormality discussed in *Le Rêve de D'Alembert* (including even a goat-man, an example of Diderot's imaginary brand of eighteenth-century genetic engineering) – all are products of the imagination, and all figure limit cases that test the theory of sensationalism, vitalism or other forms of empirically based subjectivism. Moreover, these imaginary creatures or creations of the imagination test theory in yet another way, for they resist being treated as functionally analogous to declarative statements, as heuristic fictions that could be reduced to a more expository, conceptual mode of presentation. These fictions or fabrications – the two words sharing a common etymology – all result from a generic *écart*, an artful practice somewhat hastily called literary. Together with characters such as Jacques, Rameau's nephew, Tahitians,

Suzanne, Julie de l'Espinasse, A and B, and so forth, these figures belong to imaginary space-times of words, bodies, and actions. They result from a kind of staging, occurring in texts classified as philosophical prose, novel, dialogue or letter. Ultimately though, these generic classifications are of little help in grasping the larger generic issue Diderot raises, which concerns the mode or manner in which to present sensations. An incident recounted in the *Lettre* makes this point in paradigmatic fashion.

Pursuing the question of the relation between spoken language and gestures, Diderot relates the following experimental fiction. Wishing to judge the appropriateness of actors' gestures to their spoken lines, he attended plays he knew by heart, sitting far from the stage, plugging his ears, and listening only when the gesture he saw threw him off. The point of this story is not only that language and gesture may be related in terms of translatability, or that language and thought may be incommensurable. Its point, rather, consists of shifting focus from stage to house, marking a change of perspective involving another stage, another scene. Diderot wishes above all to recount the utter surprise of those seated around him upon viewing him shed tears during the most touching of scenes, his ears plugged all the while. Questioned as to his singular behavior, he responded coolly, " 'que chacun avait sa façon d'écouter, et que la mienne était de me boucher les oreilles pour mieux entendre,' riant en moi-même des propos que ma bizarrerie apparente ou réelle occasionnait" (IV, 149). This shift from the stage of theater to the theatrical scene Diderot makes exemplifies the larger displacement the *Lettre* effectuates, and which involves a particular manner of philosophizing about the senses. The real scene staged here is Diderot's own, a scene of reception, transformation, and production, in which one text comes into being in and through its linkage with another. Diderot's performance – the plugged ears, the cool rejoinder, the tears, the inner laughter at his audience – indeed resembles a textual scene, which his fellow playgoers can only misinterpret, and which the *Lettre* presents to its readers for our response. This theatricalized text presents no translation of the text-performance of actors on stage, its refusal to do so figured by Diderot's gesture of plugging his ears. Instead it resituates the place of performance, transforming the "original" text, theatricalizing it into another textual performance occurring on another stage.

In relation to the epistemological issues engaged in the *Lettre*, this episode completely reworks the hierarchical relation between thought and language. Just as the actor's gestures allow Diderot the spectator to receive and be touched by the play's energy, so too language provides the medium of thought and not simply its representation. The potential energy of both words and gesture can be liberated only in a spectatorial response, just as the dynamics of thought can be realized in the material form it receives, in language.[20] Consequently, the notion of translatability, whether between thought and language, or between original and artwork, turns out to be a false issue, as misleading as the "common principle" of identity or mimesis founding Batteux's sensationalist esthetics. What intrigues Diderot is the creative process of transformation, not the reduplicative act of translation. His goal is not to judge the success of a putative re-presentation but to explore and engage himself in the dynamics of a theatricalizing performance.

This resituating of both epistemological and esthetic issues explains why, referring to the sublime experience of watching Shakespeare and Corneille, Diderot stages a sublime scene, with himself as privileged spectator. To be sure, like the idea the sublime can be analyzed and made comprehensible through the conceptual discourse of theory. This is not Diderot's objective however. In linking up with the sublime scene by staging his response to it, he suggests that the sublime can be *sensed* only by being transformed. The sense of sublimity must be theatricalized, performed, and replayed anew, by being written into the philosophical text that is the *Lettre*, for example. This explains why Diderot does not purport to treat the sublime, as do esthetician-philosophers from Longinus to Kant and beyond, and why instead he refers to "le sublime de situation." However much the sublime can be conceived of and treated as concept, the sense or sensing of sublimity is first and foremost an experience, an instance of intense sensation. This intensity can be grasped only by presenting sublimity *en situation* so to speak, according to the dynamics of a genre of presentation that actualizes the "situatedness" of the sublime, the fact that it cannot be grasped without replaying its tangible effects upon the viewer's or listener's very body. Proposing no general theory of the sublime, Diderot wishes instead to instantiate the sublime, not *in general*, for it does not occur thus, but in particular, nongeneralizable instances. The *Lettre* thus displays more than it proves, for these examples of sublimity are sublime instants or instances that play out the sublime, presenting it as (a) play taking place on the stage of theater and also on a stage set in the text.

This play of sublimity cannot occur in conceptual, theoretical discourse. As my own metaphors suggest, theater provides a compelling model for understanding artistic experimentations with other manners of representation. Terms such as "scene," "staging," and "performance" help identify the *opérateurs* or discursive mechanisms Diderot employs in enacting the phrasing of sensation. His enduring attraction to theater notwithstanding though, such terms should not be taken to refer only to a specific literary genre. A far larger kind of theatricality characterizes all Diderot's art of philosophizing. His experimentations with a manner of presenting things take place on the stage proper as well as off it. In fact, the theatrics of Diderot's art involves no stage proper, but rather multiple stages or space-times, where various events, enactments or stagings occur.

The event experienced repeatedly in Diderot's text is that of intense sensation. In (re)enacting that experience and seeking to phrase it Diderot invariably reaches the limits of analytical, theoretical discourse. In other words his text constantly works to arrive at its own "sublime de situation," a way of presenting the thinker's perhaps most intense of sensations, that of conceptual limits and the impossibility of overcoming them in the theoretical idiom. There is no hint of tragedy in Diderot's sense of these limits, for the tragic genre marks limits in the hope of getting beyond them by comprehending and thus transcending them (even if the tragic hero cannot). Sensing for Diderot is instead a poetic act, which can be phrased by means of a poeticized epistemology, as the following often quoted passage suggests.

In poetry Diderot senses what he calls "un esprit qui en meut et vivifie toutes les syllabes." But just what is the "spirit" of poetry?

> J'en ai quelquefois senti la présence; mais tout ce que j'en sais, c'est que c'est lui qui fait que les choses sont dites et représentées tout à la fois; que dans le même temps que l'entendement les saisit l'âme en est émue, l'imgination les voit, et l'oreille les entend; et que le discours n'est plus seulement un enchaînement de termes énergiques qui exposent la pensée avec force et noblesse, mais que c'est encore un tissu d'hiéroglyphes entassés les uns sur les autres qui la peignent. Je pourrais dire en ce sens que toute poésie est emblématique (IV, 169).

To describe the poetic sensation, Diderot distinguishes from the outset between *savoir* and *sentir*. Understanding (*l'entendement*) provides but a partial "grasp" of the poetic text, and treating poetry as an object of cognition cannot account for poetic sensation. This is because the poetic text works not only upon understanding, but also upon hearing, vision, feeling, and imagination. To explain this multiple sensation, the very notion of the poetic text must be reworked. Accordingly, Diderot refers to a commonplace understanding of poetic mimesis ("termes énergiques qui exposent la pensée"), only to redefine the poetic text as a hieroglyph. Like Roland Barthes' venture into "the empire of signs," the title of his speculation on Chinese ideograms, Diderot turns to an exotic "other" form of representation to figure the poetic text and the poetics of language.[21] The hieroglyph consolidates a series of figures in the *Lettre*, which include syntactical inversions, the metaphorical gestures of the deaf mute, "expressions énergiques," and the sublime gesture of the actor. Like these other forms, the hieroglyph presents – at least to Diderot's Western eyes – an instance of sublimely intense materiality, a network or overlay that depicts thought not by translating but by transforming it.

The hieroglyph vivifies thought, unleashing its dynamic energy, making it into "un tissu," a text, a web of energetic figures.

The dynamics of the poetic hieroglyph work not only within the poetic text but also upon its readers, who experience the poetic sensation and are thus incited to transform the hieroglyph's energy once again. Diderot continues, taking up the question of reading the poetic text.

Mais l'intelligence de l'emblème poétique n'est pas donnée à tout le monde; it faut être presque en état de le créer pour le sentir fortement. Le poète dit:

Et des fleuves français les eaux ensanglantées
Ne portaient que des morts aux mers épouvantées.
Voltaire, *Henriade*, chant II, vers 356–7.

Mais qui est-ce qui voit dans la première syllabe de *portaient*, les eaux gonflées de cadavres, et le cours de fleuves comme suspendu par cette digue? Qui est-ce qui voit la masse des eaux et des cadavres s'affaisser et descendre vers les mers à la seconde syllabe du même mot? l'effroi des mers est montré à tout lecteur dans *épouvantées*; mais la prononciation emphatique de sa troisième syllabe me découvre encore leur vaste étendue (IV, 169).

Reading (the poetic text) is a transformational process involving the (re)staging of sensation. Understanding poetry as mimesis, judging it an imitation of "la belle nature" as Batteux (and classical esthetic theory) had proposed, cannot suffice to account for what Diderot senses in the poetic figure. His own idea of nature and the material determination of thought through sensation leads him to imagine a different kind of esthetic judgment, based moreover upon how the body is worked upon by art. A discussion of music in the *Lettre* exemplifies this corporal esthetics.

"La peinture montre l'objet même, la poésie le décrit, la musique en excite à peine une idée . . . Comment se fait-il donc que des trois arts imitateurs de la nature, celui dont l'expression est la plus arbitraire et la moins précise, parle le plus fortement à l'âme?" (IV, 207). At least interrogatively, Diderot frees himself (and esthetic judgment) from the primacy of the image. Refusing to reduce the esthetic subject to a body defined primarily by its sense of vision, he departs from the traditional hierarchy of the arts in which painting is the noblest because it is the most mimetic. Instead he imagines an esthetic judgment based not on intrinsic, internal properties of the artwork, but upon the constitution of particular bodies.

> En musique, le plaisir de la sensation dépend d'une disposition particulière non seulement de l'oreille, mais de tout le système des nerfs. S'il y a des têtes sonnantes, il y a aussi des corps que j'appellerais volontiers harmoniques; des hommes, en qui toutes les fibres oscillent avec tant de promptitude et de vivacité, que sur l'expérience des mouvements violents que l'harmonie leur cause, ils sentent la possibilité de mouvements plus violents encore, et atteignent à l'idée d'une sorte de musique qui les ferait mourir de plaisir (IV, 206).

Highly musical, the figure of "fibres oscillantes" or resonant nerves relates esthetic judgment to individual anatomy. However, music is not the only case where the body plays a determining role in esthetic judgment. Music's "effet tumultueux" upon the sensing body serves as a model pertaining to all works of art, suggesting as well the manner in which such judgment can best be presented. If the esthetic experience involves the harmonic or resonant linking of artwork and sensing body, then esthetic judgment itself can best be presented in a manner resonant with the esthetic experience of the artwork. Such a mode or manner of judgment prolongs the artwork, as an echo prolongs a sound. It may increase the artwork's intensity, like a kind of sympathetic vibration. Above all it consists of a maximal response to the work of art, designed to realize, in the sense of electrical resonance, the greatest flow of energy between artwork and subject.

Redefining the artwork in terms of its capacity to effect the entire body, Diderot elevates esthetic judgment to a status equal to that of the artist. For if in order to sense the poetic hieroglyph most intensely, one must almost be able to create it oneself, then judging the artwork is itself an art. This artful judgment does not derive from rules and skills that must be learned. It is not the legislative judgment of connoisseurship. It involves rather a poetic creativity, which is a given, just as the body is.

This is why Diderot does not cite Voltaire's couplet in order to interpret it analytically, just as he refrains from translating any of the other examples of art in the *Lettre*. No Rosetta Stone unlocks the enigmatically untranslatable hieroglyph of poetry, music or painting. Instead, he interprets in another, more artful way, as one interprets a musical score or performs a written play, and as his own text's "hieroglyphic" manner suggests. In commenting on Voltaire's text, Diderot performs it, staging his own highly theatrical scene of carnage, in which, with the shift from "tout lecteur" to "me découvre," he himself becomes the privileged spectator. Once again, Diderot's goal is not to reproduce through analysis an original poetic scene. Rather, he seeks to stage a scene of sensation, one as moving and as energetic as the poetic text. This theatrical displacement involves two scenes related not by the logic of identity or analogy, but rather by an artistic practice marked by the transfer and transformation of energy. The second scene in no way translates or reduplicates the first. Artistic interpretation (in Diderot) analyzes nothing, properly speaking. Rather this second scene is related metaphorically to the first, which it reconfigures and performs. We should be careful not to recontain Diderot's insight into the art and act of interpretation by reducing it to his theory of metaphor or of poetic language. The poetics of his own work involves the dynamic, performative, transformational relation between text and reader, the artful manner of figuring the relation between artwork and the sensual experience it produces upon the receptive body. This is the real *enchaînement* or material linkage characterizing the theory of *rapports* or relationships proposed in the article "*Beau*" and which is involved in Diderot's presentation of the corporal esthetic experience.

What are the consequences of the *Lettre* for interpreting Diderot and for our own esthetic judgment of his texts? This text on knowledge, language, and art takes the form of a letter, a genre in which, as Diderot puts it, "les écarts sont permis, surtout lorsqu'ils peuvent conduire à des vues utiles" (IV, 139). As I have argued, the major *écart* of this text shifts the epistemological issue of cognitive judgment towards esthetics. If the theoretical imperative driving Diderot the philosopher of sensationalism is to link epistemology and esthetics via a notion of judgment common to both, this being the challenge posed by Batteux's *Beaux-arts*, what we discover in his philosophical manner, in the artwork that is the *Lettre*, is the incommensurability of these two types of judgment. For Diderot, interpretation can never be a completely cognitive act or art; as his stagings of esthetic experience show, it is an esthetic one in its own right. The *Lettre* displaces the primacy of the artwork, according equal status to that of interpretation, which is no longer a hermeneutic enterprise designed to produce and represent knowledge. Instead the *Lettre* presents interpretation as an artful act of transferring energy, a creative, performative, and poetic practice. Consequently, the *Lettre* reworks the temporal and hierarchical relation between artwork and interpretation. In the scenes of esthetic experience Diderot stages, he does not rewrite a primary, anterior experience, translating it into another idiom, representing it to consciousness so as to judge what in the artwork has produced that effect. This type of esthetic judgment would involve a memorative, commemorative activity occurring at a temporal remove from the esthetic event. Able to affirm the fact of having been touched only after the fact, this kind of esthetic judgment attempts to recapture or represent the original, primary, and anterior esthetic event, together with the sentiment to which it gave rise and from which it derives. But this way of posing things is not Diderot's. He links the esthetic work, the event of its experience, and the critical language referring to them in relational terms not governed by a temporal logic. His text does not relate an account of a prior experience remembered after the fact. It relates in a different sense, by linking one fictional scene and one theatrical space-time to another. Diderot's way of posing the question of esthetics, indeed the ultimate esthetic question, consists of marking in nontemporal fashion the passage from one stage to another, be it the more obviously esthetic stage of theater, music, poetry, or the no less esthetic stage of interpretation.

The consequences of Diderot's interpretive practice extend to the very genre of esthetic judgment, to interpretation's material form. By questioning the determinate role played by the body of the sensationalist subject in the act of judgment, he reworks the matter in and through which that judgment occurs. In theoretical terms, Diderot's materialism may not provide an adequate explanation of thought. Yet esthetically, his textual experiments question the limits of any theoretical explanation. The *Lettre* refutes Batteux's esthetic theory most effectively perhaps by refusing its theoretical genre, transforming the latter by theatricalizing it, just as Diderot stages his encounter with Batteux by performing it as a scene of reading, an esthetic event itself. The theoretical genre of Batteux and others will always miss that event by refusing to acknowledge its own theatricality and its own art.

Ultimately, Diderot's art of philosophizing about what matters displaces the very genre of interpretation by figuring and (re)presenting it at one remove. At one point in the *Lettre* we read, "Mais je laisse ce langage figuré . . . et je reviens au ton de la philosophie *à qui il faut des raisons et non des comparaisons*" (IV, 161, Diderot's emphasis). What is called philosophy here, and which can be taken to refer to the theoretical genre exemplified by Batteux's *Beaux-arts*, is not an esthetic genre, for it requires reasoned analysis and demonstration, which cannot rely on poetic proofs and the language of metaphor. The artistic practice consisting of images, forms, and figures that are comparable to truth without being truth has no proper place in philosophy, except, as we have seen, as a restricted rhetoric. But there is more. "Ce langage figuré" cannot be left behind as simply as that. Voltaire indeed sensed that from the sensationalist perspective "tout est devenu métaphore," as he put it in the article "*Langue*" of the *Dictionnaire philosophique*. Yet it is Diderot who more forcefully explores how this generalization of metaphor destabilizes and reenergizes the very discourse of philosophy in which understanding is phrased. The philosophy to which he "returns" is of a different sort, one reworked through an apparent departure from it. This philosophy possesses a "ton," not just a particular style but a tonality, a musicality. Craftily, at least with regard to the philosophy of reason, Diderot does not abandon "ce langage figuré" after all. The figure of philosophy's tone artfully displaces philosophy, musicalizing it by comparing it to that other esthetic genre of artworks that are capable of producing the most "tumultuous" even crazy of effects. What one *hears* in this passage, in the sonorous play between *raisonner* and *résonner*, is that the act of judgment can indeed be performed, but most forcefully and most dynamically only by a kind of reason that fully embraces the resonance of its art.

CHAPTER 4

Critical narratives: Diderot's Salons

> La sotte occupation que celle de nous empêcher sans cesse de prendre du plaisir, ou de nous faire rougir de celui que nous avons pris! C'est celle du critique.
>
> Diderot

> Il faut apprendre à lire et à voir.
>
> Diderot, *Salon de 1767*

Begun in 1759 and spanning some twenty-two years, Diderot's reviews of the biennial exhibitions organized by the Royal Academy of Painting appeared during a time of marked transformation in the fine arts in France. As the principle of a classical, courtly style gradually lost its regulative force, painters enlarged the domain of the real that was judged presentable in art. The appeal of flamboyant rococo artifice steadily waned, displaced by the desire for scenes expressing classical high seriousness and exemplary morality. Around mid-century a mixed, hybrid style emerged, as artists experimented with ways to make visible new spaces and times, and to articulate esthetic and ethical values that would provide them with meaning.

Art historians have amply described the stylistic and thematic differences between eighteenth-century painting and that of the *Grand Siècle*.[1] Description alone though cannot account for what causes these artistic experimentations, their purpose or their effects. If the descriptive idiom is monotonous, parasitic, and uncritical, as Diderot will realize,[2] it is because description idealizes and essentializes the artwork, treating it as if its significance were immanent to form. Moreover, the formalism of descriptive discourse rests on the assumption that esthetic issues can be treated independently of supposedly nonesthetic ones, a decision that brackets, if not denies, whatever exists "outside" the work of art, located on "this side" of a supposedly essentially esthetic space. The most serious consequence of this denial is that in severing the linkage between the artwork, other representational practices, and the subjects involved in them, formalism abandons the means to articulate any effectively critical function, in either the artwork or the discourse pertaining to it.

The critique of formalism's refusal of the "nonesthetic" has been made often enough that it need not be rehearsed here.[3] To counter the closure of formalism though, one cannot simply "open" the work of art onto the supposed exteriority of the real. Injecting the real and the concrete (back) into the pictorial image may seem to infuse it with the life of the historical context. Yet this gesture assumes the existence of a putative "inside" and "outside," conceptual categories whose existence is more rhetorical than real. It is not at all certain that what the closure of formalism seems to exclude can best be grasped independently of the way art positions itself in relation to that supposed exteriority. Indeed, any hierarchical linkage of artwork and context breaks down once artistic means are recognized in the very operations of presenting the context that is claimed to open the artwork to understanding. To illustrate this point, let us consider one such opening in the presentation of eighteenth-century art in Arnold Hauser's *The Social History of Art*.

As his title indicates, Hauser takes the work of art to reflect the social-historical events responsible for the transformation of artistic forms. He thus attributes the "revolutionary change" occurring in art after 1750 to the ever increasing influence of a middle-class viewing public with its own specific sensibility and taste, a public whose emergence signals the larger restructuring of power relations in eighteenth-century France.

> In the whole history of art and culture, the transfer of leadership from one social class to another has seldom taken place with such absolute exclusiveness as [in the eighteenth century], where the aristocracy is completely displaced by the middle class, and the change of taste,

which puts expression in the place of decoration, could not possibly be any clearer.[4]

The forms and meanings of eighteenth-century art come to be shaped by "bourgeois subjectivism," the belief that individuals may freely represent things according to their own individual values, a belief that for Hauser still dominates the contemporary concept of art (at least that of the 1950s, when *The Social History* was written).

Recent quantitative analyses of eighteenth-century social milieus have shown that the advent of the bourgeois mentality Hauser identifies cannot be understood in terms of a traditional Marxist definition of class.[5] Instead, this event is better understood in terms of new viewing practices, one of the effects of which is to produce a particular spectatorial subject, whose "point of view" can be adopted by members of various social groups. Thus, instead of taking eighteenth-century painting to reflect something called bourgeois interests and values that preexist the painting, we might analyze more pertinently how painting *produces* a spectatorial subject. Whatever we name this subject, "the citizen" for instance,[6] it entails a particular way of evaluating the painted image. Paintings are judged less and less in terms of represented objects' nonpictorial status, their conventionally determined signification prior to their representation. Instead, esthetic judgment bears increasingly on the effects pictorial representation produces,[7] and which are characterized as values. Although the effects of viewing the so-called perfect illusion always depend on the painter's technique, no purely technical, perspectival, objective explanation can adequately account for these effects. In the *Salons*, these effects will be presented in terms of an act of will on the spectator's part, the will to take the image to depict a state of affairs more desired than real. Mimesis can never be considered objective, and it must never be separated from the working of desire. A particular configuration of this imbrication takes shape in the eighteenth century, in a spectatorial practice that articulates the desired knowledge the image is believed to represent.

One of the most promising ways to (re)write the social

history of art would be by analyzing various instances of this spectatorial practice and its relation to other, less apparently esthetic representational practices. Instead of cataloging multiple stylizations of a pregiven reality, as does an idealizing formalist art history, one would turn to social contexts in order to make esthetic form newly legible. At the same time, such an analysis must consider what makes these contexts legible, given that they too come to us only as the result of specific representational practices. To grasp what takes place outside the space of pictorial representation in the eighteenth century, in events readily characterized in sociohistorical terms, we cannot merely define the artwork as directly reflecting an immediately comprehensible social reality, replacing a mirrored beauty and esthetic essence with class taste and social transformation. Simply reversing the spatial metaphorics of "inside" and "outside" provides no critical view of art's relation to "real" history. The danger of such a reversal is that the sociohistorical knowledge apparently visible in the pictorial image may remain just as much an illusion, and an unexamined theoretical one, as the esthetic knowledge concerning the essence of art produced by formalism's descriptive analyses.

In the rush to contextualize, historicize, and politicize, one should not lose touch with art as a technical practice employing specific techniques whereby context and history are represented and made real, in other words knowable. Trying to grasp such a practice may necessitate doing away with the notion of art as being essentially distinct from other arts and other representational practices. Perhaps this means losing what is fine and beautiful about the fine arts, *les beaux arts*. This loss – if it is one though – hopefully is counterbalanced by the chance to grasp critically the work(ings) of art, and in other genres as well. This use of representational practices to present things as real defines not only pictorial art but also that of historical discourse for instance, which is to say that the knowledge produced by historical discourse must be understood more as an effect of its art than as a reflection of things as they are.[8] The historical narrative is but one discursive idiom among others, enjoying no natural superiority over other arts.

In this sense, any knowledge of that reality exterior to art doubtless results from yet another attempt to master the real by presenting it as representation.

The masterful knowledge of the real one may wish to see in images and texts rests on shaky ground. Theorists of the literary text, and more recently of the pictorial image, have rejected the traditional understanding of realism, reworking the notion of mimesis on which it is based. As Roland Barthes argued, the text cannot properly be understood as the mimetic reduplication of a model reality. The text as such reduplicates nothing, however much it presents something that may be taken *for* an exterior reality existing prior to its representation. For Barthes, textual realism depends instead on the text's success in producing the *effect* of the real, which means that any realism is but the codified articulation of what a given reader or reading community takes to be the real. Literary realism serves to represent values that any society constructs in order to display its existence to itself in discursive and symbolic form.[9]

Barthes' critique of realism does not deny any knowledge of the real. Rather, it regrounds such knowledge upon a critical awareness of its conventional determination, its constructedness. One might wish to call this construction of the real an ideological process, the text – and all artistic and cultural products – serving to represent the imaginary relations that members of a social group have of their real conditions of existence.[10] The more these imaginary relations are taken to be natural ones, the more effective the work of ideology has been. As Norman Bryson puts it, in an analysis of pictorial realism inspired by Barthes', the "success of the image in naturalizing the visual beliefs of a given community depends on the degree to which the image remains unknown as an independent form."[11] This formulation suggests that the visual image (and the literary text) can be apprehended as material form, that is, as existing prior to or at least separable from the interpretive act or ideological process whereby form is taken to signify something and the materiality of the artwork is transformed into the idea of what it means. Something in what Bryson calls form (and Barthes the text) resists the gesture whereby the artwork is taken as the reflection of what is exterior to it, and in this resistance lies the possibility of critical knowledge of that exteriority. In this case, the question to be raised is the following: what does it mean to "know" the image or the text as an "independent form"? What type of viewing or reading, and what theoretical idiom, can produce this knowledge? Furthermore, is the theoretical idiom as such the privileged source of such knowledge?

These questions bear upon the epistemological claims made in the name of general theory, and it is in terms of such questions that the intellectual history of poststructuralism might well be written. Although these questions have helped shape this book, I shall leave it to others to write that history. But I do wish to propose that these are precisely the questions Diderot himself confronts as spectator-critic. Breaking with parasitic description, uncritical formalism, and doctrinaire esthetic theory, Diderot adopts a personal narrative idiom to account for the artwork, both experientially and experimentally. In so doing, he becomes one of the first art critics, inaugurating the modern genre of art criticism. The *Salons*' modernity lies, then, in Diderot's constant grappling with the problem of producing theoretical discourse. Questioning self-reflexively the critical act of judging a painting, the *Salons* push the genre of theoretical discourse to its limits. Here as elsewhere, Diderot's art of philosophizing is excessive with respect to that genre, and in this excess exists a resistance to the paradigms and premises designed to contain this art of philosophizing theoretically. Only by attending to Diderot's manner in the *Salons*, his experimentation with his own critical idiom, can we grasp how the discourse of Enlightenment critique turns to art, that of the fine arts and its own, in order to pose the problem of articulating critical knowledge concerning whatever there is "outside" art. How then might we read this contestatory excess in Diderot's text and the kind of critical knowledge it produces?

First, one must refuse the kind of underreading that the *Salons* consistently have received since their publication in France in 1857. This reading history is marked not so much by errors as by sophisticated containment policies designed by commentators, critics, and art historians to defuse the challenge and threat this text poses. One such approach consists of reading the *Salons* as the discursive analogue of the paintings Diderot comments upon, that is, as the text *of* the image. The *Salons* would simply give voice to what is there upon the mute canvas; both text and painting would be the eminently readable expression of the visible shifts in style, taste, and form that took place between 1715 and 1789, for instance, between the Regency and the Revolution. A second approach takes the *Salons* not as the discourse *of* painting but as a discourse *on* painting. Along with other texts by Diderot, such as the *Encyclopédie* articles "*Génie*" and "*Beau*, " the *Eloge de Richardson*, *Entretiens sur le Fils naturel*, *De la poésie dramatique*, *Lettre sur les aveugles*, and the *Paradoxe sur le comédien*, the *Salons* would be primarily about esthetic theory, generically comparable to the work of estheticians such as Crousaz, Dubos, Roger de Piles, Batteux, and even the later *salonnier* Charles Baudelaire. Readings of the second sort typically limit themselves to rehearsing Diderot's arguments concerning master concepts of esthetic theory such as beauty, verisimilitude, the natural model, etc. Thus they necessarily misapprehend how the *Salons* contest the meta-critical discourse of theoretical knowledge to which such concepts belong, a discourse claiming to express the laws of pictorial representation that guarantee the symbolic mastery of reality and the production of truth.[12] Both approaches seek to contain the *Salons* by underreading their self-reflexivity, Diderot's probing questioning of the relation between language and image, what is said about what is seen. Recently the most innovative examinations of esthetic theory and art history have elaborated critical perspectives outside the traditional boundaries within which esthetic theory and art history have cantoned themselves, perspectives exposing the linguistic, philosophical and ideological implications at work in the limits both disciplines impose upon themselves and their texts.[13] Diderot's writing too establishes such a perspective, beginning with his questioning of the seemingly most simple of enterprises, namely, describing a painting.

The breakdown of description

Diderot begins the *Salons* apparently unconcerned by the possibility of a disparity between the visual idiom and the written one. Critical sensibility and artistic style are sufficient to ensure adequate description. The critic's pen simply must be as expressive as the painter's brush.

Pour décrire un Salon à mon gré et au vôtre, savez-vous, mon ami, ce qu'il faudrait avoir? Toutes les sortes de goût, un cœur sensible à tous les charmes, une âme susceptible d'une infinité d'enthousiasmes différents, une variété de style qui répondît à la variété des pinceaux; pouvoir être grand ou voluptueux avec Deshays, simple et vrai avec Chardin, délicat avec Vien, pathétique avec Greuze, produire toutes les illusions possibles avec Vernet (XIII, 341).

This comment concerning descriptions implies that the linguistic functions like the pictorial not only in terms of style and effects but also mimetically, each idiom capable at least ideally of reproducing its absent model. This notion of an ideal equivalence between image and writing hearkens back to seventeenth-century esthetic theory, encapsulated in the dictum *ut pictura poesis*.

As the following passage indicates though, description in the *Salons* soon becomes a more complicated affair than this general theoretical perspective allows for. "Je vous décrirai les tableaux," Diderot writes, "et ma description sera telle qu'avec un peu d'imagination et de goût on les réalisera dans l'espace et qu'on y posera les objets à peu près comme nous les avons vus sur la toile" (XIV, 26).[14] Description reproduces the absent painting, translating the pictorial image for the readers of Grimm's *Correspondance littéraire* in which the *Salons* first appeared. Significantly though, Diderot places two limiting conditions on description. First, it can only *almost* reproduce the painting ("*à peu près* comme nous les avons vus"). Second, it cannot do even this unaided, for supplementary participation from a reader is required ("un peu d'imagination et de goût"). Through reference to this *à peu près*, a linguistic insufficiency, excess or even undecidability with regard to the image, Diderot suggests that commentary cannot be understood as producing a mimetic reduplication of the painting. What commentary does produce is the occasion for subjective intervention, characterized here as the exercise of taste and imagination. While reference to taste might imply the art criticism of élitist connoisseurship, in which taste serves as a floating signifier promoting social (self-)recognition more than esthetic judgment, reference to the imagination here involves a quite different viewing practice.

The importance accorded to the imagination in eighteenth-century esthetics and epistemology sharply distinguishes them from those of the previous age. Enlightenment philosophers turn to the imagination to solve problems involving perception that crop up once the latter is no longer treated as a secondary and inferior mode of cognition, as Descartes had maintained it was. To what extent, they will ask, can the imagination provide a basis for valid judgments in the realm of both esthetics and epistemology? For Diderot, imagination functions by analogy, creating relations between otherwise disparate entities. It is the mark of the genius, the poet, and the madman. In a more present-day vocabulary, the supplementary activity of imagination Diderot locates on "this" side of the canvas can be characterized as involving a poetics of subjectivity. Critical commentary does not reproduce the painting for the *Salons*' reader; rather, Diderot's literary-poetic recreation of the experience of viewing the painting permits the subject – be it the reader or Diderot himself – to invent a particular idiom that in fact produces the imagined – and imaginary – image.

The heightened significance attributed to subjectivity leads Diderot to rework completely a theory of imitation that defines the relation between artwork and model to the exclusion of the individual subject. This reworking takes place conceptually, in theoretical terms. It also involves Diderot's own critical practice and idiom. For once imagination becomes the limiting condition of the critic's discourse, no longer can it be claimed that discourse reduplicates the image in a strictly mimetic sense. One practical result of this is that Diderot's confidence in his own descriptive abilities soon begins to erode.[15] Referring to two landscapes by Vernet, he writes, "il n'est presque pas possible d'en parler, il faut les voir. Quelle immense variété de scènes et de figures! Quelles eaux! Quels ciels! Quelle vérité! Quelle magie! Quel effet!" (XIII, 386). Two years later his reaction to a set of some twenty-five Vernet paintings is similar: "Il est impossible de rendre ses compositions, il faut les voir" (XIV, 135). And again, referring to landscapes by Robert, he states, "il est presque impossible de faire concevoir cette composition et tout aussi malaisé d'en transmettre l'impression" (XVI, 349).

This "il faut les voir" returns with increasing frequency in the *Salons*. But does it merely reflect critical coquetry, Diderot's inability to describe being more feigned than real? He has no difficulty describing the intricate spatial arrangement of the crowd of figures in Greuze's *Le Paralytique* for instance. Elsewhere, his playing out an inability to describe the complexity of Casanove's *Une marche d'armée* serves in fact as a fairly obvious rhetorical vehicle for presenting the painting.[16] The question though is not whether Diderot can write anything about a given painting, for even silence says something. At issue is his desire for a critical idiom that would make the artwork comprehensible by effectively transmitting the effects it produces.

Does such an idiom even exist? Perhaps not. "La meilleure description dit si peu de chose" (XVI, 405), Diderot laments. "A tout moment, je donne dans l'erreur, parce que la langue ne me fournit pas à propos l'expression de la vérité . . . J'ai au fond de mon cœur une chose, et j'en dis une autre" (XVI, 274–75). By its very nature, the linguistic cannot replicate the pictorial, a commonplace of esthetic theory Diderot frequently casts in sensationalist terms. "Autant d'hommes, autant de jugements. Nous sommes tous diversement organisés. Nous n'avons aucun la même dose de sensibilité. Nous nous servons tous à notre manière d'un instrument vicieux en lui-même, l'idiome qui rend toujours trop ou trop peu et nous adressons les sons de cet instrument à cent auditeurs qui écoutent, entendent, pensent et sentent diversement" (XVI, 118). Such passages suggest that the breakdown of description in the *Salons*, which involves the relation between critical commentary and painting, the linguistic and the pictorial, sign and referent, can be explained by a general theory of language, knowledge, and subjectivity.

In this sense, Diderot's esthetic texts too are marked by a displacement already witnessed, whereby the universal subject of linguistic and epistemological theory is replaced by the individual sensing subject of empiricism and sensationalism.[17]

The point I wish to make though is somewhat different. In reading the breakdown of description in the *Salons* in terms of a general theory, that of (Diderot's) linguistics, epistemology or esthetics for instance, one risks misapprehending the most critical aspect of Diderot's text, which pertains to the idiom of general theory itself. The breakdown of description in the *Salons* is linked to a questioning of the mimetic function of art, a questioning that also extends to the applicability of a general theory of mimesis in other idioms, notably that of theory. Can the theoretical idiom succeed in describing, representing, and thus making comprehensible what Diderot seems able to sense only in terms of nongeneralizable particularity, which he can define only in terms of each person's unique dosage of sensibility and language's uncontrollable capacity for saying too much or too little? So long as this sensing of the particular is phrased in general theoretical terms (involving the subject, language, painting, etc.), we will misjudge the particularity of the specific idiom he invents in the *Salons*, its resistance to general theory, and the critical knowledge it does produce. Turning to what I would call his short-circuiting of mimesis, we see that Diderot can realize this critical resistance only by breaking with a general theory of mimesis in order to fashion a different critical idiom. Refusing ultimately to define the relation between image and model, as well as critical discourse and its object, in terms of imitation, he reformulates questions concerning the nature or essence of the esthetic object by relating them to the intensely personal activity of the particular subject of viewing and of writing in this text. It is through this activity, moreover, that a critical linkage between artwork and historical context will be effectuated.

The short-circuiting of mimesis

A barrage of texts suggests that Diderot takes over unquestioningly the principle of art as imitation, which had become

4. Jean-Baptiste Chardin: *Raisins et grenades* (1763).

esthetic doctrine in France some hundred years earlier.[18] Like the estheticians of French classicism, he defines imitation as the relation of veridical identity between esthetic object and natural model. His initial response to Chardin's still lifes for instance is one of unmitigated admiration for the mimetic illusion their plasticity creates. Referring to paintings such as *Pièces de gibier*, *Raie dépouillée* or *Fruits*, he writes, "C'est la nature même. Les objets sont hors de la toile et d'une vérité à tromper les yeux" (XIII, 379). "C'est toujours la nature et la vérité; vous prendriez les bouteilles par le goulot, si vous aviez soif; les pêches et les raisins éveillent l'appétit et appellent la main" (XIII, 76). Chardin's appeal for Diderot, his technical skill in depicting grapes "qui appellent la main," might remind us of another *appel*, that of the Greek painter Apelles (in French, Apelle), who was supposed to have painted fruit so real even birds were deceived. It is as if Diderot too delights in being deceived, tricked into taking colored oils for real objects. For the moment, he is content to take his pleasure, believing it legitimate enough given the imitative finality of art.

While Diderot's praise of Chardin, Vernet, and Vien for their paintings' naturalness and veracity may seem subjective, impressionistic, even naïve,[19] the scenes of delighted deception he stages reenact nothing less than the ancient view of pictorial representation as the artful double of an absent model.[20] Despite his invocation of this traditional, even founding notion of representation, simple delight in mimetic illusion becomes harder to come by in the course of the *Salons*. Diderot realizes moreover that the pleasure he does experience in viewing a painting cannot be accounted for by the notion of pictorial representation as imitation. Consequently, he slowly disengages himself from the esthetic theory of classicism he initially took over, attempting to articulate a different manner of phrasing the relation between artwork, natural model, and the subject. This is not to say simply that Diderot's understanding of pictorial imitation becomes more refined theoretically, although such an argument is not unfounded. Rather, the very manner in which he phrases the effects of pictorial representation effectively displaces the classical theory of mimesis, marking in the process the limits of the theoretical discourse of art in general.

This displacement begins with a questioning of the relation between painting and its model. Instead of positing the existence of a real model existing prior to the act of painting and whose reality determines artistic production, Diderot claims no such model exists. If painters' goal is to represent beauty, nature provides them with no perfect models. "[La nature] produit tous ses ouvrages viciés" (XVI, 69). Consequently, the artist's model can only be an ideal one, perfect yet imaginary, one that never existed and never will.

Convenez donc que ce modèle est purement idéal, et qu'il n'est emprunté directement d'aucune image individuelle de nature dont la copie vous soit restée dans l'imagination, et que vous puissiez appeler derechef, arrêter sous vos yeux, et recopier servilement, à moins que vous ne veuillez vous faire portraitiste. Convenez donc que, quand vous faites beau, vous ne faites rien de ce qui est, rien même de ce qui puisse être (XVI, 67–68).

Diderot is not just belatedly adopting the position of the previous century's estheticians, who maintained that pictorial imitation involves the painter's observing not one but numerous models, then selecting the most beautiful elements of each. His insight is more far-reaching. In affirming "quand vous faites beau, vous ne faites rien de ce qui est, rien même de ce qui peut être," he effectively unleashes art from the determinate priority of objective reality and of objects – however "real" – existing "outside" and prior to the act of representation. Such objects exist only as ideal models, created as part of the working process.

This undermining of the determinate role attributed to an anterior, nonpictorial, and model reality already begins in the *Encyclopédie* article "*Beau.*" Diderot appears to argue here that beauty does indeed exist in an objective sense, independently of the individual subject's relative perception of things. Thus beauty can be understood in two ways, existing "hors de moi" and "par rapport à moi." Yet if we consider how this formulation distinguishes between two types of beauty, it becomes clear that subjectivity cannot be delimited so easily. Beauty can be defined objectively "hors *de moi*" only in relation to "*par rapport à*" – a subject, which is the very definition of subjective beauty. Commentators have noted the instability of this dualism, taking it to reflect the hesitant, probing nature of Diderot's earliest theoretical formulations in the area of esthetics. If this dualistic definition of beauty does hold together through the article, it is due primarily to the latter's level of theoretical abstraction. Once this definition is applied practically, in the context of the viewing practice the *Salons* describe, it falls apart. Diderot comes to realize that while art and esthetic judgment indeed involve relations or *rapports*, there exists no absolute, objective relation on the basis of which art can be judged. The objective existence of beauty, and with it the truth of pictorial representation, increasingly depends upon, and hence is definable only in terms of, their relation to an individual subject. One result of Diderot's insight is that beauty cannot be treated as a technical question alone, and still less as an affair of theoretical abstraction. For the act of perceiving beauty testifies above all to the work of affectivity in techniques of representation, the affective nature of the relation between artwork and the subject judging it.

Diderot repeatedly invokes the faculty of the imagination to account for this affectivity, elaborating what has been seen as a post-Classical, pre-Romantic definition of the artist and the artwork. This valorization involves a thorough reworking of the concepts of mimesis, the truth function of pictorial representation, and esthetic judgment. "L'imitation rigoureuse de nature rendra l'art pauvre, petit, mesquin, mais jamais faux ou maniéré. C'est de l'imitation de nature soit exagérée soit embellie que sortiront le beau et le vrai, le maniéré et le faux; parce qu'alors l'artiste est abandonné à sa propre imagination. Il reste sans aucun modèle précis" (XVI, 534). Far different from a technique of "rigorous" reduplication, imitation resulting from the excessive work of the imagination involves no "precise model," that is, no object outside pictorial representation whose truth the latter could be judged to depict. Hence, when viewed as resulting from the work of the imagination, pictorial representation no longer can be reduced to the truth it depicts, for the imagination produces both truth *and* falseness, the beautiful *and* the mannered. This is why Diderot elsewhere defines painting as "un tissu de faussetés qui se couvrent les unes les autres" (XIII, 373).

The faculty of the imagination is not invoked to explain how artworks create illusionary effects that subsequently must be judged in terms of their truth. Rather, Diderot suggests that something is involved in the work of art that cannot appropriately be judged according to the criterion of truth. This is why he repeatedly characterizes the imagination in terms of its unbounded dynamism, its poetic capacity to represent.

L'imagination passe rapidement d'image en image; son œil embrasse tout à la fois. Si elle discerne des plans, elle ne les gradue ni ne les établit. Elle s'enfoncera tout à coup à des distances immenses. Tout à coup elle reviendra sur elle-même avec la même rapidité, et pressera sur vous les objets. Elle ne sait ce que c'est qu'harmonie, cadence, balance; elle entasse, elle confond, elle meut, elle approche, elle éloigne, elle mêle, elle colore comme il lui plaît (XVI, 151).

The imagination does not know the rules of classical composition, if indeed it *knows* anything at all, properly speaking. Rather, it works, performs, and acts. Hence, Diderot insists on distinguishing the work of the imagination from the supremely philosphical act of judgment, instead of subordinating one to the other or joining them synthetically.

L'imagination et le jugement sont deux qualités communes et presque opposées. L'imagination ne crée rien. Elle imite, elle compose, combine, exagère, agrandit, rapetisse. Elle s'occupe sans cesse de ressemblances. Le jugement observe, compare, et ne cherche que des différences. Le jugement est la qualité dominante du philosophe. L'imagination, la qualité dominante du poète (XVI, 214).

This description of the work of the imagination not only redefines the nature of pictorial representation, it reworks the relation between painting and spectator, representation and the subject, art and the discourse of esthetic theory. For Diderot, being a philospher means suppressing the imagination and the poetic, and thus he cannot be said to propose yet another philosophical theory of art. Instead he seeks to elaborate a practice of spectatorship as imaginative, as artistic, and as poetic as what is at work upon the canvas.

Initially, Diderot senses that practice only negatively, as that which is precluded by classical esthetic theory and the philosophical view of art. "Il y a dans la poésie, toujours en peu de mensonge. L'esprit philosophique nous habitue à le discerner, et adieu l'illusion et l'effet" (XVI, 222). The philosophical perspective limits the spectator to interrogating painting in terms of its truth, to asking "mais est-il vrai?" as Diderot does at one point concerning a particular detail. Such a viewer or viewing of pictorial representation limits its capacity to represent truly and thereby short-circuits its effects. To ask the supremely philosphical question "but is it true?" means bringing an end to illusion and its effects, unless we speak of the illusionary nature of truth itself, its artful artifice.[21] "Il y a des passions bien difficiles à rendre. Presque jamais on ne les a vues dans la nature. Où donc en est le modèle? où le peintre les trouve-t-il? qu'est-ce qui me détermine, moi, à prononcer qu'il a trouvé la vérité?" (XIII, 236). When Diderot asks how he, as art critic, can decide whether the painter has "found the truth" by faithfully reproducing his model, he also questions a particular type of viewing and the limitations it places upon the spectator. To account for the illusionary, imaginative, and poetic work of the spectator, and above all his own viewing practice, finally he must reject the prescriptive discourse of legislative esthetic theory.

Diderot shows himself well aware that in refusing this type of viewing, he undermines his own critical discourse and esthetic judgment in general. He writes, for example, referring to Casanove's battle scenes,

> grande variété d'incidents; beau et effrayant désordre, avec harmonie. C'est tout ce que je puis dire. Mais quelle idée cela laisse-t-il? aucune. On composerait d'après cette description, cent autres tableaux différents entre eux et de celui de Casanove . . . Quelle est la description d'un tableau de bataille qui puisse servir à un autre que celui qui l'a faite, les yeux devant le tableau. Plus vous détaillerez; chaque petit détail ayant toujours quelque chose de vague et d'indéterminé; plus vous compliquerez le problème pour l'imagination (XVI, 280, 285).

The following remark concerning a Vernet marks the high point of skepticism concerning critical discourse. "Voilà à peu près toute cette prodigieuse composition. Mais que signifient mes expressions exsangues et froides, mes lignes sans chaleur et sans vie, ces lignes que je viens de tracer les unes au-dessous des autres. Rien, mais rien du tout. Il faut voir la chose" (XVI, 225).

As Michel Foucault has argued, the goal of classical age epistemology is to *faire tableau*, to present knowledge as representation.[22] The breakdown of description in the *Salons*, which stems from the ultimate incommensurability between word and image, indicates symptomatically that this goal is unattainable. Nothing guarantees that the painting the critic presents through description in any way resembles the painting the spectator views. "Un coup d'œil supplée à cent pages de discours," Diderot writes, affirming the primacy of vision over language, and the powerful immediacy of an ineffable visual experience. In the need "to see the thing," the kind of viewing Diderot calls for is not a preview or review of the image that captures it better than language ever could. Rather, he refers to a particular kind of viewing, the *coup d'œil*, whose function is to *suppléer*, that is, to supplant and replace language, yet at the same time to supplement and complete it. The visual *supplément* is thus distinct from the kind of epistemological discourse that seeks to comprehend its object, to succeed in representing it as an object of knowledge; yet simultaneously and paradoxically this *supplément* of vision completes the work of epistemological discourse. If anything is revealed by the kind of viewing Diderot refers to here, it is that the seen cannot be displayed for knowledge (*fait tableau*) except by being phrased (*fait récit*). The problem of viewing becomes enmeshed with that of phrasing, of inventing a way to tell the story of viewing a painting. The *coup d'œil* as *supplément* of and to vision does not mark a "return" to the visual image, but rather a way of presenting – in language – the relation of the eye/I to an image, a relation that the *Salons* repeatedly stage.

All paintings are based on the convention that they are meant to be viewed. In the *Salons*, however, it is from the painting's "other" side, that of spectator, that a viewing is staged which becomes a constitutive part of the work. This is why Diderot cannot characterize painting solely in terms of technical and mimetic accuracy involving only the relation between image and model, and why above all he privileges pictorial effects as they are registered in the spectatorial act. "La peinture est l'art d'aller à l'âme par l'entremise des yeux; si l'effet s'arrête aux yeux, le peintre n'a fait que la moindre partie du chemin" (XIV, 226). Or, defining painting more melodramatically: "Touche-moi, étonne-moi, déchire-moi, fais-moi tressaillir, pleurer, frémir, m'indigner d'abord; tu recréeras mes yeux après, si tu peux" (XIV, 389). Art historians frequently take such statements to reflect Diderot's personal art preferences, and his contemporaries' excessive sentimentalism – if not their bad (and bourgeois) taste. More significantly, such passages suggest nothing less than a complete revision of a solely ocular relation to painting. What Diderot calls for here is an intensification of painting's ability to work not only upon the eyes but upon the entire body. In this sense the body becomes the truly critical text that judges the painting's success by transcribing and performing its effects. Only through this performance or performativity of the spectatorial body can a revision of art be produced.

This emphasis on spectatorial response seems paradoxical in the light of Diderot's claim that the spectator's presence must be ignored, even neutralized. "Lairesse prétend qu'il est permis à l'artiste de faire entrer le spectateur dans la scène de son tableau. Je n'en crois rien; et il y a si peu d'exceptions, que je ferais volontiers une règle générale du contraire. Cela me semblerait d'aussi mauvais goût que le jeu d'un acteur qui s'adresserait au parterre. La toile renferme tout l'espace, et il n'y a personne au delà."[23] Or elsewhere: "une scène représentée sur la toile, ou sur les planches, ne suppose point de témoins" (XVI, 127). Or again, in his advice to actors and playwrights: "Soit donc que vous composiez, soit donc que vous jouiez, ne pensez non plus au spectateur que s'il n'existait pas. Imaginez, sur le bord du théâtre, un grand mur qui vous sépare du parterre; jouez comme si la toile ne se levait pas" (AT VII, 345). This "great wall" Diderot would erect to separate stage and house does not deny the presence of the real spectator however. The spectatorial presence he refuses is that of the virtual or implied spectator, a subject constructed by the rules and conventions of acting, staging, and dramaturgy in eighteenth-century high theater.

The real object of Diderot's critique is a theatricalized type of spectatorship. As the art historian Michael Fried has argued, for Diderot this way of viewing plays and paintings produces "dislocation and estrangement" within the object–beholder relationship rather than "absorption, sympathy, and self-transcendence." Accordingly, Diderot was led to experiment with techniques and strategies for overcoming that alienation, to "de-theatricalize beholding" in order to create through painting and theater "a mode of access to truth and conviction."[24]

Fried's argument is helpful for understanding the technical and generic reforms Diderot proposes, which are clearly designed to revitalize theatrical representation's capacity to produce intense effects upon the spectator. The *Entretiens sur le Fils naturel* and *De la poésie dramatique* propose the hybrid theatrical genre of the *drame bourgeois*,[25] which entails a complete reworking of the traditional relation between audience and actor, house and stage. Diderot maintains, for instance, that writers must not be satisfied with stringing together witty, well-turned phrases: "ce ne sont pas des mots que je veux remporter du théâtre, mais des impressions ... Le poète excellent est celui dont l'effet demeure longtemps en moi" (AT VII, 314). Actors must be given freer rein to perform instead of merely reciting:

> nous parlons trop dans nos drames; et, conséquemment, nos acteurs n'y jouent pas assez ... Qu'est-ce qui nous affecte dans le spectacle de l'homme animé de quelque grande passion? Sont-ce ses discours? Quelquefois. Mais ce qui émeut toujours, ce sont des cris, des mots inarticulés, des voix rompues, quelques monosyllabes qui s'échappent par intervalles, je ne sais quel murmure dans la gorge, entre les dents (AT VII, 104–6).

Actors should avoid the declamatory, emphatic style of the tirade, employing instead a more expressive, emotive vocabulary of gesture and pantomine. Writers should dispense with the expedient *coup de théâtre* to advance the plot, and instead let action freeze from time to time into tableaux that arrest spectators' attention and intensify their experience.

Recalling Diderot's own distrust of formalist description, we might ask whether describing techniques and genres in this manner can help us comprehend this newly intensified spectatorial experience. More specifically, can one locate in Diderot's critique of an alienating theatricality the link to an "outside" of the painting, a theoretical joint between image and context? Closer consideration of how Fried puts Diderot's theatrical theory to use provides an answer.

Fried's concern is to explain the structural or formal logic of mid-eighteenth-century French painting, and in particular the "master theme" of absorption. This theme appears in scenes depicting persons oblivious to their surroundings, intensely engrossed in what they are doing.[26] Displaying no awareness of being seen, these figures turn their sight "inwards," and eye contact with an implied viewer, such as one finds in full or three-quarter face portraits, is absent. As Fried reads them, these scenes of absorption depict more than a certain style, for they present a formal solution to the problematic relation between painting and viewer that emerges in the eighteenth century. Absorption designates precisely that pictorial technique that by offsetting and refusing the conventional viewer's presence provides the real viewer with a less determined, less theatricalized way of viewing the painting, and thus a supposedly more authentic comprehension of what it presents.

For Fried, Diderot's theory of spectatorship makes absorption legible as a pictorial technique for overcoming the self's disjunction from the objects of its beholding. What Fried views in Diderot is a theory of viewing stemming from the need of both painters and viewers to involve themselves in scenes of absorption, scenes that amount to the pictorial quest for a means of "self-transcendence." These scenes, as well as their understanding, would originate in the ontological desire to locate oneself in and through a viewing, to find the desired and imaginary self in the image. Thus, the master theme of absorption (as well as its masterful theory) amounts to yet another version of a more masterful "theme," that of self-representation.

It is significant that Fried suggests his view of absorption can be understood not only formally and ontologically, but historically as well. The role of beholding, he claims, both stabilized and undermined "a new consciousness of the self" that emerged in the eighteenth century. As for the causes that produced this consciousness, they are to be found in "the social, political and economic reality of the age – in all that bears on the history of the self." With this explicit reference to an extrapictorial reality, Fried holds open the tantalizing promise that his study of absorption presents at least a chapter in a new history of the self, of the self as historical product. Yet surprisingly enough, he does not make good on this promise. The introduction to *Absorption and Theatricality* contains the following disclaimer: "Nowhere in the pages that follow is an effort made to connect the art and criticism under discussion with the social, economic, and political reality of the age" (p. 4). Why this categorical denial, this almost defensive foreclosure of the possibility of linking painting, a theory of art, and "reality"? Why also does this theory of art reveal a process whereby self-consciousness is constructed, and simultaneously invoke a division of labor designed to preserve art history within familiar disciplinary boundaries, thereby limiting the disciplinary self-awareness art history might derive from such a theoretical investigation?

The answer to these questions lies in Fried's understanding of theatricality. For him, it is a conventional, artificial, and thus alienating form of representation, one moreover that can be comprehended and countered by a theory of representation. Such an understanding is not Diderot's however. Certainly he criticizes the alienating conventionality of eighteenth-century high theater. Yet what he proposes in its stead is precisely *another* theatricality, that is, another set of theatrical mechanisms better able to produce the effects he desires. Like Rousseau, who in the *Lettre à D'Alembert* mounts a scathing attack on the alienating effects of theater and at the same time presents its antidote in the most theatrical of figures, Diderot criticizes theatricality only to employ and deploy it in both his plays and prose texts. When he states, concerning Le Prince's *Pastorale russe*, "Un tableau avec lequel on raisonne ainsi, *qui vous met en scène*, et dont l'âme reçoit une sensation délicieuse, n'est jamais un mauvais tableau" (XIV, 226, my emphasis), he suggests nothing other than a highly theatricalized viewing and writing event, a staging that contains the narrative of his own absorbed beholding of the painting. If Diderot breaks with the descriptive discourse of the conventional *salonnier*, and with the judgmental discourse of classical mimetic theory, it is precisely because these discourses are not theatrical enough. And if the *Salons* are marked by any kind of "disjunction," "alienation" or "estrangement," it is in the distance Diderot takes from a certain kind of theoretical genre that willfully or blindly ignores its own theatrical potential, its own capacity to "make a scene."

This, one senses, is what *Absorption and Theatricality* attempts to comprehend and contain. Calling the *Salons*' genre "criticism and theory" seems designed to preclude considering whether this text involves not only a theory of spectatorship but also its practice. A twentieth-century theoretician of absorption would have to exclude (or cover up) this practice, lest the desires driving the quest for spectatorial and critical self-absorption be revealed as precisely that, as desire. Diderot does not necessarily claim to comprehend this desire. But he certainly does not claim ignorance of its driving force in the process of self-representation, the production of spectatorial self-consciousness. To read the *Salons* otherwise is to fall into the trap this text sets, for its readers and even its author, that of a pleasure-taking that feigns ignorance of its own mechanisms.[27] It is far from certain the theory and practice of spectatorship the *Salons* articulate can be understood on the basis of the "social, political and economic reality of the age," at least not until one comes to terms with the real issue, namely, "reality," whether of the self or the age whose history one would write.

The *Salons* constitute a primary document in that history, and to write it Diderot must be read not solely as a spectator-critic who produces a new theory of viewing, but also as a spectator-writer. One may admirably describe the "great wall" of theory erected to separate actor and spectator, painting and viewer. Yet this theoretical construction precludes grasping the role of one particular spectator, the writing subject of the *Salons*. Instead of accepting as pregiven the notion of reality, be it the historical reality of the event or the ontological reality of the self, one must consider the discursive mechanisms whereby terms such as "event" and "self" come to signify the presence of natural, independent, self-contained entities. Certainly, one must not discount what is historically specific to a given period, including its "social, political and economic reality," by disregarding real persons and making everything into fictions, or by excluding the event and reducing everything to language, if such oppositions remain meaningful. However, only by examining the discursive mechanisms that make things knowable *as* events and subjects, can one grasp that reality in its discursive determination. This is why we shall now consider these discursive mechanisms at work in the *Salons* in privileged scenes of beholding. One of the effects of these stories of viewings that Diderot narrates will be to produce a critical sense, if not the knowledge, of the discursive, cultural, historical, and ideological product that is the self.

"Du plaisir tout pur et sans peine"

At one point, Diderot compares sketches and paintings. "Pourquoi une belle esquisse nous plaît-elle plus qu'un tableau ... L'esquisse ne nous attache peut-être si fort que parce qu'étant indéterminée, elle laisse plus de liberté à notre imagination qui y voit tout ce qu'il lui plaît" (XVI, 358–59). Of interest to Diderot are the particular effects each genre produces, and which cannot be explained by the degree of nobility each genre's subject matter possesses. This is the criterion Félibien had proposed a century earlier in defending the doctrine of the hierarchy of the genres, which placed the historical painting above all other genres.[28] Here though, Diderot discards this overarching theoretical explanation. What attracts him to the sketch is not its formal nature, which distinguishes it from other genres, but its indeterminacy, its capacity to afford the viewer's imagination a play of interpretive possibilities. In this sense the sketch exemplifies the relation between imagination and the visual in general. If imagination can see in the sketch "whatever it pleases, whatever it desires," then the question of vision cannot be separated from that of desire, or what Diderot calls "passion." A kind of critical pleasure principle is involved here, located in the ways the pictorial can serve as pretext for producing an imaginative response, an imaginary pleasure. How does such pleasure come about? What kind of viewing does it presuppose, and what kind of writing? Diderot's commentary on Le Prince's *Pastorale russe* provides one answer.

The painting depicts an old man holding a balalaika, a young woman, and a young man playing a reed pipe. But the painting itself is not the object of Diderot's commentary, which does far more than simply describe the painting's rustic scene. The old man, his daughter, and the young man become characters in an imaginary scene, a fictional event Diderot narrates and in which, curiously enough, he himself participates.

> Cette composition va droit à l'âme. Je me trouve bien là, je resterai appuyé contre cet arbre, entre ce vieillard et sa jeune fille, tant que le jeune garçon jouera. Quand il aura cessé de jouer et que le vieillard remettra ses doigts sur sa balalaye, j'irai m'asseoir à côté du jeune garçon, et lorsque la nuit s'approchera, nous reconduirons tous les trois ensemble le bon vieillard dans sa cabane (XIV, 226).

It would be reductive at best to understand "je me trouve bien là" as simply meaning that Le Prince's scene is a pleasant one. For it is there indeed (*bien là*) that Diderot finds himself (*je me trouve*), but where? "There" (*là*) refers to the scene depicted in "this composition," yet also to the scene Diderot composes and in which he leans against "this tree." Thus, there indeed where Diderot finds himself and takes pleasure is not in the act of viewing the painting, but in the act of writing. Two different scenes or spaces are linked by the deictic, as a theatricalizing micronarrative shifts reference from the visual to the written, from the pictorial to the fictional, and from the time of an eternal present to that of a deferred future.

This referential linkage allows Diderot to write himself into the painting, by viewing in it what he pleases, namely, himself. For the harmonious scene in which he participates, however banal, is coded in familial terms ("ce vieillard et sa jeune fille"). Significantly, the scene Diderot describes himself seeing in and through Le Prince's painting bears a curious and distorted resemblance to two elements of his own family story, involving his relationship with his father, sister and brother, and with his only daughter. Versions of Diderot's family romance are recounted elsewhere, most accurately perhaps in letters to his confidante-mistress Sophie Volland, and most interestingly in the *Entretiens sur le Fils naturel*. In the latter's play within a play, the character of Diderot-Moi is written into the spectacle as a hidden observer of the bourgeois drama of family reconciliation, rewarded virtue, wealth, and happiness that ritualistically plays itself out before him.[29] Just as the *Entretiens* privilege a position of viewing that can only be read (by the text's readers), not seen (by the play's actors), so too in Diderot's narrative (re)creation of Le Prince's scene he wishes to see himself – or rather writes himself – as unable to be seen. Referring to the old man in the painting, he states, "je le crois aveugle, s'il ne l'est pas, je voudrais qu'il le fût." In (re)writing the painting as he desires it, Diderot blinds the gaze of the father, canceling the authority of the visual given, in order to allow his own image-making, scriptural gaze to reach out towards the object it wants.

More than a personal psychodrama, this narrative, imaginary pleasure-taking offers one criterion for esthetic judgment, as a concluding remark concerning Le Prince suggests: "un tableau avec lequel on raisonne ainsi, *qui vous met en scène*, et dont l'âme reçoit une sensation délicieuse, n'est jamais un mauvais tableau" (XIV, 226). This praise of paintings that stage their viewer would seem to contradict the rule formulated elsewhere, namely, that painting must distance, even negate spectatorial presence. This apparent contradiction reveals in fact a tension that informs esthetic judgment throughout the *Salons*, and which involves on the one hand a theoretical discourse that signifies the viewer as an anonymous *on*, a limited, idealized, effaced presence, and on the other a more "subjective" discourse whose critical potential stems from a "mise en scène." This staging is what theoretical discourse tends to overlook, a staging of the subject of esthetic judgment. Writing moreover, not vision, operates this staging, producing the "sensation délicieuse" to which Diderot refers. The case of Chardin illustrates this point.

In the early *Salons*, Diderot's praise for the naturalness and veracity of Chardin's still lifes is unbounded. Judged in terms of an esthetics of imitation, Chardin's works portray "nature itself," captivating and transfixing their viewer.[30] These paintings' power diminishes however, and eventually Diderot wearies of the very predictability of a Chardin still life. This eventual disinterest stems above all from these paintings' narratability. Even at the high point of his admiration for Chardin, Diderot stops short of inserting an imaginary scene in his commentaries, a nonresponse that cannot be explained by the paintings' subject matter alone. If Diderot does not take delight in writing into Chardin's still lifes what is not there to be seen, it is because he cannot break with a pictorial rule created by a precise aspect of Chardin's technique, namely, perspective. Diderot explains: "On n'entend rien à cette magie. Ce sont des couches épaisses de couleur, appliquées les unes sur les autres, et dont l'effet transpire de dessous en dessus ... Approchez-vous, tout se brouille, s'aplatit et disparaît. Eloignez-vous, tout se crée et se reproduit" (XIII, 380). "Le faire de Chardin est particulier. Il a de commun avec la manière heurtée que de près on ne sait ce que c'est, et qu'à mesure qu'on s'éloigne l'objet se crée et finit par être celui de la nature" (XIV, 123). Chardin's "magic" consists of a chromatic layering effect, which establishes a point of perspective from which the painting appears to be an exact copy of the thing itself. But this mimetic illusion can occur only if the painting is viewed from one particular position. The rules of Chardin's perspective are unyielding, providing the viewer no freedom or play in the viewing. In a broader sense, Diderot's reaction to the inflexible positioning of the viewer figures a clash between the laws of perspectivism and the dynamics of the scriptural. Chardin's perspective rigidly determines not only a point of view but also a point of writing. The sole critical perspective these paintings afford is the discourse of description, which is bound moreover by a law of imitation that reins in the pleasure of imagination, the writing of imaginary pleasure. Chardin's technique limits the viewer's imagination, restricting the desire to narrate and the narration of desire. This above all is what painting must not foreclose. "Quand on écrit, faut-il tout écrire? Quand on peint, faut-il tout peindre? De grâce, laissez quelque chose à suppléer par mon imagination" (XIII, 356). The need for the supplemental activity of spectatorial imagination explains why Diderot's judgment of Chardin changes from transfixed admiration to forced appreciation and finally to simple boredom.[31]

The case of Chardin exemplifies a more general critical project, and whose effective force should be gauged in terms of the supplementary activity of spectatorial imagination. In describing painting, Diderot seeks to "faire concevoir [la] composition" by producing a secondary form of representation based on the assumed legitimacy of rules and principles whereby painting makes the real comprehensible by representing it. At the same time, however, he also wishes to recount and stage the particular effect of viewing the painting, "en transmettre l'impression." Because of this concern with the "impression," with the effects of representation upon a given subject, the pleasure experienced before the painting becomes increasingly autonomous, unrelated to the theory of pictorial representation as imitation that Diderot initially takes over from classical esthetic theory. The 1761 *Salon* begins, "voici, mon ami, les idées qui m'ont passé par la tête à la vue des tableaux qu'on a exposés cette année au Salon" (XIII, 215). Can such comments justify calling Diderot's art criticism impressionistic? Perhaps, but only once his impressionism has been correctly understood. "Ideas" can start "coming to mind" only once the descriptive project has begun to break down, only once Diderot counters the law of imitation with the imaginative play of the written. Through narrative intervention, Diderot frames his reaction to the painting, (re)creating an experience and producing a discursive event in which the significance of the visual event takes place.

This last point must be stressed. Narrative in the *Salons* should not be judged in terms of its accuracy, for its function here is not to translate into language an essentially nonnarrative object, experience or event. It is beside the point, for example, to ask whether the *Salons*' narratives tell how Diderot really felt when he saw Robert's Roman ruins or whether Vernet's landscapes are as magically enticing as Diderot's story makes them out to be. At work in these narratives is the production not of truth, *le vrai*, but of *le vraisemblable*, not what really is but rather what appears believable and desirable to a particular subject, what this subject wants to believe to be.

In Diderot, artistic production takes place as much on the page as upon the canvas, dislocating in the process the very concept of art and the esthetic theory that founds it. As Jacques

Chouillet perceptively notes, "[Diderot est] celui par qui s'est opéré la transmutation du concept d'art en une activité productrice: le discours sur l'art, dans lequel s'accomplit, avant de s'abolir, l'esthétique théorique."[32] Reworking the place and function of representation, the *Salons*' critical discourse on painting does not aim to make its object comprehensible by presenting itself as a substitute for it; nor does critical discourse even claim itself able to attain such understanding. Rather, in these narratives of pleasure-taking we find what Jean-François Lyotard has called, in a redefinition of representation that would short-circuit the question of mimesis, "concentrations of libidinal energy on the surface of the visible and the articulatable."[33] These intense moments of narrative pleasure-taking suggest that any claim to universal truth made through esthetics is determined and limited by the essentially libidinal desire that produces them. The question that remains concerns how Diderot's text itself reveals that determination, and whether in the text alone that truly critical understanding can be said to occur. To develop these questions, let us turn to the paintings of Jean-Baptiste Greuze and Diderot's commentary on them.

Often viewed as inaugurating bourgeois realism in painting, Greuze's innumerable scenes of moralizing sentimentality mark a key moment in the revolt already begun by 1750 against a pleasure-seeking and frivolous rococo, and which leads eventually to the propagandistic art of the Revolution. Diderot spares no praise for these scenes, which for him exemplify the morally didactic function of art at its best.[34] To grasp just what is involved in Greuze's art, and in Diderot's commentary, we should approach the moralizing Greuze somewhat obliquely though, by way of one of Diderot's not entirely innocent responses to one of Greuze's not entirely innocent paintings.

Commenting on *Le Baiser envoyé*, also called *Une jeune fille qui envoie un baiser par la fenêtre, appuyée sur des fleurs, qu'elle brise*, Diderot writes,

Il est impossible de vous peindre toute la volupté de cette figure; ses yeux, ses paupières en sont chargés. Quelle main que celle qui a jeté ce baiser! Quelle physionomie! quelle bouche! quelles lèvres! quelles dents! Quelle gorge! On la voit cette gorge et on la voit tout entière, quoiqu'elle soit couverte d'un voile léger. Le bras gauche ... Elle est ivre, elle n'y est plus, elle ne sait plus ce qu'elle fait, ni moi presque ce que j'écris ... (XIV, 276).

Once again description is said to be unable to reproduce what the painting figures, in this case voluptuousness. But here least of all does Diderot write off the inadequacy of descriptive discourse with a simple "il faut le voir." Instead he proceeds to disassemble the painting, transforming it into a fragmented series of newly eroticized signs whose signification results from the narrative repositioning that occurs in the discourse of commentary. Voluptuousness may be unrepresentable; its experience or effect is not. Thus, Diderot breathlessly piles one expression of desire upon another, until at last he can produce another scene. At this moment the figure of the painting quite literally is no longer there ("elle n'y est plus"), for the figure has been displaced onto the imaginary scene produced by commentary. One could imagine this one scene (of writing) completely dispossessing the other scene (of painting). Abruptly though Diderot forecloses this playing out of desire by claiming he is "almost" unaware of what is going on. But what does Diderot "almost" not know? Or rather, how do these not so innocent commentaries provide (us) knowledge of how desire represents its object?

Considering Diderot's commentary on another of Greuze's paintings, *La Jeune fille qui pleure son oiseau mort*, one notes that this painting is thematically related to *Le Baiser envoyé*. Greuze's use of dead birds, shattered flower pots, and broken mirrors is part of a more general sociocultural encoding of the feminine.[35] Far from being unaware of what is signified here, Diderot comments on the painting by way of an invented fiction. In a three-page dialogue with the young girl, he tells the story of an absent mother, a hesitant girl, the persistent and finally successful entreaties of a young lover, a story bathed abundantly in the tears of Diderot's melancholy partner of fiction. Somewhat banal, or at least designed to banalize seduction, this first fictive dialogue is abruptly branched onto a

5. Jean-Baptiste Greuze: *L'Oiseau mort* (1800).

second. Addressing himself to Grimm and to any reader whose complicity could be coded as masculine, Diderot protests,

Mais, mon ami, ne riez-vous pas, vous d'entendre un grave personnage s'amuser à consoler une enfant en peinture de la perte de son oiseau, de la perte de tout ce qu'il vous plaira? Mais aussi voyez donc qu'elle est belle! qu'elle est intéressante! Je n'aime point à affliger, malgré cela, il ne me déplairait pas trop d'être la cause de sa peine (XIV, 182).

If Diderot damns a Loutherbourg with faint praise by saying, "enfin c'est un très beau tableau où il y a peu à désirer" (AT XI, 500), then Greuze's *Jeune fille* seems on the contrary to provide much to be desired, and through an essentially narrative process.

Prior to the invented fiction, Diderot comments on a particular element of the painting, the young girl's hand. "On s'approcherait de cette main pour la baiser, si on ne respectait cette enfant et sa douleur" (XIV, 180). This reference to the painting has a curiously double status, since the deictic ("cette main") marks the reality of the painting as such, and at the same time refers to an imaginary scene into which Diderot enters or is drawn ("on s'approcherait"). In this second scene, that of the fictional dialogue, spectatorial desire plays itself out as it turns the visual image into a discursive partner and transforms the object beheld (the painted image) into a discursive subject (I/you). This transformation through dialogical invention also allows Diderot to give both Grimm and his reader a sly poke in the ribs and say he would not mind being the cause of all those tears. This fictive dialogue allows for a real visual image to be replaced by a fictional, discursive subject, if not *the* subject as such. For it is through the dialogical potential of discourse that Diderot as the "I" of this text can be phrased. The pictorial space of "she" and "it" becomes the discursive locus of an "I" and "you." In making the painting speak (to him), Diderot stages through writing the phantasmic projection of an other who, because of the way it can be made to speak, to say "you," allows Diderot to say and be "I." Once again the self is constructed through the invention of an imaginary other.

It might seem hazardous to locate positive critical understanding in Diderot's commentary on Greuze's paintings. Yet his text not only blatantly displays the discursive and libidinal mechanisms whereby subjectivity is constructed, it provides a way of understanding how this very process is what defines Greuze's art in its most ideologically suspect of dimensions.

Consider, for example, Diderot's commentary on Greuze's preparatory sketch for his *La Mère bien-aimée.*

Once again, Diderot is drawn to the sketch because of the genre's vague and indeterminate character, which gives free rein to the spectator's imagination.

Plus l'expression des arts est vague, plus l'imagination est à l'aise. Il faut entendre dans la musique vocale ce qu'elle exprime. Je fais dire à une symphonie bien faite presque ce qu'il me plaît . . . Il en est à peu près de même de l'esquisse et du tableau: je vois dans le tableau une chose prononcée; combien dans l'esquisse y supposai-je de choses qui y sont à peine annoncées! (XIV, 193–94).

An all but blank screen, the sketch permits the projection of "presque ce qu'il me plaît," almost whatever imaginary image is desired. Helpful in understanding the spectatorial practice of the *Salons*, this remark also frames and legitimates a particular response to Greuze's work. What this sketch portrays, or rather what Diderot has it show, is feminine pleasure. Depicted is a "belle poissarde avec son gros embonpoint, qui a la tête renversée en arrière, dont la couleur blême, le linge de tête étalé, en désordre, l'expression mêlée de peine et de plaisir montrent un paroxysme plus doux à éprouver qu'honnête à peindre" (XIV, 188). Causing women to blush and men to linger, this sketch provides a "spectacle de volupté forte." Most significant about this "spectacle" is that it reappears in Greuze's *La Mère bien-aimée*. In the complete painting however, the figure of the woman in the preliminary sketch. is shown surrounded by six clinging children, a grandmother, a servant, and returning from the hunt a husband, whose look expresses, as Diderot understands it, "la vanité d'avoir produit toute cette jolie marmaille." The image of autonomous feminine pleasure is indeed made visible in Greuze's sketch, yet only to be recontextualized, inscribed in a context that effectively transforms feminine pleasure into maternal joy and eliminates orgasm in favor of bourgeois bliss.

Diderot phrases thus the moral lesson provided by the domestic scene of *La Mère bien-aimée*:

Cela est excellent et pour le talent et pour les mœurs; cela prêche la population, et peint très pathétiquement le bonheur et le prix inestimable de la paix domestique; cela dit à tout homme qui a de l'âme et du sens: Entretiens ta famille dans l'aisance, fais des enfants à ta femme, fais-lui en tant que tu pourras, n'en fais qu'à elle, et sois sûr d'être bien chez toi (XIV, 196).

To understand the place of this bourgeois credo in Diderot's commentary, one should not assume disparagingly that once again sentimentality has led him astray in judging Greuze's pathetic, preaching scenes. However much he seems to identify with the painting's privileged subject – "tout homme qui a de l'âme et du sens" (father/husband) – he also exposes the process that makes this identification possible. Referring to the sketch, he states that those (men) who linger before it are "ceux qui s'y connaissent." Man can call himself knowledgeable, he can come to know himself through this sketch, but only by covering the orgasm it sketches with a veil of morality, only if the image of feminine pleasure is changed into one of bourgeois production. Insofar as Diderot attributes to the spectator (and claims for himself) the freedom to read into the image whatever he desires, he comes to occupy the position of the painting's male character; both become spectators who can say what Diderot reads on the father's face: "c'est moi qui ai produit tout cela." Both the *père de famille* and the male viewer take over the scene, reading its constitutive elements as so many signs of their own autonomous identity. But precisely by focusing on the passage from sketch to painting, Diderot reveals how representation inscribes its object, encoding it within a system of values and viewing practices designed to determine that object's meaning for a particular subject. In his commentary on *La Mère bien-aimée* Diderot displays how Greuze (and bourgeois representational practices) effectively render invisible (the image of) woman as subject of autonomous pleasure.[36] Diderot's text reveals how this elimination takes place, shows its cost, and exposes the body that the law of bourgeois morality rewrites.

For Diderot, Greuze is "le premier qui se soit avisé parmi nous de donner des mœurs à l'art, et d'enchaîner des événements d'après lesquels il serait facile de faire un roman" (XIV, 177). Traditionally, Diderot's praise for paintings such as *Un père qui vient de payer la dot de sa fille*, *Père qui lit l'Ecriture sainte à ses enfants*, *Le Fils ingrat* or *Le Mauvais fils puni* is seen as reflecting the questionable taste of the bourgeois critic, who admires Greuze because the latter's style is both moral and literary, because his paintings tell an edifying and easily accessible story. As Diderot's commentary makes manifest, however, less important than the moralizing story the painting tells is how pictorial representation provides viewers with material to tell their own story. The question of these paintings' narrative subject concerns less their subject matter than their relation with a spectator, a narrating subject. The narrative instance is located on *this* side of the canvas, in the discourse of a Diderot for whom Greuze's deflowering paintings lend themselves to narration as easily as scenes of bourgeois moralism. Diderot's response to the painting is determined not by their intrinsic morality but rather by their desirability, which is intimately bound up with their narratability. Narration here is the story told by a subject situated in relation to an other – a viewer and a painting, a man and a woman, to take examples we have considered – a story that recounts and amounts to the attempt to capture that object, thus affirming the subject and its forceful desire.

As is especially evident in Diderot's commentary on Greuze, this narrativizing spectatorial practice involves nothing less than the production of ideology, forms of representation that make it seem that what is said or seen is in fact what is. Yet Diderot's spectatorial practice also demonstrates that nothing could seem less harmless, yet in fact be more powerful, than thinking that what the viewer sees is what the painting shows. To be sure, Diderot's spectatorial practice in the *Salons* participates in that ideological act, but at the same time it situates that act as a thoroughly ideological one. In the numerous narratives the *Salons* play out, all versions of the story Diderot has to tell about painting, we cannot fail to understand that the story we hear the painting tell is always one we wish to tell ourselves. We reach this understanding through Diderot's text, which testifies to the drives and discursive mechanisms whereby the esthetic object acquires the seemingly autonomous power to situate a subject, a power stemming above all from the object's status as a willed and desired image, the subject's own phantasmic projection.

For Diderot, the viewing subject is always linked to the object viewed, and thus the knowledge gained from any viewing cannot be abstracted from the narrating subjectivity and the subjectivizing narrative that drive vision. This is why the *Salons* present a kind of speculative esthetics, which sets up the esthetic object as *speculum*, a mirror of projections capable of representing the desired self's other. Yet Diderot constantly seeks to make manifest the enabling conditions of the knowledge derived from viewing, thereby empowering that knowledge as a means of comprehending not just painting but numerous other instances of representation. He finds the discourse of a generalizing theory of mimesis unsuited to such an empowering of knowledge, and he turns instead to a more literary, subjective, and ultimately more artistic form of critical discourse. By focusing on the critical art deployed in the *Salons*, we have probably not succeeded at last in opening art onto the real, in contextualizing and historicizing either painting or theoretical prose. Such an opening of art would reveal but other instances of art, in and through which the representation of the real occurs. The *Salons* themselves reveal no more than this, yet certainly no less. They are a marginal text with regard to more canonical texts identified with the Enlightenment. But theirs is a constitutive marginality, for what we read here is the narrativization of critical knowledge which occurs as the Enlightenment turns to art in order to comprehend its representation of itself.

CHAPTER 5

Embodying knowledge

> Si quelqu'un a aboli la distinction platonicienne-chrétienne entre le haut du corps qui contemple et le bas du corps qui désire, c'est bien Diderot.
>
> Elisabeth de Fontenay

In her study of modern scientific discourse, E. F. Keller argues that any discourse of knowledge, including that of science, is libidinally determined. "Without mediation, commonality, or intercourse between subject and object, knowledge is not possible. One of the most common metaphors in Western history for such mediation has been the sexual relation: knowledge is a form of consummation, just as sex is a form of knowledge. Both are propelled by desire."[1] Moreover, modern scientific knowledge does not reflect upon what drives it as desire. Rather, to found its values, criteria, and practices, it appeals to an "objectivist ideology" designed to preserve the scientist's anonymity, disinterestedness, and impersonality, as well as the neutrality of his or her discourse. But in doing so, it reveals all the more its desire to become a totally "objective" science, possessing an ideal knowledge of objects that would transcend the body and the material in general. Science dreams of an autonomous and objectified subject of science, a subject disconnected from the world of other subjects and from their own subjectivity by the discursive act that represents them as "objects." In sum, the objectivity of modern scientific knowledge results from its sublimation of a body of desires and its refusal to consider the discourse through which they are channeled.

The Enlightenment's development of techniques for mastering the objects of nature marks one of the beginnings of the scientific modernity Keller analyzes. The first chapter of my own study located that beginning in the words and images of the *Encyclopédie*, which portrays "man," the encyclopedic subject of reason, at the expense of the bodies and labour of the men and women its plates depict. Starting from this constitutive tension between knowledge and the material form of its representation, I have sought to show how it informs Diderot's texts, which to a certain extent stem from the theoretical imperative driving a search for truth. This search ultimately reaches its limits, however, in an artful displacement of a theoretical, cognitive genre towards another genre, in which truth could more "resonantly" be presented. In Diderot, the limits of speculative, theoretical discourse are always marked by a shift towards esthetic issues, which involve above all the language, genre or art of phrasing the truth. This shift never leaves truth untouched, which is to say that the displacement from cognitive questions to esthetic ones, from an objective, mimetic description of things to theatrical, narrative accounts of how they are desired, in short, the shift from reason to passion, irremediably alters the way the relation to truth can be stated.

Pursuing the consequences of this shift, I wish now to gauge the critical potential of Diderot's art of philosophizing by relating it to what Elisabeth de Fontenay calls his "enchanted materialism," an ongoing reflection on the subject of knowledge whose privileged reference point is the materiality of the body. As we have seen, Diderot's experimentation with presenting the subject of writing leads to the presentation of exemplary bodies in the two *Lettres*. These bodies are models for a different way of grasping the determinate role the body plays both conceptually, with respect to metaphysical-ethical theory, and textually, involving the way ideas are presented. From the *Lettres* onward, the body in Diderot's texts is that place where theory and practice converge, in a discourse on the material in which what is presented cannot be dissociated from the art and manner of its presentation. The visit to the blind man of Puiseaux in the *Lettre sur les aveugles* is a theoretical-performative gesture repeated incessantly, a centrifugal, eccentric movement out towards another, another body, and also the embodiment of difference.[2] The *Lettre* prefigures Moi's potentially promiscuous encounter with Lui in *Le Neveu de Rameau*, the European's encounter with the Tahitian body in the *Supplément au voyage de Bougainville*, Suzanne's encounter with the religious body as well as her own in *La Religieuse*. The bodies through which the world is known in the *Lettres* announce many other bodies in the Diderotian corpus: innumerable bodies of colored oils, the paintings he speaks of and to in the *Salons*; countless textual bodies, the intertexts of his writing; the body of the dreaming geometer D'Alembert and the loquacious Julie in *Le Rêve de D'Alembert*, that of the actor in the *Paradoxe*, that of Sophie . . . Invariably Diderot's text effectuates a *mise en rapport* with others – both persons and things – involving embodiment. Ideas and feelings are incorporated in a way that attaches them to points of difference constituting the sensual, oftentimes sensuous materiality of a body.

A statement from the *Commentaire sur Hemsterhuis* expresses the desire underlying the philosophical work in all Diderot's texts: "le philosophe veut être vrai." With its copulative function, the infinitive *être* brings the philosopher into greatest proximity to truth by phrasing that relation as an affective one. Philosophizing for Diderot amounts to a libidinal act, much more than the mental, mechanistic, and solid operations of cool reason. It also involves the organic, at times orgasmic flux of a body of desires. These philosophical desires take shape as the voluptuous urge to join with truth, to spring forth and seize it, as well as to rest in wait, receptive, for its coming.

As my own metaphors suggest, the body plays a privileged role in Diderot's philosophical desire "to be true." Consequently, it is tempting to use the body as a structuring master metaphor in the enterprise of making sense of the entire Diderotian corpus, whether conceptually, thematically, existentially, generically or poetically. Such readings would amount to the attempt to embody Diderot, to give material form in the text of interpretation to what seems to be signified by the body in and of texts called "Diderot." Diderot's readers too would play out a libidinal act of philosophizing, driven by desires that cannot circumvent the body and that pass through and throughout it in the attempt to establish their own relation between being and truth.

The corporal tropology that seems so apt for understanding Diderot is of course part of a larger rhetorical-epistemological tradition of representing knowledge of all kinds, a tradition perhaps coextensive with philosophy itself. Indeed, the very idea of tradition, that bedrock of continuity and reassuring repetition, is materially figured in a body trope: that which is given over and handed on, hence something tangible, graspable, comprehensible, and that can be preserved. Of course, such a trope possesses no natural motivation, a characteristic it shares with (figural) language in general.[3] Tradition could just as well be figured via another body trope, as that which is manufactured or even fabricated. Any form of understanding, be it of tradition or anything else, must rely on figuration, which is to say that no one understanding of tradition is more legitimate than another, and certainly not an etymological one.

However certain it is that a metaphorics of the body plays an essential role in figuring knowledge, one should not seize on such metaphors' literal meaning too quickly. In Diderot's case, the attempt to grasp the body cannot be separated from a figural and artistic practice involving what I call embodiment. Historians of (Diderot's) ideas may disembody them, but Diderot never does. Thus, when Diderot refers to the body, it is often to represent an object of understanding, something that can be apprehended cognitively and conceptualized. In this sense, the materiality of the blind man's body in the *Lettre*, for example, is ultimately translatable into significance, coming to figure the idea of sensationalism, materialism, even atheism. This at least is how Diderot wishes to imagine the body of the blind man, which he reduces to a voice or a text, in short to a set of signs he can comprehend as a figure standing for ideas in the mind.

The body's significance would depend, then, on its being semioticized, viewed as a sign that signifies nothing less than thought.[4] Embodiment, as I use the term here, involves that practice more than its ultimate result though, for it pertains to presentation itself, the event or act whereby the body is presented. Although we might characterize the result of that process as an object of cognition, the event or act of embodiment need not, perhaps cannot, be grasped in cognitive terms. Thus, we need not ask what we can understand of it. Indeed, it is not certain that the cognitive and the esthetic, that is, a theory of the body and the presentation of a theoretical body, belong to the same order. Hence, one can imagine engaging embodiment not solely as a cognitive act but as an esthetic one as well, asking for instance what effects embodiment produces and how, to what play of affects it gives rise and why. This at least is the direction Diderot takes as he responds to bodies of oils and of words in the *Salons*, a shift of emphasis suggesting that the body *means* nothing at all, properly speaking, its significance resulting only once it has been figured.[5]

In *The Will to Power*, Nietzsche asks the following question: to what extent is the truth susceptible to embodiment (Verköperlichung)? Involving not only the human body as the classically privileged figure for truth, but also embodiment, a materialization or material presentation, Nietzsche's question pertains to philosophy as well as to literature, for at stake is the art or genre of truth's presentation, the artful, artistic way that truth can be embodied in the artwork that is the text. Diderot's philosophical desire for truth, and Nietzsche's critical questioning of the limits of truth's artful embodiment – these are the two poles between which we shall move in considering Diderot and the question of embodiment.

A jewel of a woman

Les Bijoux indiscrets recounts the story of a magic ring so powerful that when directed towards women it forces them to speak the most intimate of truths, voiced by the most intimate part of the female body, their "jewel." The sultan Mangogul receives this ring from his magician Cucufa, and with it he is freed from merely imagining the innermost secrets of the women in his court, for now he can know them. If Mangogul stands for a subject driven by the desire to know, then then ring is that magical instrument which realizes desired knowledge by making it audible, in other words by producing it as representation. The ring's real power is that of representation itself, which presents things *as if* they were real, appearing to require no intervention and no interpretation in order to be understood. To know, Mangogul believes he has but to listen. Yet what he does not know, and all the while is driven by, is that he does not know enough and never can. Diderot's story narrativizes this state of affairs by telling how Mangogul, once he realizes the ring's power, is tempted to turn it upon his favorite, Mirzoza, in order to assure himself of her total fidelity, which before receiving the ring he had never questioned.

As James Creech has argued, *Les Bijoux indiscrets* recounts a "theoretical fable." Representation contaminates direct and unmediated experience (of Mirzoza), causing Mangogul to question that prior experience and to seek a form of supplementation, a doubling or repetition, which mediates that experience and allows it to be known. Consequently, Mirzoza becomes less a presence than a woman for the sultan, more precisely a metaphor for Woman. "What she represents is no longer the same as what she is. Whereas the sultan, in Mirzoza, previously dwelt in the bosom of a totality – the totality of Woman, of Meaning, where self and Other were in perfect coalescence – he is now confronted with a figural, synecdochical part, signifying a whole only because it no longer *is* the whole."[6]

For Creech, *Les Bijoux indiscrets* recounts in fictional form no less than the entire Enlightenment's theory of knowledge, if not a problematic of representation extending from Plato to Derrida (two other major figures in his study). Let us imagine putting one more spin on this story by asking an ethical question, or, in more Diderotian terms, a melodramatic one. Turning the title of one of Diderot's plays towards Mangogul, let us ask, "est-il bon? est-il méchant?" Is this sultan the involuntary victim of the representational set-up in which the ring places him, irremediably imprisoned by the impossibility of knowing otherwise? If so, then Mangogul is a victim of language as much as his women are, victimized by an inexorable logic of representation that grants no reprieve, no return to a prior, unmediated experience of things, short of denying the workings of representation itself. This Mangogul could not do, just as he cannot – or will not – remove the ring. Perhaps then Mangogul's actions take place beyond the ethical dualism of *bon* and *méchant*, beyond good and evil. Perhaps any judgment of his acts can only evaluate their efficacy and their power, the power of the will to know through representation. And yet can one not wonder whether such a reading is not in some sense an exculpatory one? If Mangogul is as much a victim of representation as his women, then no one is a victim. The very notion of victimization ceases to obtain, and with it the possibility of ethical judgment. Perhaps Diderot's text only raises this question, allowing us to ask whether Mangogul's idiom is the only one possible, whether we can do no more than listen to what the magic ring makes audible, spectators of the world as seen from this magical perspective. Such questions imply the possibility of another idiom, a different or differential way of phrasing the dispute between Mangogul and Mirzoza in *Les Bijoux*. For there exists between them what Jean-François Lyotard calles a *différend*, "a case of conflict between (at least) two parties, that cannot be equitably resolved for lack of a rule of judgment applicable to both arguments." If we rely on a universal rule of judgment for settling such a *différend*, we may in fact perpetrate upon one (or both) of the parties what Lyotard calls a wrong (*un tort*), which occurs when "the rules of the genre or discourse by which one judges are not those of the judged genre or genres of discourse."[7] How then are we to judge the "phrases in dispute" in *Les Bijoux indiscrets*, on the one hand the powerful desire for knowledge that wills representation, a *faire parler*, and on the other the silence imposed upon women's mouths so that their "jewel" can speak, a *faire taire* that results in another idiom, silence, yet a way of phrasing nonetheless. Perhaps more than anything else, that silence states that power not knowledge is at issue, that *Les Bijoux indiscrets* is more an ethical-political text than an epistemological one (assuming such distinctions can be maintained). In any event, for Mangogul woman signifies a disquieting nonsubmission, and thus a loss of control, identity, and mastery. The ring lets him master that gnawing fear by providing him with truth, a universal idiom his women must speak and in which he hears confirmed his power and his knowledge. Mangogul seeks to acquire by force the knowledge he lacks, confident he can thus allay the greater terror of a lack to which his very name points. Knowledge and power are indeed entwined in *Les Bijoux indiscrets* in a desire for the power of knowing, a *pouvoir/savoir* that like the magic ring is constantly directed towards the body of woman. Forced to speak the truth as Mangogul wills it, the truth that can be phrased only in his royal idiom, this body cannot speak otherwise except in silence.

In many respects, the female body made audible and knowable in *Les Bijoux indiscrets* belongs to an ancient dream of Western (masculine) imagination: presenting the body in such a way as to find there access to truth. This dream is also a very modern one, at least concerning knowledge about the sexualized body. "We all have been living for quite some time in the kingdom of Prince Mangogul," claims Michel Foucault, who calls his *History of Sexuality* an "historical transcription of the fable of *Les Bijoux indiscrets*." For Foucault, *le sexe* (sex, the sexualized body) is the embodiment of truth as Western culture demands to know it.[8] Diderot's text rewrites in slightly off-color fashion the semioticization of the body produced by new and powerful discourses designed to make that truth known.

The sexualized, symptomatic body in *Les Bijoux* resembles other more exotic bodies, which populate a "new world" so fascinatingly yet threateningly different that to be known it must be inscribed in a preexistent *savoir* or narrative of knowledge. These other bodies may figure a natural order and the purity of human origins, or, at the other extreme, a state of ignorance, idolence, and savagery. In either case they become knowable only by being phrased in a familiar European idiom. In that idiom the other's body and the body of others become a sign (or always already are one), a mute marker whose significance is determined by a colonizing, imperial consciousness seeking above all to resolve its own problems of identity and history, self and becoming.[9] The great voyages of discovery during the Renaissance and Enlightenment brought European consciousness into confrontation with the phenomenon of alterity. In representing that other and narrativizing the experience of alterity, European consciousness sought a self-reflexive vantage point from which to view critically the values, customs, and institutions of European culture. Europe put the other and the other's body to work in order to think its place in a unified historical, scientific, and ethical system. The knowledge thus produced is far from innocent, however. Not by chance do modern medicine and the great voyages of discovery dovetail with the cultural "rebirth" of Europe and humanism, as well as religious wars, territorial expansion on the continent, and the colonization of new space.

These remarks require a cautionary note, however. We may well wish to take Diderot's tale as a symptom or narrative of this enlightened, empowering quest for knowledge, and the real exploitation of others to which it leads. Yet *Les Bijoux indiscrets* does not seriously present itself as such. Blending the philosophical with the erotic, the tale is cast in a hybrid genre that is not analogous to explorers' and evangelizers' travelogs or doctors' medical treatises. Or rather, reading these different genres involving knowledge of the body as referring to the same body of knowledge and its production might amount to taking Diderot's story too seriously. The reading of *Les Bijoux* Michel Foucault proposes, this serious philosopher who gets no closer to laughter than sardonic wryness, is indeed helpful for grasping the conjunction of power and knowledge in the Enlightenment, and especially upon a feminized other body. But Foucault's reading has no place for the possibility that *Les Bijoux indiscrets* presents both an emblematic narrative of knowledge and its satire. Diderot's text remains a fiction, a literary artwork that stages the entwining of power and knowledge, as well as its limits.[10] In reality, such powerful knowledge is impossible, which is to say its sole reality is as magical as Mangogul's ring. The real limit of such knowledge perhaps consists, then, in its inability to know why this should be so. Once again, Diderot's text turns knowledge back upon itself and its own genre. *Les Bijoux* provides speculative and specular knowledge concerning the sexualized body; at the same time its idiom phrases that knowledge and embodies it in a way that disputes the legitimacy not only of a Mangogul and his sultanic, white, male, European idiom, but also of any universalizing idiom that claims to resolve conflict and tension, to settle disputes, and to judge differences.

Les Bijoux indiscrets appeared well before Diderot turned more directly to the question of sensationalism and materialism in *Le Rêve de D'Alembert*, *De l'interprétation de la nature*, the *Commentaire sur Hemsterhuis*, the *Réfutation d'Helvétius* and the *Eléments de physiologie*. Yet *Les Bijoux indiscrets* already foregounds the determinate role the body plays in the enterprise of producing knowledge, a role shaped by Diderot's affinity with and exploration of materialism. Through its hybrid, satiric, artful genre, this tale prefigures other literary texts that seem less overtly connected with Enlightenment materialist theory. The scenario of loquacious jewels and muted women whose silence states their protest uncannily resembles that of *Le Rêve de D'Alembert*, in which the discourse of a dreaming geometer challenges interpretation by a waking reason (D'Alembert awake but also the all-knowing Dr. Bordeu). Or the scenario of *Jacques le fataliste*, in which the stories told by Jacques, the text's fictive narrator, defy an interpretation that seeks to master them by imposing other criteria for judging their veracity. Or the scenario of *Le Neveu de Rameau*, in which the pantomimic art of the Nephew disputes "Mr. Philosopher's" efforts to comprehend it and thereby contain its challenge. In sum, it is by juxtaposing two seemingly different types of texts – one articulating the conceptual discourse or theory of materialism, and the other more literary, presenting a fictional encounter between characters and bodies – that the relation between a theory of materialism and the artful embodiment of the material can be grasped in differential terms. Diderot's writing stages this relation with increasing urgency as he turns to the problem of formulating knowledge about the body otherwise.

"Pas de livres que je lise plus volontiers, que les livres de médecine," writes Diderot in the *Eléments de physiologie* (XVII, 510). This disposition towards medical knowledge stems from the fervent conviction that only through knowledge of the body can anything else be known, an epistemological condition stated in the most categorical of terms: "Je défie qu'on explique rien sans le corps," (XVII, 334). In his own attempts to explain things with the body, Diderot challenges materialist thought to account for nature without relying on metaphysical finalism, such as divine causality, or reducing living and material bodies to abstract geometrical figures and movements explained in purely mechanistic terms. The bodily existence of Saunderson in the *Lettre sur les aveugles* effectively refutes such finalism. Similarly, the countless examples of biological deformation and monstrosity discussed by Bordeu, D'Alembert, and Julie in *Le Rêve de D'Alembert* deny the existence of any harmonious natural order devised according to some divine plan. Indeed, Diderot asks whether the monstrous itself is not the normal order of things, "l'univers ne semble quelquefois qu'un assemblage d'êtres monstrueux" (XVII, 444), imagining that a dynamics of natural formation could explain both the normal and the apparently monstrous abnormal. The eccentric staging of biological materialism in *Le Rêve* and elsewhere challenges Enlightenment materialist theory to explain material organization not in terms of a static, mechanistic model but rather as a dynamic process of becoming, and moreover to relate this dynamic model of matter to the body, not as one manifestation of the material, but rather its privileged instance.

The most subversively troubling aspect of Diderot's materialism may well consist in his claim that the material organization of life is the only kind of causality that exists.[11] This determinism extends far beyond the biological, encompassing the social aspect of existence as well. "Regardez-y de près, et vous verrez que le mot liberté est un mot vide de sens; qu'il n'y a point, et qu'il ne peut y avoir d'êtres libres; que nous ne sommes que ce qui convient à l'organisation, à l'éducation, et à la chaîne des événements. Voilà ce qui dispose de nous invinciblement" (IX, 256–57). One of Diderot's most forceful experimentations with presenting this "invincible" brand of material causality is *Jacques le fataliste*, in which the servant Jacques' attempts to comprehend the cause and sense of things end up in his fatalistic acceptance of a situation in which the order of events is "written up yonder." Of course, one must question exactly what it means "to be written," be it "up yonder" or in this text, which foregrounds the act of storytelling, narration, and thus an artful causality in a way that precludes *Jacques* from being read as a treatise on determinism (unless one reductively discounts the significance of the specifically esthetic genre in which Diderot philosophizes here). For the moment though, one can imagine that Diderot's theoretical, formulaic, prosaic rejection of any possible notion of freedom, in the name of an all-encompassing physical and material determinism, expresses the desire of Enlightenment materialism to extend the consequences of a theory of matter to include morality as well. Metaphysics and morals would constitute two sides of the same coin, analogous insofar as both can be understood in terms of the body.[12] Ultimately, Enlightenment materialism applies this unifying vision of physical determination to the social-political sphere. "Quoique l'homme bien ou malfaisant ne soit pas libre, l'homme n'en est pas moins un être qu'on modifie. C'est par cette raison, qu'il faut détruire le malfaisant sur une place publique" (IV, 257). Physically determined, human behavior may be modified, at least in the more utopian versions of eighteenth-century reformist materialism.

Viewed in an intellectual historical perspective, eighteenth-century materialist thought seems ultimately unable to account for reason, the lynchpin of Enlightenment. Henri Lefebvre, for example, has argued that the eighteenth-century materialists fail to treat human nature in terms of the kind of dynamic change and transformation they attribute to material nature.[13] Instead, in passing from material nature to human nature they ground the ethical side of materialism on the faculty of an abstract, universal, and impersonal reason, thereby reintroducing into ethical theory the very idealism they seek to avoid. "La perfectibilité de l'homme," writes Diderot, "naît de la faiblesse de ses sens dont aucun ne prédomine sur l'organe de la raison" (AT IX, 271). It is not obvious how the metaphor of "the organ of reason" accounts for an historical, dynamic apprehension of rational self-consciousness, and still less how reason can be related to "perfectibility" through a dynamic theory and practice of meliorative individual and social transformations.

Nonetheless the eighteenth-century materialist philosophers did believe they could explain self-reflexive knowledge, and moreover that social institutions could be reformed according to the idealized, universal human faculty of reason. Yet this enlightened reason has a darker side, as critics of the Enlightenment's legacy have argued. As in the case of the *Encyclopédie*'s plates, the Enlighteners' viewing the world ideally in rational terms carries with it the imperious urge to rationalize the real world, to systematize, order, and dominate it. Similarly, Diderot's comment that the individual, whether good or evil, can be "modified" points to the instrumentalization of rational ethics to which materialist theory can lead. By accepting the material determination of thought, eighteenth-century materialists came perilously close to arguing not only for the material determination of behavior, but also for the need to control and reform modes of behavior in a rational, orderly way. Insofar as the Enlighteners' world appeared as "la maison du plus fort" (XVII, 516), their cautious fascination with the so-called enlightened despotism of a Frederick the Great or a Catherine of Russia becomes more comprehensible. They wished to believe that representatives of real social and political power could be instrumental in modifying the conditions of existence for individuals and nations. Deriving political principles from those of rational philosophy was the Enlighteners' goal. It was also their stumbling block, as a brief discussion of Kant reveals.

In his essay *What is Enlightenment?*, Kant links reason and politics by maintaining that the "natural" faculty of reason promotes "the propensity and vocation to free thinking" and thus must lead to more rational and ethical political systems and practices. Rational free thinking, he claims, "finally ... affects the principles of government, which finds it to its advantage to treat men, who are now more than machines, in accordance with their dignity."[14] Kant's optimistic belief in gradual, evolutionary progress contains without dispelling the very threat of instrumentalization and mechanization that critics of Enlightenment have insisted upon. In this essay at least, he skirts the issue by eliding the relation between rational philosophy and politics: "This is the age of enlightenment, or the century of Frederick." Kant distinguishes between a public use of reason, which must always be free, and the private use of reason an individual makes in a particular civil post, a use that must be restricted. Does "civic" life ever lead to the "barbarity" from which society is supposedly freeing itself? The essay provides no answer. No dialectic joins the Kantian public and private spheres, the *sapere aude* of triumphant Enlightenment and the "one must obey" of the Prussian state. The two spheres coexist harmoniously.

> So far as a part of the mechanism regards himself at the same time as a member of the whole community or of a society of world citizens, and thus in the role of a scholar who addresses the public (in the proper sense of the word) through his writings, he certainly can argue without hurting the affairs for which he is in part responsible as a passive member (p. 265).

However appealing this optimistic belief in humanity, the world community, and the intellectual's place within it, one must not overlook the way this belief is figured. What exactly is this "part of the mechanism" that determines whether the individual may speak in the role of "scholar" and thus that regulates his or her discourse? Curiously enough, the metaphor of the machine describes the barbarous, preenlightened age as well as the regulative instance of enlightened government, which suggests the extent of the problem the Kantian notion of Enlightenment fails to resolve, at least in this essay.

Enlightenment rationalism, especially its materialist version, reaches its limits in its failure to link reason and politics, to formulate a rational philosophy that could resist being translated into the kind of instrumental reason Catherine, Frederick, and others practice. These limits, then, are paradoxical ones, in that the extreme limit of reason is also its own limitation, where reason borders on raw power, mastery, violence, and terror. Do the philosophers retreat from such a paradox, that darker side of what Horkheimer and Adorno call an "eclipsed" reason? Do they proclaim their faith in the ideal of humanity, progress, and the future precisely so as not to confront reason's potential instrumentalization? Such a position may well characterize a Voltaire, but not a Diderot, whose reflection on knowledge and power was far more searching. An event that intensified this reflection was Diderot's extended stay at the Russian court, which resulted in two explicitly political works, *Entretiens avec Catherine II* and *Observations sur le nakaz*. These works testify to the reformist philosopher's high hopes for influencing directly the course of progress towards enlightenment. Yet as events soon proved, Catherine's *raison d'état* would not and could not yield to the philosopher's *raison humaine*. Apparently no amount of well-intentioned rational reform could counterbalance real political power. But if Diderot learned a lesson from his experience with Catherine, it was one he already knew, namely that the ultimate limitation of reason depends more upon the power of the genre in which it is affirmed than upon its intrinsic logic. That lesson is laid out in an earlier text that examines the empowerment of reason. The question Diderot asks is whether there exists a way to affirm the rational without immediately falling victim to its empowerment by others, despots for instance? Can the rational be artfully phrased, embodied in an art of philosophical discourse, and thereby escape such entrapment?

The power of paradox

Pages contre un tyran responds to the critique of Baron d'Holbach's *Essai sur les préjugés* made by Frederick II.[15] D'Holbach's *Essai* mounts a harsh attack against religion, maintaining it to be of little moral usefulness, politically dangerous, inimical to the advancement of scientific reason, and perverted in its origin, dogma, and representatives. The reign of religion must be replaced by that of truth, which would better serve the interests of the individual, society, and state. Only through the philosophical education of the people moreover can the reign of truth be realized. Frederick rightly perceived that d'Holbach had pitted the cause of truth against the authority of both political and religious institutions. In his critique he argues that d'Holbach's notion of truth is vague and ill-founded, and that even had d'Holbach defined truth properly, it remains an ideal far too lofty to be aspired to by everyone.

The short text with which Diderot joins the fray may be read as a philosophical one, in which he argues the cause of truth, its utility, and its attainability. But as its title indicates, *Pages contre un tyran* conjoins philosophy and politics in that Diderot speaks out for philosophical truth and against political tyranny, especially of the despotic Prussian variety. In these three texts, truth and power are entwined both thematically and discursively, for this three-part joust involves a struggle for discursive legitimation and the authority to speak the truth. The social positions of these three writers cannot adequately explain their dispute however. Eighteenth-century philosophers may speak to princes concerning the enlightened exercise of power, but what of the power of these philosophers' discourse and of philosophical discourse itself? Writing against political tyranny, and despite his personal and intellectual sympathy for d'Holbach, Diderot asks whether philosophical discourse just as much as the political discourse of a despotic sovereign might not have a tyrannical side that makes it too an instrument of power, control, and domination. As long as competing and conflicting statements claiming to present the truth are judged in terms of their legitimacy, there exists no escape from entrapment by a dialectic of power. That dialectic itself must be disputed, Diderot will suggest, and illegitimately, by means of something to which all three authors refer, namely, paradox.

Countering Frederick's objection that he is arguing in paradoxes and thus against common sense, d'Holbach replies by affirming that common sense is simply what makes sense to common people ("le vulgaire"). If they fail to comprehend the truth of paradox, it is due to their opinions, prejudices, and ignorance. "Mais qu'est-ce qu'un paradoxe, sinon une vérité opposée aux préjugés du vulgaire, ignorée du commun des hommes, et que l'inexpérience actuelle nous empêche de sentir? Ce qui est aujourd'hui un paradoxe pour nous sera pour la postérité une vérité démontrée."[16] Today's paradox is tomorrow's truth, which we philosophers can grasp although common people, *le vulgaire*, cannot. Despite its élitist tone,

D'Holbach's definition of paradox corresponds to the classic eighteenth-century understanding of the term.[17] More interestingly, from the point of view of argumentation this definition overlays reference to truth with a discursive structure designed to check response by simultaneously legitimating the philosophical position and weakening all others. The addressee of this statement is presented the choice between, on the one hand, silence or social weakness (the position of posterity or *le vulgaire*) or, on the other, the position of *nous*, we philosophers. Paradoxically, the strength of d'Holbach's materialist critique is determined – produced but also limited – by the latter's way of being phrased. Regardless of the particular nature of truth, however paradoxical it may seem, the real assertion d'Holbach wishes to make concerns a metaposition from which and in terms of which truth can be stated and a statement's truth or falseness can be judged.

Taking issue with this definition of paradox, Frederick warns "would-be philosophers" against such egregious errors. More significantly, he parries d'Holbach's discursive set-up, but not with another definition of paradox, which would effectively validate the metaposition of we-philosophers. Instead he seeks to delegitimate that position, warning d'Holbach that the power of those who speak in the name of philosophy derives solely from the name given to the discursive position from which they speak. In response to those who take the name of philosopher, another We, in other words I, a prince whose power is otherwise discursive, need but question your name, your authority to take the name of philosopher, in order to neutralize the critical force of your discourse. *Baron, vous êtes du vulgaire.*

Responding to Frederick's challenge, Diderot provides his own definition of paradox, which sidesteps the skirmish between prince and philosopher by reworking their discursive set-up. "Le paradoxe n'est point une opinion contraire à une vérité d'expérience, car le paradoxe serait toujours faux; or il arrive assez souvent que c'est une vérité. Le paradoxe n'est donc qu'une proposition contraire à l'opinion commune, or l'opinion commune pouvant être fausse, le paradoxe peut être vrai."[18] More cautious than d'Holbach, Diderot does not claim that paradox is or will be true, either for philosophers or for posterity. Rather it *may* be true. But under what conditions? How might truth be presented so as to realize the potential of paradox? Diderot's definition sticks close to etymology, suggesting that paradox is a type of statement or discourse located beside and/or beyond (*para*) commonly accepted beliefs, values, and opinions (*doxa*). Neither intrinsically true nor false, unable to be judged according to a hierarchical opposition (we versus they, the present versus the future of posterity, "absurde en apparence" versus "vrai au fond," etc.), unresolvable by any dialectical operation, paradox simply runs counter to the convictions and persuasions of the majority ("l'opinion commune"). Paradox thus exemplifies an oppositional discourse, always in conflict with the majority opinion (the *doxa*), which it disputes. A response to both d'Holbach and Frederick, Diderot's treatment of paradox suggests public opinion cannot be discounted, which is to say that one cannot ignore the real or potential addressee of one's discourse, nor that addressee's power. (This lesson Diderot learned early as editor of the *Encyclopédie* and as unwilling guest in the Chateau of Vincennes.) In strategic terms, this means the outcome of speaking in paradoxes – at least as far as truth is concerned – is unpredictable. For only when public opinion is false can paradox be true. But vice versa. Everything depends on timing, which might explain why *Pages contre un tyran* was not published during Diderot's lifetime. In any event, the temporality Diderot attaches to paradox in no way resembles d'Holbach's. There is no utopian "tomorrow" when the truth of paradox will be self-evident. The belief in an enlightened posterity constitutes a trap, and a difficult one to avoid, since it well may result from Enlightenment's self-entrapment, its ideal goal and end. At any rate, to speak truth paradoxically, one must choose one's moment, which is the political lesson drawn by the interlocutors A and B in the *Supplément au voyage de Bougainville*.

The consequences of this three-way dispute involving paradox extend well beyond the discursive event linking Diderot, d'Holbach, and Frederick. Diderot's remarks concerning paradox suggest the shape of his attempts to fashion a materialist critique resonant with d'Holbach's virulent and inflexible materialism yet far more artfully effective at disputing and defusing the powerful, authoritarian, and political discourse represented by Frederick's despotic gesture to police philosophy. Like the aphoristic *Principes de politique des souverains* written during the same period, *Pages contre un tyran* contains numerous themes that mark it as a political text. The most effective political aspect of Diderot's writing resides in its art, however, the manner in which critique is embodied. *Pages contre un tyran* helps us grasp that art of critical embodiment as paradoxical, in other words as a conflictual, nondialectical manner of presentation. The most powerful of Diderot's texts are those in which he experiements with this philosophical art as a means of formulating a materialist critique that could escape or at least sidestep the entrapment of truth, in other words the self-deceptive illusion of being able to speak (for) it, to which d'Holbach falls victim as is pointed out to him by the savvy representative of Prussian *Realpolitik*.

Paradox is clearly central to any global understanding of Diderot's writing. This is all the more true now that Diderot studies seem finally to have shaken off a tenaciously residual nineteenth-century positivism that reduces the question of paradox to one of style and authorial proclivity. This reduction was part of the larger attempt to "humanize" Diderot so as to defuse the more threatening aspects of his writing (and of Enlightenment materialistic philosophy in general). Now that paradox is treated instead as a particular brand of logic, textual form, and philosophical investigation,[19] it is easier to see why this attempt to neutralize Diderot ideologically was made in the first place. But to pursue that less humanized understanding of paradox, one must do more than simply resolve the paradoxical by providing an explanation of the riddle individual paradoxes seem to pose. Phrased in terms of the œuvre or the text, the person of the writer or the creative subject, Diderot's ideas or (his) thought in general, such explanations implicitly attempt to rescue paradox from itself. We have been told, for instance, that Diderot's esthetics can be formulated *sans paradoxe*, that there is a "secret unity" hidden within *Jacques le fataliste*, that *Le Neveu de Rameau* contains a "true meaning," that Diderot's "mystification" can be demystified, and that his "language of absence" can be made audible, and so forth.[20] These well-trodden paths of Diderot interpretation all begin from the assumption that contradiction can be resolved by dint of critical intervention. Interpretation can express a higher, synthetically unified truth or meaning, which for some reason – a point seldom pursued – the text cannot.

What then of paradox itself? First of all, paradox is an implicity self-referential statement about how statements function. By its very nature, paradox challenges the logic of interpretation. Serving to mark boundaries, to hover between and cross over them, paradox operates "on the limits of discourse,"[21] on the margins of what is acceptable according to regulative rules of argumentation, logic, and thought. Possessing a potentially threatening undecidability, paradox exposes the limits and limitation of such regulative instances by affirming *both* this *and* that. It constitutes an affront to the logic whose paradigm is that of either/or, yes/no, true/false. Consequently, however legitimate it may seem to judge paradox in terms of its improper, transgressive nature, it continues to challenge precisely the regulative logic grounding the judgment of what is and is not proper, legitimate, and nontransgressive. Such a judgment in fact seeks to neutralize the power of paradox, to settle its dispute with logic (or rather with another logic), and to attain the ultimate satisfaction of believing it possible to decide between oppositions and contesting parties. But even silenced, paradox challenges the authority of whoever attempts to contain and defuse it. Far more than a linguistic or poetic riddle to be answered, or an irregular use of logic that must be reordered to be made acceptably meaningful, paradox stages contradictions and oppositions whose intractability results from the absence of a third term or position that would enable a dialectical resolution of the constant doubling paradox involves.

In a major essay on the *Paradoxe sur le comédien*, Philippe Lacoue-Labarthe argues that through a paradoxical logic – or a logic of the paradoxical – Diderot "aura ouvert . . . cette énigmatique possibilité de penser l'identité sans identité des contraires."[22] Lacoue-Labarthe calls this logic hyperbolic, a hyperbologic "par lequel s'établit – probablement sans jamais *s'établir* – l'équivalence des contraires, et de contraires eux-mêmes poussés jusqu'à l'extrême, infini en droit, de la contrariété . . . Le paradoxe se définit par l'échange infini ou l'identité hyperbolique des contraires" (p. 270). Despite its uncanny resemblance to speculative logic, this hyperbologic is unresolvable and cannot be stopped by any dialectical operation. If Lacoue-Labarthe insists on the nondialectical nature of paradox, it is because he wishes to short-circuit the apparatus of speculative philosophy and Hegel in particular. For Hegel, art provides a reflection of and for the rational subject, a mediating representation of self-consciousness. Art's production – at least that of beautiful art – is determined moreover by the finality of consciousness becoming manifest to itself, its taking successively more perfect, beautiful forms with which to embody the idea of the beautiful. For Lacoue-Labarthe it is that finality Diderot's notion of paradox contests, and with it Hegelian esthetics, according to which philosophy claims the right to judge art, to translate its manifestation of the idea into conceptual knowledge.[23]

Not unsurprisingly, Lacoue-Labarthe turns to the question of art, arguing that the logic of paradox is none other than that of mimesis, a "mimetologic" whose law can be stated only in the form of a paradox: "L'art, en tant qu'il se substitue à la nature, en tant qu'il la remplace et mène à terme le procès poïétique qui en constitue l'essence, produit toujours un théâtre, une représentation. Ce qui veut dire, *une autre présentation* – ou la présentation d'*autre chose*, qui n'était pas encore là, donnée ou présente" (p. 274). Art, like the great actor, can imitate anything, and does so all the better because it (and the actor) have no properties or qualities proper to it (him). In Diderot's text which traditionally has been read as proposing a limited theory of acting, Lacoue-Labarthe articulates a more general theory of mimesis and art, one that strips a limited theory of esthetic imitation of any regulative finality according to which art could be understood in terms of a preexisting and ideal nature it embodies. No longer can art be said to possess the determinate finality of presenting once again what is already there, for it is not governed by the eidetic structure determining the production of knowledge. Instead the artwork – the working of art – involves nothing more – yet nothing less – than a presentation. It results from a "pure gift or giving," a gift or giving of nothing, in other words of the thing itself. Lacoue-Labarthe explains: "Je veux dire: le don que la nature fait d'elle-même, non en tant qu'elle est elle-même déjà là ou déjà présente . . . mais en tant qu'elle est plus essentiellement . . . pure et insaisissable, poïésis: force productrice ou formatrice, énergie au sens strict, perpétuel mouvement de la présentation" (p. 276).

In *De l'interprétation de la nature* Diderot characterizes nature's "perpetual vicissitude" as the very limit of philosophy: "si la nature est encore à l'ouvrage; malgré la chaîne qui lie les phénomènes, il n'y a point de philosophie" (IX, 94). Lacoue-Labarthe's discussion of the paradoxical logic of mimesis suggests that what Diderot saw initially as the limit of philosophy will become the very condition for articulating a paradoxical materialist esthetics (or an esthetic materialism). A dynamic nature may indeed be uninterpretable and unknowable for philosophy, at least until philosophy takes an esthetic turn, engaging the manner in which it presents nature. Only by seeking to embody nature in an artful, even theatrical way, which may be paradoxical according to a properly philosophical logic, can philosophy become coextensive with nature's *don*, its own presentation. This is how Diderot will attempt to embody nature in his most artful of materialist texts, *Le Rêve de D'Alembert*.

The art of a dream

It has been well established that *Le Rêve de D'Alembert* reflects the leading edge of the Enlightenment life sciences.[24] From the outset in the "Entretien entre D'Alembert et Diderot," the interlocutor Diderot takes direct aim at the residual metaphysical underpinnings of mechanistic materialism, rejecting any divine, spiritual or otherwise idealist explanation of matter and its dynamic transformations. He proposes instead the all-explicative notion of *sensibilité*, a general property of matter and a product of biological organization. A materialism is articulated here that goes well beyond the static, mechanistic understanding of matter and movement personified by D'Alembert. He too rejects deist causality, but he cannot espouse the notion of *sensibilité* and total material determination. Retreating from the brink to which Diderot leads him, he entrenches himself in the compromise of a skepticism that rejects idealism without embracing a consequential materialism. "Sceptique je me serai couché, sceptique je me lèverai," he affirms, to which Diderot responds, "Sceptique! Est-ce qu'on est sceptique?" (XVII, 111).

Ironically foreshadowing the experience of the dream D'Alembert soon undergoes, Diderot suggests that the doubt of a vigilant, alert reason inevitably must yield to the evidence of the material body. Sleep will free the mind of this all too lucid geometer from the constraints of mathematical logic as he discovers that the body has reasons reason does not know. D'Alembert will dream the mad dream of a nature that manifests itself in constant and ongoing acts of creation, its laws unhampered by first causes and final principles. In images of polyps or clusters of bees, nature is figured as a transformational, regenerative material universe made up of heterogeneous and continuously rearranging molecular composites.[25] Nature presents itself in D'Alembert's discourse as well, in convulsive bursts of oneiric mutterings, and also through his very body, in seminal ejaculations containing "l'histoire du monde." D'Alembert the dreamer is as much a part of nature's presentation as he is its spectator, belonging to a dynamic nature in a way that literally embodies materialism. Significantly, this extravagant biological materialism assumes the shape of a dream, one that recalls the noble genre of the philosophical dialogue and at the same time blithely and exuberantly oversteps its limits.[26] To explain why Diderot formulates medical-scientific theory in *Le Rêve* in a wildly literary, theatrical fashion, one must begin by asking what aspect of his materialism matters esthetically?

As philosophical topos, the dream has long served to figure deceptive appearances, a state of illusion and imaginary sensory perceptions that challenge reason's capacity to affirm the truth and reality of things. The dream has been taken to stand for the mind's inability to free itself completely from the body, to distinguish itself consciously and cognitively from a dreaming body and thereby comprehend if not master it. For Descartes, the dream state signifies that realm of false appearances and error so threatening to the waking desire for dazzlingly clear truths that it borders on utter madness.[27] Only for the philosopher of consciousness though, concerned with comprehending the truth of reality in cognitive terms, is the dream irremediably opposed to reality. As if to reply to the stern philosopher afraid to nod off, Diderot writes:

> C'est un état bien singulier que celui du rêve. Aucun philosophe que je connaisse n'a encore assigné la vraie différence de la veille et du rêve. Veillé-je, quand je crois rêver? rêvé-je, quand je crois veiller? qui m'a dit que le voile ne se déchirerait pas un jour, et que je ne resterai pas convaincu que j'ai rêvé tout ce que j'ai fait et fait réellement tout ce que j'ai rêvé (XVI, 229),

For Diderot, the dream is by no means the terrifying nightmare from which Descartes seeks escape. Diderot willingly imagines that the state of dream and waking may be reversible, even to the point of being undecidable. Does this undecidability amount to madness? Perhaps, but only if the dream and waking perception are both understood as representations of the real, as images or ideas that possess varying degrees of accuracy yet are determined ultimately by the law of mimesis that makes them and the real itself comprehensible.

But Diderot does not approach the question of the dream and thus of reality and truth in cognitive terms alone. The above passage occurs in the *Salons*, in the context of pictorial illusions, or rather the artful, esthetic presentation of nature. In such a context it makes no more sense for Diderot to seek escape from a dream than from a painting, into whose "illusion" and magical effects he willingly enters.[28] His materialism involves the attempt to grasp nature esthetically instead of comprehending it cognitively, to seize its paradoxical manner or art of presentation without attempting to resolve the opposition between illusion and reality, falsehood and truth. Perhaps Diderot's ultimate dream takes place in the linking of the two theatrical and discursive spaces in *Le Rêve* between which D'Alembert's dream and its echo-extension-interpretation circulate. This paradoxical joining of two scenes brings together two stages or manners of presentation, yet without relating them hierarchically or explaining one in terms of the other and thereby resolving their difference.

Like the bizarre couplings between dissimilar species Julie and Bordeu discuss in the "Suite," this paradoxical coupling takes a theatrical form in *Le Rêve*'s staging of this "extravagant" dream. Called to the bedside of the delirious D'Alembert, Julie overhears and witnesses his dream. She transcribes his "radotage," then reads it to Bordeu, the experienced medical practitioner and theorist who undertakes to analyze the dream. Curiously though, Bordeu's explanation prolongs the dream as much as it interprets it. He "knows" so well what D'Alembert dreamed and what Julie wrote that he can repeat the dream and complete it, doubling it yet without establishing its precise confines.[29] His commentary thus short-circuits the logic opposing dreaming to waking thought, madness to reason. Hearing Bordeu's continuation of D'Alembert's dream, Julie asks, "Docteur, délirez-vous aussi?", finally exclaiming, "c'est cela, et presque mot pour mot. Je puis donc assurer . . . qui'il n'y a aucune différence entre un médecin qui veille et un philosophe qui rêve" (XVII, 122). Even Bordeu himself later admits, "je rêvais de mon côté."

Le Rêve seems to suggest that the materialist philosopher dreams what the eighteenth-century biological scientist already knows. Yet this text's manner of presenting that knowledge makes it difficult to reduce it to pure concepts. It is especially significant that Bordeu's comments double and prolong the dream rather than analyze it or translate it into finally comprehensible scientific discourse. The dreamer's position does not differ from that of the dream's waking witnesses and commentators: none of the characters is in a privileged position of knowing. As Elisabeth de Fontenay suggestively puts it, Julie and Bordeu, as much as D'Alembert, are "travaillés et comme parlés par la même matière exubérante, extravagante. Leur unanimité batailleuse est celle d'un unique grand corps qui fait l'amour avec lui-même."[30]

The way nature embodies itself here, presents itself and is presented, cannot be thought by the skeptical waking D'Alembert, for it cannot be represented in terms of a mechanist science and philosophy. Nor, more generally, can this presentation be contained by any dualistic logic, which the dream's extravagant madness undoes as it circulates from mouth to mouth, destabilizing all oppositions between dreaming and waking, the dream and its analysis, male and female, the normal and the monstrous, and of course matter and mind. For Diderot, the discourse of medical science, like that of all the nonmathematical life sciences, provides no ultimate and absolute epistemological certainty. Required is a scientific manner, yet also an artistic one, more attuned to and resonant with the manifold ways in which nature presents itself. This explains why Bordeu's countless examples of physical abnormalities display no less extravagance than D'Alembert's dreams of human polyps, both being embodiments of nature's manifestation. In dramatizing D'Alembert's dream and the undecidability it states, *Le Rêve* paradoxically presents the life sciences as the necessary supplement to a philosophy of materialism. At the same time it disputes the claim to knowledge made in the name of the language of science. Ultimately, then, *Le Rêve* disputes theoretical discourse claiming to represent nature as object of cognition, to analyze and interpret it, and thus formulate its ultimate truth. The way things are staged here suggests that nature presents itself and is embodied in manners incomprehensible in cognitive terms alone. These manners simply cannot be represented to consciousness, at least not unless one engages in the most extravagant philosophical illusion imaginable, that of situating consciousness somewhere outside the stage on which nature presents itself, attributing to it the status of some kind of privileged spectatorial presence, somehow uninvolved in the acts of nature's presentation.

Le Rêve resists this detheatricalizing, dematerializing idealism. It also stages the material presentation of things in a way that resists being understood as the expression of Diderot's theory of materialism. Unlike other less literary and more expository texts, *Le Rêve* blocks the drive of the intellectual historian bent on translating it into a conceptual theoretical statement to be integrated within a coherent historical narrative. Literary interpreters, generally more attuned to a text's formal properties, have better sensed *Le Rêve*'s resistance to the theoretical imperative. Yet they tend to characterize that resistance in terms designed to overcome it. Jean Mayer for instance refers to *Le Rêve* as "philosophie lyrique, avec tous ses excès poétiques."[31] Yvon Belaval extends the interpretive problem of *Le Rêve*'s hybrid genre to the mobile, essayistic nature of the eighteenth-century materialists' writing, arguing that in the absence of a consolidated theoretical doctrine, interpretation must "démêler la part du rêve d'avec celle de la réflexion positive."[32] Reading *Le Rêve* with more nuance and insight, Aram Vartanian stresses how Diderot frees mechanical science from the demands of mathematical certainty, transforming science into a figural, poeticized discursive and literary form. Diderot's philosophical dream, Vartanian argues, like real dreams has the role of rendering "the 'unthinkable' somehow thinkable," thus providing a "phenomenological awareness" of biological doctrines by giving them "embodiment" and thereby filling the "cognitive void" of that which could not be thought by Diderot or by his materialist contemporaries.[33]

It is not certain that embodiment, tangible in the text's theatricalizing, poetic workings, makes things thinkable the same way that Diderot's interpreters do. The poetic, both here and in general, may fill the metaphorical "void" of the unthinkable with thoughts, properly speaking, but only insofar as it can be translated into and reduced to a series of ideas, something by no means assured. Perhaps interpretation can disentangle the positive historical significance of *Le Rêve* from its "poetic excesses," and perhaps Diderot's apparently groping efforts are meaningful in terms of the larger story of developing scientific theory. But such finalizing unity is produced by contemporary interpretation's attempt to fill its own "cognitive void," to defuse (Diderot's) poetics' challenge or threat to cognition by rewriting *Le Rêve* as the scientific version of a narrative of self-consciousness, one that Diderot's text continues to resist.

Situating *Le Rêve* in the history of scientific thought, Ilya Prigogine and Isabelle Stengers define the challenge to interpretation it poses. Diderot "souligne, à l'époque du triomphe newtonien, qu[e la question de l'organisation vivante] a en fait été refoulée par la physique: il l'imagine qui hante le sommeil des physiciens incapables désormais de la penser éveillés, c'est-à-dire dans le cadre de leurs théories."[34] Not only is the question *Le Rêve* raises unthinkable within the framework of Newtonian physics, the theoretical discourse of the mathematical sciences represses that question, which erupts elsewhere, in this philosophical dream on the periphery of theoretical consciousness. Extending the scope of Prigogine and Stenger's comment, one can ask whether what *Le Rêve* presents is equally unthinkable for, and equally repressed by, the interpretation that seeks to overcome the resistance to interpretation posed by Diderot's literary-poetic manner of presenting materialism. What exactly then constitutes this resistance, and what are we to think of it?

Diderot himself states that these three dialogues result from "le plaisir de se rendre compte à soi-même de ses idées" (AT II, 104). Suggesting a notion of writing as specular self-representation, this comment is of limited help in interpreting *Le Rêve*, in which the unity of the self is far from pregiven, to say nothing of how to attain such self-consciousness. Another remark written to Sophie Volland suggests a more promising perspective. "Cela est de la plus haute extravagance et tout à la fois de la philosophie la plus profonde; il y a quelque adresse à avoir mis mes idées dans la bouche d'un homme qui rêve: il faut souvent donner à la sagesse l'air de la folie, afin de lui procurer ses entrées ... Il n'est pas possible d'être plus profond et plus fou."[35] This joining of the philosophically profound with the madly extravagant recalls Lacoue-Labarthe's definition of the hyperbolic, infinite extremes. The "narrow bounds of ancient philosophy" cannot contain what *Le Rêve* presents, but not because the traditional genre of the philosophical dialogue is not plausible or modern enough for Diderot's taste. Rather, this staging of nature's presentation must be of the moment, contemporaneous with the dynamic of nature it embodies. *Le Rêve* presents nothing ancient, nothing that already was. Indeed, no temporal or logical finality governs what presents itself here. If the organization and transformation of matter *Le Rêve* presents can be formulated theoretically, the manner of matter's presentation here resists any such theoretical metadiscourse that seeks to comprehend its object.

In the drama of theory *Le Rêve* stages, this paradoxical state of affairs is most manifest in the role played by Bordeu. Consummate and all-knowing pedagogue-philosopher, Bordeu recalls the teacher of the Socratic dialogue through whose questions the pupil is brought to formulate latent ideas and connect them to reality. Yet Bordeu's role is not merely maieutic, and he does more than play philosopher-midwife to Julie. Presenting a physiological theory of animate matter, he purports to explain the development of life itself. Beginning with imperceptible molecules, a metamorphosis of nerve fibers occurs that results in organs, appendages, and finally the entire body. The latter's sensory network receives sensations, compares and recalls them, thereby producing thought, reason, memory, and self-consciousness, "l'idée de mon unité, de mon moi," as Julie puts it.[36]

Whatever the scientific validity of Bordeu's theory of epigenesis, in which Buffon's notion of organic molecules is replaced by Haller's notion of fibers, we should note its epistemological status in this text. Bordeu invites Julie to "[faire] par la pensée ce que la nature fait quelquefois," to imagine mutilating the nerve network in order to produce an imaginary mutant or monster lacking a certain organ or appendage. Analogously, his own thought would explain the workings of nature, including its so-called leaps or skips, its abnormalities and monstrosities, precisely insofar as his theoretical discourse is able to "do" discursively what nature itself does. It is a performative language that doubles nature's self-production, providing a comprehensible albeit imaginary image of nature itself. Through Bordeu, theoretical thought imagines nature, embodying it and comprehending it in an imaginary form.

But what kind of nature does Bordeu's and Julie's discourse

represent? Is such a performativity or performance possible? Can thought or language in fact "do" what nature does, given that for Diderot and an eighteenth-century atheist materialism that resolutely refutes all idealist transcendental principles there exists no metaphysical position guaranteeing the unity and comprehensibility of nature and the material? The encyclopedists' question reappears: how can one know the world and represent that knowledge if one lacks or refuses precisely the transcendental principle enabling such knowledge and such representation? The encyclopedists turn to their own language, finding there an arbitrary yet ultimately more effective means of representation. Bordeu too takes up the question of language in *Le Rêve*, marking the limits of knowledge of nature, and also the enabling condition for such knowledge, in its material and artistic embodiment.

Having laid out his theory of matter, D'Alembert and Julie press Bordeu to explain how it could possibly account for concepts such as free will and ethics, imagination and artistic genius, in other words precisely those aspects of a deterministic materialism most resolutely contested by its critics. Bordeu's response thus merits scrutiny. Concerning free will, he replies,

> Est-ce qu'on veut de soi? La volonté naît toujours de quelque motif intérieur ou extérieur, de quelque impression présente, de quelque réminiscence du passé, de quelque passion, de quelque projet dans l'avenir. Après cela je ne vous dirai de la liberté qu'un mot, c'est que la dernière de nos actions est l'effet nécessaire d'une cause une, nous, très compliquée, mais une (XVII, 185–86).

He extends this physiological determinism to the ethical realm, arguing as Diderot does elsewhere that only by modifying the individual can the inclination to perform harmful actions be redirected towards the good. For D'Alembert and Julie these statements affirm more than they prove, and D'Alembert presses on, asking Bordeu to explain imagination and abstract thinking. The imagination Bordeu defines as "la mémoire des formes et des couleurs," and abstractions as "des ellipses qui rendent les propositions plus générales et le langage plus rapide et plus commode" (XVII, 189–91). In the elliptical language of abstraction, as Bordeu characterizes it, the sign has been separated from the physical object, thereby eliminating the idea itself, in other words the possibility of conceptualizing and signifying the thought of the physical object. "On n'a nulle idée d'un mot abstrait . . . Toute abstraction n'est qu'un signe vide d'idée" (XVII, 192).

Recalling comments Diderot makes elsewhere concerning other "abstractions" of idealism such as freedom or the soul, Bordeu's critique of abstract language contaminates language in general, to the point of rendering problematic all communication. D'Alembert exclaims, "Le langage plus rapide et plus commode! Docteur, est-ce qu'on s'entend, est-ce qu'on est entendu?" to which Bordeu responds,

> Presque toutes les conversations sont des comptes faits . . . Je ne sais plus où est ma canne . . . on n'y a aucune idée présente à l'esprit . . . et mon chapeau . . . et par la raison seule qu'aucun homme ne ressemble parfaitement à un autre, nous n'entendons jamais précisément, nous ne sommes jamais précisément entendus; il y a du plus ou du moins en tout: notre discours est toujours en deçà ou au delà de la sensation (XVII, 192–93).

Bordeu's hurry to take his leave of D'Alembert and Julie suggests that in reaching the question of language, he reaches as well the limit of his physiological theory, and perhaps of the theoretical representation of nature in general, materialist or otherwise. The representation that theoretical discourse performs, and consequently the knowledge it provides, always risks being "elliptical," resulting from a discourse of abstraction from which "the physical object" has been abstracted and the material excluded. Appropriately, at the very moment Bordeu becomes most theoretical and abstract, his own speech becomes most elliptical, as if to indicate that the language of theory, or language in theory, cannot in fact double sensation and thus nature. "Toute science abstraite n'est qu'une combinaison de signes. On a exclu l'idée en séparant le signe de l'objet physique" (XVII, 192). Abstract knowledge can only represent nature abstractly, at one remove, and thus it cannot account for nature's presentation. Like abstract science, theory too could never be concrete enough, never material enough. It can offer only a view onto nature, a viewing that only can claim to know nature but never double it.

And yet Bordeu continues, proposing the possibility of a materialist science, or, more precisely, a kind of knowledge that paradoxically takes the impossibility of direct knowledge of nature as the enabling condition for its presentation.

> On exclu l'idée en séparant le signe de l'objet physique; et ce n'est qu'en rattachant le signe à l'objet physique que la science redevient une science d'idées; de là le besoin . . . d'en venir à des exemples. Lorsqu'après une longue combinaison de signes vous demandez un exemple, vous n'exigez autre chose de celui qui parle sinon de donner du corps, de la forme, de la réalité, de l'idée au bruit successif de ses accents, en y appliquant des sensations éprouvées (XVII, 192).

The abstraction of idealism can be avoided only by turning to the concrete, by returning to things themselves. Materialist science would thus correspond to the "philosophie expérimentale" called for in *De l'interprétation de la nature*. It is significant that this return takes place in language, through a particular way of linking words and things, "the sign [and] the physical object." The idea must be realized by materializing it, by giving it "body, form, and reality," which can occur moreover through examples. Now the example, like the abstraction, involves removing one element from a larger set. But unlike the abstraction, the example does not exclude the remaining elements of that larger set, to which it remains logically, organically, and materially connected. Bordeu's definition of an exemplary discourse that provides the basis for "une science d'idées," a material embodiment of nature, helps us grasp Diderot's philosophical and esthetic wager, which is to produce a text that stands in an exemplary relation to the nature to which it belongs.

Le Rêve is not a metaphysical text. It presents no ideal, metadiscursive position from which nature can be known. Rather, this theatricalizing, performative artwork exemplifies nature, embodying it and thus realizing it, just as nature realizes itself.[37] Consequently, the scientific position Bordeu personifies and the epistemological position *Le Rêve* presents is a paradoxical one, from which the attempt is made to conceptualize a nature in which there exists no position outside nature where such a conceptualization and representation could possibly occur.

The examples of the workings of nature and matter in *Le Rêve* are part of an embodying discourse that does produce an imaginary doubling of material nature. Yet this discourse functions paradoxically, by means of an undecidable, unresolvable joining of opposites. For instance, in Bordeu's and Julie's discussion of the most monstrous of physical abnormalities, these are taken to prove the physiological rule of the normal, all the while remaining such a deformation of the normal that they cause a complete restructuring of dualistic logic.[38] The distinction between animate and inanimate is characterized as one of degrees and not opposition ("il faut que la pierre sente"). Examples are given of medical anomalies that alternate between life and death. Minds witness the workings of nature in *Le Rêve* only to discover that mind and body double that nature and are continuous with it, a part of matter and not its spectator. At one point "une idée bien folle" occurs to Julie, namely, "l'homme n'est peut-être que le monstre de la femme, ou la femme le monstre de l'homme" (XVII, 153). Even the norm determining sexual identity is undeterminable. Just as the material universe to which *Le Rêve* refers is one of dynamic transformation ("tout change, tout passe, il n'y a que le tout qui reste," exclaims the dreaming D'Alembert), so too the discursive, theatrical form in which such reference occurs is marked by passages from one position or stage to another. Moreover, there exists no discursive position or stage that can absolutely master, control, and comprehend all the rest, except that of paradox, which undoes any such mastery and ultimate comprehension.[40]

Diderot's paradoxical materialist esthetics (or his esthetic materialism) involves the matter of theory in a way that suggests the consequences of this materialism extend to the political as well. At one point, referring to the various deformations the "nerve bundle" can undergo, Bordeu describes the sensitive person ("l'être sensible") as one whose emotions, thoughts, and actions are governed by the diaphragm.

Un mot touchant a-t-il frappé l'œil? et voilà tout à coup le tumulte intérieur qui s'élève, tous les brins du faisceau qui s'agitent, le frisson qui se répand, l'horreur qui saisit, les larmes qui coulent, les soupirs qui suffoquent, la voix qui s'interrompt, l'origine du faisceau qui ne sait ce qu'il devient; plus de sang-froid, plus de raison, plus de jugement, plus d'instinct, plus de ressource (XVII, 179).

In the body of the sensitive person an insurrection occurs, as the nervous system contests the authority of the "origin of the nerve bundle," which is the "organ of will." One consequence of this insurrection may be anarchy, which produces either madness or else poetry and art. Unlike *le sensible* and *le fou*, however, *le grand homme* and *le sage* succeed in weakening and dominating this natural disposition towards sensitivity. An individual such as these

sera grand roi, grand ministre, grand politique, grand artiste, surtout grand comédien, grand philosophe, grand poète, grand musicien, grand médecin; il régnera sur lui-même et sur tout ce qui l'environne . . . [Il] se sera affranchi de toutes les tyrannies du monde. Les êtres sensibles ou les fous sont en scène, il est au parterre; c'est lüi qui est le sage (XVII, 180).

This notion of the wise man, whose greatness in whatever domain he acts stems from his ability to dominate and liberate himself from a dispositional sensitivity, would seem to represent the one remaining possibility for freedom in a materially determined world. In a sense, this characterization of the wise man replays an ideal of humanist philosophy, and one Diderot invokes elsewhere in the character of Cléobule, the wise philosopher who retires to the countryside to meditate, or Moi in *Le Neveu de Rameau*, who claims that the philosopher alone can rise above the world's falseness and hypocrisy to become a disinterested observer of "la pantomime du monde." In *Le Rêve*, this struggle for freedom is described in explicitly political terms – domination, mastery, rule, liberation, tyranny. It is situated moreover within the very body. The metaphorics of Diderot's text suggests that the body provides a way to figure a biopolitical drama involving not only the individual, the wise philosopher, but also the nation.[41]

Has the body finally been understood, as a master metaphor for a notion of subjectivity so extensive it includes even a political philosophy? Even as we gain such understanding though, the body slips away, literally to another stage. "Les êtres sensibles ou les fous sont en scène, [le grand homme] est au parterre; c'est lui le sage." This shift to theatrical metaphors repeats the idea of the wise man's capacity to free himself of his own sensitivity by removing himself from its tyranny. In this sense, wisdom derives from the ability to place oneself in that privileged spectatorial position, in the "parterre" and not on the stage of the worldly theater.[42] But to understand the "great individual" this way, together with the political relation between philosopher and society such an understanding implies, the metaphor of theater must be understood as allowing *scène* to be distinguished and distinguishable from *parterre*. In other words there must exist a non-theatrical position that somehow frees the individual from the drama of sensibility as well as from the tyranny of the emotive body. As I have sought to show in the context of *Le Rêve*, no such position exists. Not only does Diderot the philosopher steadfastly reject Cartesian dualism (in the case of materialist theory), Diderot the artist produces a literary-scientific text designed to dispute the existence of any metadiscursive, theoretical position. *Le Rêve* proposes another grasp of theater in the interpretation of the body this theatricalizing text performs. Just as this text stages a dream and also its contamination of all other spaces (that of those who witness it, analyze it, comprehend but also prolong it), so too the stage "the great individual" views is double. Two types of theatricality are at work here, one restricted, the other general and all-inclusive. And thus, while it may be possible to get off one stage, one cannot get out of the theater. There exists no extratheatrical position, no metadiscursive position absolutely guaranteeing freedom, wisdom, and greatness. According to Diderot's materialism, the subject does not exist independently of matter; similarly the philosophical subject cannot be removed by an act of will from the "tyranny" of the theatrical, the ungovernable and at times anarchical ways that matter presents itself in and through the body.

Perhaps the real issue then is not a deterministic materialism but art. Diderot's materialism takes on its most extensively political dimension when it intersects with esthetic concerns, when it engages or is engaged by the question of presenting or embodying the material. In Bordeu's discussion of "the great individual," *Le Rêve* displaces a biopolitical theory by means of a bioesthetic metaphorics. Disputing the "proper" domain of the political, *Le Rêve* suggests the most extensive political gesture may be an esthetic one, consisting of acts that reveal how art can double the political, all the while resisting being subordinated to it and reduced to its metaphor or analogue. Art then would be capable of contesting any absolute judgment or regulative finality that might be couched in the political idiom, by doubling that idiom and presenting it on another stage, where the political appears as but one idiom among many, no more legitimate than other idioms to make its claims for judging things. To explore further the critical consequences of this esthetic doubling, the next chapter takes up other examples of Diderot's embodying materialism, examining how they delimit claims made in and for the political idiom, both in their own time and that of their reception.

CHAPTER 6

Portraying Diderot: the aftermath

> Quand je parle de la voix publique . . . je parle de ce petit troupeau, de cette église invisible qui écoute, qui regarde, qui médite, qui parle bas et dont la voix prédomine à la longue et forme l'opinion générale; je parle de ce jugement sain, tranquille et réfléchi d'une nation entière, jugement qui n'est jamais faux . . . [et] qui assigne à toute production sa juste valeur.
>
> Diderot, *Le Pour et le contre.*

Arguably, the history of Diderot's reception amounts to a series of misreadings that stem in large measure from an unavoidable ignorance of many of his major and now familiar texts. Far more complicated than most, the publishing history of this *œuvre* is one of constant additions, discoveries, and revisions, as it moved slowly and circuitously from one state of completion to another between 1798, when Naigeon published his edition of the *œuvres complètes*, and 1970, when the first volumes of the Hermann edition appeared. Naigeon's "complete" portrayal was highly partial, an inevitable misapprehension that was not to end soon. The next major edition was published by Brière (1821–23), followed by the Paulin edition of 1830. Only in 1875 would Assézat and Tourneux present the most complete portrayal of Diderot in what for a century would remain the standard edition. Yet even Assézat-Tourneux now appears incomplete, given Herbert Dieckmann's discovery of the Vandeul manuscripts in 1951, the publication of the *Commentaire sur Hemsterhuis* in 1964, and the ongoing appraisal of Diderot's contribution to Grimm's *Correspondance littéraire* and to Raynal's *Histoire des deux Indes*.

6. Louis-Michel Van Loo: *Diderot* (1767).

The story of *Le Neveu de Rameau* illustrates that when generations of readers said "Diderot," they were referring to something quite different from what we refer to today. Begun in 1761, *Le Neveu* remained unpublished during Diderot's lifetime, circulating among a small group of friends as did many of his writings. Naigeon chose not to include *Le Neveu* in his 1798 edition, and only in 1805 did Gœthe's German translation appear. *Le Neveu* was not published in France until 1821, and then as an inexact translation from the fairly faithful German version. Brière would present a version based on a manuscript supposedly obtained from Diderot's daughter, Angélique Vandeul, as would Assézat in 1875, based on another manuscript, and Tourneux again in 1884. Only in 1891, roughly a century after Diderot's death, did an edition appear based on a manuscript written in the author's hand.

In his 1803 *Eloge philosophique de Denis Diderot*, Eusèbe Salverte spoke at least a century too soon when he remarked, "la postérité a commencé tard pour Diderot."[1] This posterity has always been a belated one though, given that the interminable history of Diderot's reception is defined by the attempt to portray him in order to represent Enlightenment and a belated relation to it. Generations of Diderot's readers, from the French Revolution to the present, have sought to situate themselves in their own present by situating Diderot in the past, more often than not (perhaps inevitably) a past of their own creation. Without a doubt, we can now evaluate better than earlier readers how the immediacy of events determined not only Diderot's writing but also its interpretation in various historical, political, and ideological contexts. But in returning to the historical moment of a text's appearance and successive interpretations in order to comprehend the determining immediacy of past contexts, we must bear in mind that this interpretive act itself is linked to a present context. The historical understanding such a return promises must not be bought at the price of grasping the relation between a particular act of interpretation, including above all our own, and the contextual immediacy of the event to which it belongs.

Reading Diderot can help us articulate this relation. Persistently outstripping attempts to delimit and comprehend it, Diderot's art displays the limits of Enlightenment and points to the limits of the discourses employed to interpret it. Whether we call it his art of philosophizing, his style and manner, or his texts' poetics or genre, a certain aspect of the Diderotian text invariably slips beyond the grasp of interpretation. Given that interpretive inevitability, the value of Diderot's texts lies in how they may be used to articulate our contemporary relation to Enlightenment, both as an historical moment and as a critical practice of interpreation. In resisting the effort to situate them, Diderot's texts ask their readers to consider whether they too have fallen victim to the self-entrapment of Enlightenment by seeking that ideal position beyond the event from which to witness the past and comprehend it finally by representing it. In an attempt to gauge that resistance, this chapter focuses on selective yet emblematic moments in what I call Diderot's aftermath, proposing one genealogy of the desire to portray Diderot belatedly.

> L'éloge de nos contemporains n'est jamais pur.
>
> Diderot, *Le Pour et le contre*

Appearing in 1798, Jacques-André Naigeon's edition marks the first major attempt to complete the works – and work – of Diderot, as understood by this first of many editors. Consolidating Diderot's image, the Naigeon edition also provided a far more authentic one than had previously existed, especially given the standard inaccuracy of eighteenth-century printing and Diderot's singular uninvolvement in prior editions. Naigeon possessed several original manuscripts or copies he had made himself, and he already had included quotations, résumés, and analyses of texts in his long article on Diderot in the philosophy section of the *Encyclopédie méthodique* of 1792. Thus he could also present a new Diderot by including works not previously published. (He did not include all he might have though. The notable omission of *Le Neveu de Rameau* suggests that the supposedly neutral criterion of completeness was by no means Naigeon's primary one.) Prior to Naigeon's edition, the eighteenth-century reader would have associated Diderot with the *Encyclopédie*, *Les Bijoux indiscrets* (perceived primarily as a libertine novel), the *Supplément au voyage de Bougainville*, two plays (*Le Fils naturel* and *Le Père de famille*), and the two tales *Les Deux amis de Bourbonne* and *Entretien d'un père avec ses enfants*. The earlier works – including two translations, the *Pensées philosophiques*, the *Lettre sur les aveugles*, and *De l'interprétation de la nature* – had appeared in print, yet their impact during the revolutionary period preceding Naigeon's edition was minimal. Immediately following 1789, as the revolutionaries sought to explain and legitimate their political program and principles, Voltaire and Rousseau were the writers most often invoked, not Diderot.

All this changed after the Thermidoran reaction in 1794, the fall of Robespierre, and the collapse of the Revolutionary Government. In the post-Thermidoran alliance between center and right, the Notables attempted to restrict the power of the sans-culottes, and during these reactionary times another Diderot emerged. A veritable offensive was launched against the writer now vilified as philosophe, one of the most perverse shapers of the Jacobin Terror in its most republican, anticlerical, antiaristocratic, and violent excesses.[2] Ammunition for such virulent hostility was found in two incendiary verses of the poem *Les Eleuthéromanes*, republished in 1796: "Et ses mains ourdiraient les entrailles du prêtre, / Au défaut d'un cordon pour étrangler les rois."[3] Diderot's notoriety immediately prior to Naigeon's edition was due above all to the trial of François-Noël (Gracchus) Babeuf, arrested in 1795 and executed two years later. Primary instigator of the Conspiracy of Equals, an insurrection against the Thermidor government, Babeuf called for abolishing private property to ensure true equality among citizens. During his trial he based his defense on Morelly's *Code de la nature*, published anonymously in 1755, which he attributed to Diderot whom he praised as "le maître du communisme."[4] Babeuf's error was understandable, since the *Code* had appeared in a 1773 error-ridden Amsterdam edition of Diderot's works.

It is against this shifting political backdrop that the 1798 edition must be situated. Taking direct aim at Babeuf, Naigeon sought to disenculpate Diderot from the attacks of a conservative right, at a time when Babouvist extremism had turned even the left away from Diderot.[5] It is as if Naigeon sensed in advance the virulent and acrimonious attacks Barruel and La Harpe would launch against Diderot a few years later, attacks whose avatars were to have a long life.[6] The most troublesome issue for Naigeon was Diderot's atheism and materialism, for these aspects of the philosophe movement were most stridently denounced as having prepared the way for the Jacobins' violent and repressive measures. As friend and disciple, Naigeon undertook to present a complete Diderot and more important to rehabilitate him. To do so, he strategically presents the double figure of a writer who is both of the moment and eternal. Situating Diderot in an historically specific combat, Naigeon also presents him as exemplifying an eternal philosophical struggle for free thought and rational knowledge, a struggle whose description is lifted directly from the *Encyclopédie*. As for Diderot's materialism, it is presented primarily in terms of medical and physiological questions. Although it may lead to atheism, Naigeon repeatedly counterbalances this philosophical position – in order to protect it perhaps, but in the process neutralizing it – with eloquent descriptions of Diderot's personal virtues as father, friend, and citizen.

Naigeon's portrait is obviously shaped by its historical context, and thus it lends itself to an analysis relying on familiar political categories (Ideologues/Thermidorans, left/right, liberal/conservative). These categories are not hermeneutical ones however. Nothing guarantees that Naigeon or any of Diderot's first generation of portraitists were more accurate or faithful to their friend, relative, acquaintance or philosophical fellow traveler than other readers on a conservative right, the ideological tenor of whose comments seems much more obvious.[7] Instead of judging the accuracy of these portraits, we should consider their potential effects and the use to which they can be put. Viewed from this perspective, the first major edition of Diderot's works sets in place a strategy of editorial portrayal repeated many times during the next two centuries. From the outset, the enterprise of editing Diderot involves more than assembling manuscripts and documents in the name of completeness and authenticity. For Naigeon's edition focuses on certain traits and leaves others in the shadows, steering its readers away from aspects of Diderot's writing that the portraitist judges improper and even dangerous. It institutes a kind of strategic containment policy, as if there resided in Diderot's works something excessive that had to be circumscribed, rephrased or channeled elsewhere. This work of the portraitist-editor should be understood neither in personal terms (such as Naigeon's biases) nor in seemingly more objective ones (the availability or lack of certain manuscripts). Rather, at issue is a rhetoric of portraiture that involves more than authenticity and falsification, truth, misapprehension, and error. It is to the portrait's rhetorical dimension that we must attend, especially since any judgment concerning the objectivity of a particular portrayal itself constitutes yet another rhetorical instance, the absoluteness of which as a standard of judgment is far from pregiven. More specifically, how does the rhetoric of portraiture in Naigeon's text effectively engage the question of history?

Naigeon's edition, like all successive ones, is inscribed in the larger enterprise of narrating events and thereby ordering the past to make the present comprehensible. In this sense, the editorial portrait is not so much a static image or fixed representation but rather a discursive act that establishes a particular relation to history. Consequently, the real issue Naigeon the portraitist-editor confronts is that of situating the event, both that of Enlightenment and of the Revolution. This task was all the more difficult in 1798, when not so distant events seemed literally incommensurable to the existing paradigms available for comprehending them. To understand the revolutionary course of raw events in the hope of determining the Revolution's meaning, it had to be represented, its eruptive immediacy translated into a symbolic order, whether iconographic, ceremonial, theatrical or narrative.[8] In linguistic terms, *discours* must produce an *histoire*, a history or narrative of the past. The symbolic (and ideological) function of such an operation is to transform the event into the past and thereby escape the event's otherwise unpredictable, uncontrollable contingency. In the case of French history, however much France sought to put the Revolution behind it, it did so above all by representing it symbolically, in forms that are inseparable from the development of the culture and institutions of the modern French democratic and bourgeois state. In such diverse events as the institutionalization of public education during the Napoleonic era, the reforming of the university curriculum toward mid-century, the development of history as academic discipline and the rise of historiography, the technical refinement of the realist novel, one sees the attempt to take in charge the means by which the event can be represented, the place and procedures whereby it can be situated in an historical narrative. All these cultural phenomena testify to the constant need felt to master and regulate the domain and manner in which the event can be mediated and its contingency limited by writing its history.

Naigeon's 1798 portrayal of Diderot also represents a particular way of mastering the event. Not belonging to a political left or right, to a philosophical idealism or materialism, the rhetoric of portraiture involves a crafting of language (as an artist shapes raw materials) in and through which the event can be referred to and represented. Rhetoric is no more liberal than conservative, and thus it can be judged only in the effects it is designed to produce, and which are never completely controlled by the portraitist-editor. Instructive in this regard is another portrayal of Diderot, contemporaneous with Naigeon's, whose position towards Diderot is one of open hostility.

Jean-François La Harpe's *Cours de littérature ancienne et moderne*, published in 1805 and reprinted well into the nineteenth century, represents twice weekly lectures given at the Lycée de Paris beginning in 1797. La Harpe's stated goal in these lectures was to "[faire] entendre . . . tout ce qui pouvait inspirer l'horreur et le mépris de la *philosophie révolutionnaire*, sans restriction ni exception."[9] Tracing a lineage of "charlatans misérables" extending from Diderot to Robespierre, the *Cours*' extensive and detailed commentary of Diderot's works is placed under the heading of "sophistes." It would be fastidious to cite at length La Harpe's venomous invective, were it not for the fact that it exemplifies a thematics of rejection that resurfaces throughout the coming century, and in precisely the same pedagogical domain. To teach what La Harpe calls the "Littérature moderne" of the eighteenth century, and to present the Enlightenment as an institutionalized object of instruction,

La Harpe must target Diderot's atheism and materialism. This aspect of his thought and character must be presented in a way that defuses the threat they pose to the institutionalization of literature and the establishment of a "modern" pedagogical discourse. La Harpe's *Cours* marks the end of the antiphilosophe reaction that sprang up to denounce the perceived threat to religion posed by the *Encyclopédie*. It also marks the beginning of a more "modern" critical reaction, located in the university, a rejection of Enlightenment instituted by critics of literature in a lineage that includes Villemain, Faguet, Brunetière, and other master teachers of Republican France.

An "esprit ardent et bizarre" possessing more imagination than "génie," the Diderot of the *Cours* is disqualified from the outset from the noble genre of philosophy. Invoking what already were commonplaces during Diderot's lifetime, La Harpe presents him as a disorganized thinker and a piecemeal writer: "Il ne pouvait s'attacher à rien, de là les disparates continuelles d'un style scabreux, haché, martelé, tour à tour négligé et boursouflé; de là les fréquentes éclipses du bon sens et les bizarres saillies du délire. Incapable d'un ouvrage, jamais il n'a pu faire que des morceaux" (p. 450). Elsewhere, the *Cours* portrays Diderot through a body simile, inaugurating a strategy of corporal metaphorics that will become a consecrated way of encoding reference to materialist philosophy and class origins.[10] The *Cours* also situates Diderot in a context larger than that of literature and philosophy. Political events of the 1790s weigh heavily over this text, as La Harpe seeks above all to contain their "horreur" and "vertige" by defining the proper relation between philosophy and the political.

Understandly, La Harpe rejects the philosophes' claim that theirs was a philosophical age. "Ce nom [le siècle de la philosophie], affecté avec tant de prétention, prôné avec tant d'emphase, répété jusqu'au dégoût, devait d'abord, par cela même, être fort suspect à la raison. La raison est ennemie du charlatanisme, et il y en avait certainement à s'arroger ainsi un titre qu'il faut attendre de la postérité" (p. 252). More important here than the opposition between reason and charlatanism is the temporal mechanism of judgment La Harpe sets up to classify particular writers. The claim to reason can be judged only after the fact, legitimated solely by the verdict of "posterity." Delegitimating the encyclopedists' claims, La Harpe invokes the discourse of posterity in a ventriloquistic gesture that presents his own pedagogical and political discourse as posterity's putative own. La Harpe's critical discourse can claim to be superior to the encyclopedists' because it is temporally posterior. He thus can situate events, be it the Enlightenment or the Revolution, in their proper place, in other words as past, by virtue of their being judged by the posterity La Harpe claims to represent. Only by means of the discursive temporal operators that crystallize around the notion of posterity can the *Cours* hope to break with the dizzying events of the Revolution.

The desire for such a break appears clearly in the following passage. By refuting "Diderot's" *Code de la nature*, La Harpe wishes to explain once and for all "toutes les causes de cette tranquille et imperturbable possession de l'absurde pendant tant d'années, de cette longue et incompréhensible impunité dont le vertige *révolutionnaire* a été la suite, *et dont il doit aussi être le remède* (p. 390, my emphasis of the last phrase). The Revolution is presented here as a political *pharmacon*, the vertiginous consequence of the atheist-materialist philosophes' absurdities as well as the latter's ultimate remedy. Hence the Revolution must be over. Or rather it has to end ("*doit* être le remède"). Only thus can La Harpe belong to the posterity whose judgment he valorizes, a posterity representing the sole way to break with the event by narrativizing it as a series of causes and effects and by portraying it through figures that render it past. But just as the exact moment of the Revolution's end is highly ambiguous in La Harpe's phrase – that which has occurred or must occur – so too is his own temporal distance from that event. For throughout his polemical commentary on Diderot and other "sophists," he returns to the question of the Revolution repeatedly and obsessively. It is as if only by locating in Diderot, Helvétius, and their "disciples" the ultimate cause of the French Revolution could La Harpe find scapegoats whose expulsion from philosophy would purge emergent modern literature of the effects of its encounter with the "incomprehensible," "absurd" immediacy of the revolutionary event. Thus, through an irony that repeats itself in Diderot's readers (and not only his hostile ones), precisely the events of the Jacobin Terror that La Harpe wishes to put behind him inscribe themselves all the more uncannily in his own text. His purging of "modern literature" doubles the purges of the Terror at its apogee, when ever-increasing numbers of scapegoats were sent to Guillotine's then recent humanitarian invention by the members of the Committee for Public Safety, including ultimately its own head, Robespierre. A kind of beheading also occurs in La Harpe's own text in the corporal simile that figuratively deprives Diderot of his head by comparing his mind to an unhealthy stomach.

In the two conflicting portrayals of Diderot that Naigeon and La Harpe produce, a struggle occurs over who will write – or right – the history of Enlightenment and Diderot's place in it, a struggle to forge a narrative that situates the event and thereby produces its history (whether of a humanitarian Enlightenment or a revolutionary and terroristic one). The stakes involved in this enterprise are high, for both Naigeon and La Harpe wish to represent their own modernity through reference to the past. This struggle continues in the Romantic reading of Diderot prompted by the appearance of another major edition of the complete works. But before examining that reading, we must consider another text that appeared in the last decade of the eighteenth century and that would be pressed into service some 175 years later to articulate another modernity, another relation to events and to history, namely, *Jacques le fataliste*.

When Buisson published *Jacques le fataliste* and *La Religieuse* in 1796, reviewers' initial reaction to the two novels was motivated as much by political views as by literary sensibilities. Perhaps though we should take the pitched battles in the various journals and newspapers of the time as signifying that from the outset *Jacques* elicited responses in which the line of demarcation between the political and the literary is hard to draw. In any case, the novels' publication was perceived as much as a troublesome political event as a literary one. Given the views attributed to Diderot, it was feared during the counter-revolutionary reaction that the appearance of his novels could itself contribute to a resurgence of political extremism. Bourlet de Vauxcelles, for example, relates – and reduces – the significance of *Jacques* to the immediate political context, claiming "quand ce serait le Public qui lirait cette *joyeuseté* du Philosophe, il est bon que le Public sache quel a été le véritable Instituteur de la sans-culotterie."[11] Political passions cool by 1798, and during the next two years attention shifts to the two novels' more properly literary aspects. Yet even when they were not dismissed outright because of their author's supposed political position, the more literary approach was equally reductive. Conventionally subordinated to the nobler genres of poetry and theater, the novel was judged according to the degree it compensated for its genre by providing serious discussion of philosophical or moral issues.[12] Consequently, readers judged *La Religieuse* more favorably than *Jacques*, taking the pathetic story of the young nun's tribulations as a *roman à thèse*, all the more topical since the high point of de-Christianization in 1793. Even the depiction of the Mother Superior's lesbianism was seen as a critical portrayal of the depravity and abuses of the religious orders. Readers had a far more difficult time finding the apparently serious side of *Jacques*. Despite its title, it could not easily be read as a scholarly discussion of fatalism, nor as a moralizing *peinture de mœurs* depicting the evils of the *Ancien Régime*, however much contemporary readers attempted to fit the novel into such conventional molds.[13] Even the readers who dismissed the novel on formal grounds as being excessively long, disorganized, and derivative, would find that it already anticipates such criticism at every turn, incorporating them in a way that flouts the conventional standards by which a novel was judged at the time.[14]

In sum, the contemporary responses to *Jacques* amount to superficial readings, determined either by a political ideology or by an esthetic one, both of which result in what now seem to be reductive, at times grossly caricatural misreadings. These eighteenth-century readers could not but remain captive to a culturally determined practice of interpretation that, according to two modern editors of *Jacques*, could produce no more than "le déchriffrement univoque des textes et leur lecture naïve," a reading based on the assumption that the novel does – or should – provide a window onto the world, a pure and simple representation of the real. Given this cultural practice of mimetic reading, eighteenth-century readers necessarily had to fail to grasp "la portée réelle [du] texte," remaining caught between "l'incompréhension pure et simple ou la dénonciation du scandale d'un sens qui semblait se dérober."[15]

However superficial, reductive or otherwise dated these early readings of *Jacques* might seem, we should not dismiss them too quickly in the name of a modern interpretive practice, especially one that claims to free us finally from the naïveté and misapprehension of prior generations of readers. In fact, the history of *Jacques*' reception amounts to a repeated playing out of a problematic already set in place by the novel's earliest readers, if not by the novel itself. In arguing, as *Jacques*' modern editors do, that the naïveté and misapprehension of eighteenth-century readers are governed all too transparently by a culturally determined interpretive practice, one discredits a particular set of readings in the name of determinism, a concept that Diderot's text presents both thematically and formally as problematic, to say the least. Before basing any judgment of a reading on the notion of cultural determinism, which happens to carry with it the notion of historical determinism (the naïveté of the past versus the insightful comprehension of modernity), we would do well to consider how *Jacques* sets up the problem of determinism, especially as it concerns the question of narrating the event.

From the novel's opening pages, determinism is thematized through the servant Jacques' constant reference to his former master's philosophy. The cause of all actions and events is predetermined, he maintains, already written in the great scroll "là-haut." "Tout ce qui nous arrive de bien et de mal ici-bas est écrit là-haut. Savez-vous, Monsieur, quelque moyen d'effacer cette écriture? Puis-je n'être pas moi?" (XXIII, 28). Jacques' master on the other hand holds just as stubbornly to his belief in free will, affirming himself to be a free subject capable of controlling himself, his servant, and events. "Mais il me semble que je sens au dedans de moi-même que je suis libre, comme je sens que je pense" (XXIII, 270). Ironically undercutting the master's belief in his own freedom, the narrator describes just how unfree he actually is. "Il a peu d'idées dans la tête; s'il lui arrive de dire quelque chose de sensé, c'est de réminiscence ou d'inspiration . . . Il ne dort pas, il ne veille pas non plus; il se laisse exister; c'est sa fonction habituelle" (XXIII, 45). At one point the master becomes separated from Jacques, which leaves this "automaton" little else to do but take snuff and look at his watch, the habitual actions that along with questioning Jacques make up his sole resources in life. And elsewhere, the master's horse is promptly stolen from him once he falls asleep holding its reins. Numerous other eminently picaresque incidents that befall the two travelers demonstrate that the master possesses as little mastery over objects and events as over himself.

Actions and events in the novel appear to illustrate a doctrine of determinism, as does the narrative relation linking Jacques and his master. While Jacques spins out the tale of his loves, the master's insatiable curiosity imprisons him ever increasingly in his role as listener. Almost without exception his comments are responses to the story he hears, and thus his place is determined by the endless narrative addressed to him, just as Jacques determines his own place as narrator. One should not translate the narrative relation too quickly into nonnarrative, narrowly thematic terms however. Admittedly, the debate between "nos deux théologiens" concerning determinism and free will can be read as a philosophical one, involving two opposing sets of principles. Yet this debate also belongs to a larger narrative contest between Jacques and his master, each vying with the other to tell his own story, to relate events and thereby establish his own version of what occurs "down here," be it the amorous relation involving a Denise and an Agathe, or a more social one involving a master and his servant. Freedom and determinism are not simply two of the novel's several themes. These two principles characterize the narrative relation between Jacques and his master, between the narrator and the fictive reader, and in a broader sense two opposing types of views of narrative in general.

A strictly thematic reading of this complex narrative opposition between freedom and determinism can only treat it reductively. For example, Jacques thematizes determinism in his constant reference to the predestination of things whose cause is already written "up yonder." Yet in the narrative relation linking him to his master he displays a remarkable ability to control events "down here," that is, to provide a plausible account of their cause and thus determine their interpretation. In one scene, Jacques' master becomes enraged at having fallen from his horse and chases Jacques for half an hour, cursing and beating him all the while. Jacques finally breaks out laughing and admits he had rigged the saddle straps and stirrups, thus taking credit for the entire incident. He presses the demonstration home, asking,

> N'est-il pas évidemment démontré que nous agissons la plupart du temps sans vouloir? Là, mettez la main sur la conscience, de tout ce que vous avez dit ou fait depuis une demi-heure en avez-vous rien voulu? N'avez-vous pas été ma marionnette, et n'auriez-vous pas continué d'être mon Polichinelle pendant un mois si je me l'étais proposé? (XXIII, 286).

No narrator intervenes to assure the reader that Jacques had actually planned the entire scene, nor does the master ever admit to being his servant's puppet. But if Jacques bests his master here, he does so as a narrator, through his account of the event's cause.

In a general sense, narrative is what determines things in *Jacques*, which explains why the novel figures the principle of determinism as a great scroll, a written narrative. Narrative is the linguistic act linking events, establishing their order and giving the impression of causality. Through narrative alone, significance and meaning are attributed to subjects and objects, acts and events. Thus, what Jacques constantly points out to his master concerning the determinism figured by the great scroll applies to narrative: there is no escape from narrative, no concept, principle or idea that could ever be situated outside narrative, except by another narrative. Consequently, if there exists any freedom in *Jacques*, it is the freedom of deciding whether or not to tell the story of narrative's determining function, which is to say that no absolute freedom exists here at all, for in telling any other story one still submits to the regulative principles of narrative. When Jacques' master takes over as narrator, for example, recounting his own affair with Agathe, Jacques continues to assert his mastery by falling asleep during the story, or pretending to. Effectively demonstrating his master's dependence on a listener, Jacques shows that whatever story his master chooses to tell, both he and the story remain determined by essentially narrative rules.[16]

The relation between Jacques and his master appears, then, to be a thoroughly narrative one, each character involved in a contest for narrative mastery. This contest is doubled by the equally conflictual relation between narrator and fictive reader. Just as Jacques proclaims that he "mène son maître," so too the narrator constantly intervenes to announce his freedom to tell his story as he wishes, regardless of the reader's expectations. "Vous voyez, Lecteur, que je suis en beau chemin et qu'il ne tiendrait qu'à moi de vous faire attendre un an, deux ans, trois ans le récit des amours de Jacques, en le séparant de son maître et en leur faisant courir à chacun tous les hasards qu'il me plairait ... Qu'il est facile de faire des contes!" (XXIII, 24–25). Storytelling is remarkably easy for this novel's narrator because Diderot uncouples narrative from its supposed determination by an extranarrative reality. Instead, the narrator bases his tale on the taunt, "Qui m'empêcherait?" Nothing in fact prevents him from telling the story as he wishes, given that fidelity to the putative truth of what actually happened no longer has any limiting, regulative function with respect either to the story he has to tell or to narrative in general. The sole reality in question in *Jacques* is that of narration, since the time and space of the narrator can easily be made coextensive with that of the characters. For the fictive reader, this uncoupling of narrative from any nonnarrative, extratextual principle only heightens the desire to re-establish that reality by asking for more information, more descriptive elements so as to make up an imaginary world that would safeguard the reality principle on which his own is founded. The narrator invariably responds to that desire for realism – and for an extratextual reality – by anticipating it, all the better to frustrate it, as in the novel's opening lines: "Comment s'étaient-ils rencontrés? Par hasard, comme tout le monde. Comment s'appelaient-ils? Que vous importe? D'où venaient-ils? Du lieu le plus prochain. Où allaient-ils? Est-ce que l'on sait où l'on va?" (XXIII, 23). Here as throughout the novel, the fictional reader personifies the conventions of a reading blind to its determination by the rules of the novelistic genre. The reader's interventions and their anticipation by the narrator foreground notions such as character, motivation, linear development, origin and end, cause and effect, in short the interpretive logic according to which the novel doubles and thus is determined by an extratextual reality.

The traditional novel attempts to render its generic conventions invisible and naturalize this interpretive logic by deploying the novelist's "techniques of illusion."[17] *Jacques* on the contrary foregrounds the arbitrary nature of these conventions, presenting the novel genre in denaturalized, parodic form and thus undermining its claim to truth. Diderot's novel uncouples from any possible grounding in the real all possible novelistic genres (historical, picaresque, romance), as well as all novelistic elements (temporality, causality, character, etc.). What this novel represents is nothing, except the novel's virtual capacity to present anything. This explains why *Jacques* has been read both as a realist novel and as its refusal. Not only does it incorporate all possible conventional means of referring to an extratextual reality, it also contains a self-reflexive commentary on these conventions, thereby displacing the mimetic relation between fiction and the real. *Jacques* plays out the desire for mimesis and simultaneously thwarts it, just as the narrator's replies to the fictive reader's questions shift attention from the story told to the act and art of its telling. *Jacques* responds to the desire for realism with another desire, one that contests the determinism of the real in the name of a narrative freedom the novel enjoys to tell any story it wishes, including its own.

If Diderot's novel is "about" anything at all, it is as much about the novelistic genre in general as any particular story of a servant and a master. Thus, this narrative's only "real" referent turns out to be narrative itself, thanks to a referential displacement that turns interpretation back upon itself. In one scene, for instance, Jacques and his master encounter a funeral procession transporting a coffin on a carriage bearing Jacques' former master's coat of arms. The picaresque event is also a semiotic one, for Jacques immediately interprets this sign as meaning the captain has died. His outpouring of grief is interrupted a few pages later however when the procession reappears heading in the opposite direction, this time with the men bound and led by armed tax officers. Unable to interpret this second event, which is a parody or travesty of the high seriousness of the first, Jacques falls silent. His master experiences no such interpretive difficulty, explaining that the men must have been bandits in disguise who were using the coffin to transport contraband. Or else, he adds, the men had borne off with a wife, daughter or nun, whom they had hidden in the coffin. Finally, though, the master's own interpretation of what these signs actually signify turns short. When Jacques asks him to explain why the carriage bore his captain's coat of arms, in other words to justify his reading of the event and his story of what it signifies, the master replies, "Ce sera tout ce qu'il vous plaira; mais achève-moi l'histoire de ton capitaine."

As this story spins itself out, the significance of the episode comes to involve the interpretive event as much as any picaresque one. As a set of signs, the components of the event (coffin, coat of arms, bier draped in black, etc.) may plausibly refer to almost anything, depending on how they are interpreted. The event's double occurrence establishes no opposition between illusion and reality, or a wrong interpretation and a correct one. Instead, it highlights the arbitrary, conventional nature of any interpretive act. Only when *Jacques* is interpreted as if the character were a real person does it make any difference whether the coffin contains his master's body or contraband or a kidnapped woman. If instead Jacques and his master are read as personifying two interpretive acts, two instances of a semiotic event, two narrative instances, then it makes little difference at all what the coffin contains, which as the master points out might be anything one wishes, given narrative's limitless capacity to generate stories. What does matter then, here and throughout the novel, is the narrative of interpretation, the way significance is attached to characters, objects, and events, through narrative linkage. Given the novel's general self-reflexivity, the most telling significance of the coffin episode lies in the way it frustrates the wish to know what in fact the coffin might contain, the desire to fix the sign's referent once and for all. Displacing that desire onto the novel, the episode suggests that the most important question concerns not *what* the coffin signifies but *how*, not any ultimate meaning but the process whereby meaning is created. Not by chance does this story of self-reflexivity concern an illicit act, the transgression of laws through ruse and deception. Marking the self-reflexive link joining this picaresque event to the interpretive one, making the novel's fictional reality coincide with that of its readers, the coffin episode recounts the "tragic" end of one kind of novel and reading, as deterministic as Jacques' captain's philosophy, and also the appearance of another kind, which seems to contain something significant yet may contain either something illicit or nothing at all. Perhaps the most illicit, transgressive novel is one whose significance stems from its containing nothing but itself, telling no other story than that of its own telling, referring to nothing besides itself. The real contraband *Jacques* transports then is perhaps itself, as it constantly marks the passage from one reality to another, from one narrative perspective to another, presenting the relation between them simply as coincidental and not hierarchical. Like the coffin, *Jacques* may turn out to be an autotelic object, doubling all reference to an extratextual reality with reference to the novel and its interpretation.

The narrative act and art of *Jacques le fataliste* do not break with mimetic conventions so much as they foreground them as precisely that, as arbitrary and constructed manners of establishing reference and producing an interpretive narrative. Both narrator and novel appear to have limitless freedom to escape these conventions by parodying them, to undermine their naturalness and determinate authority. Narrative acquires this freedom only by setting up a kind of counter-convention, an interpretive protocol that explicitly and self-reflexively contests the generic rules of the novel form in the name of a different yet equally determined novelistic truth. At one point, for example, the narrator anticipates the fictive reader's expectations concerning what will happen to Jacques and his master. Uncoupling these expectations from any possible grounding in an extratextual reality, he affirms,

> il ne tiendrait qu'à moi que tout cela n'arrivât; mais adieu la vérité de l'histoire, adieu le récit des amours de Jacques . . . Il est bien évident que je ne fais pas un roman, puisque je néglige ce qu'un romancier ne manquerait pas d'employer. Celui qui prendrait ce que j'écris pour la vérité serait peut-être moins dans l'erreur que celui qui le prendrait pour une fable (XXIII, 35).

By the 1750s, readers had grown accustomed to denunciations of the novel genre for being more "fabulous" and hence less truthful than other, nobler genres such as historical narrative. Experimentation with different narrative techniques such as those of the first-person memoir, the epistolary novel, and the historical novel marks the attempt to stake a new claim for the novel's veracity, to win esthetic recognition for this developing genre and social recognition for its practitioners. Diderot pushes this experimentation to its limit by suggesting that the novel can have access to truth only by displacing it. Contesting the traditional novel's claim to present the truth of an extratextual reality, *Jacques* reworks the notion of novelistic truth by defining it as "la vérité de l'histoire," the truth of the story, of storytelling, and of narrative. Constituting a thorough refusal of the novel through its constant parody of the genre's artificial conventionality, *Jacques* at the same time lays claim to being a truthful account, yet of itself, of writing and reading, of the text and its interpretation.

Diderot's novel occupies a limit position with respect to the rules governing the relation between narrative and the real by repeatedly producing a metaleptical displacement or transfer of significance from one order to another. Through narrative metalepsis, the time and space of narration are made coextensive with those of the narrated story, producing a linkage between two otherwise heterogeneous temporal-spatial and logical orders. At one point, for instance, the narrator suggests he may go and lie down while Jacques and his master are sleeping. Elsewhere, the narrator proclaims his power to make the reader wait two or three years – Jacques' time or the reader's? – for the story of Jacques' love, while Jacques and his master continue to travel. These instances of narrative metalepsis eliminate any fixed boundary separating *histoire* and *discours*, the story and its telling. The narrator's interventions and the dialogical relation they establish with the fictive reader exemplify the most explicit instance of such transgressive metalepsis, effectively displacing the object of the act of reading. The fictive reader's act of reading becomes coextensive with the reality of the story being read, as narrative constantly foregrounds its destination, the reality of its reception. Real readers of *Jacques* have little difficulty in distinguishing their own reading from the mystified one performed by the fictive reader. For whenever any narrative stages its reading, it opens up a stage of potential difference between this self-generated reading and actual readings it will receive and which it cannot totally control. At one point a more general metalepsis occurs, inscribing in the text not just a fictive reader and his mystified, convention-bound interpretation, but reading in general, and in a far more problematic way.

Pressing the narrator to name where the two travelers are heading – place names being one of those descriptive elements powerfully capable of producing what Barthes calls "the effect of the real" – the fictive reader's questions reveal how he remains imprisoned by his teleological understanding of narrative. For him, narrative is always determined by its end, by the moment of revelation, knowledge, and comprehension towards which it should be directed, by the structural and logical closure an ending should provide. Frustrating that desire for closure, Diderot's novel parodies the teleological narrative by supplying not one ending but three possible ones. Breaking off his story because he has told all he knows about the two characters, the narrator suggests that the reader finish the story as he wishes, or that he question Jacques or even Denise concerning its outcome, thereby taking over the master's position. The narrator further suggests that a set of memoirs of dubious authenticity may contain some clue as to the ending the narrative lacks. At this point another narrator intervenes, whose persona as editor marks the story's textual status as book and the mode of its reception as reading. Supplying three paragraphs containing three possible endings, one of which is copied from Sterne's *Tristram Shandy* (unless, the editor notes, Sterne was the one guilty of plagiarism), the editor provides no metanarrative perspective. Once again metalepsis undoes any possible interpretive hierarchy between writing and reading, between *Jacques*' narratives and those of its interpretation. If the editor grants the reader the freedom to finish the story as he wishes, adding that "de quelque manière que vous vous y preniez, je suis sûr que vous finirez comme moi," it is because there is no end to narrative, just as there exists no metanarrative that could contain and control all other narratives. Endings are as arbitrary as any descriptive detail, since no principle determines their significance absolutely.

Consequently, when the narrator satisfies the fictive reader's curiosity concerning the two travelers' destination, he does so only to subvert all the more effectively the type of reading that produces it:

> Oh, Lecteur, vous êtes d'une curiosité bien incommode! Et que diable cela vous fait-il? Quand je vous aurai dit que c'est à Pontoise ou à Saint-Germain, à Notre-Dame-de-Lorette ou à Saint-Jacques-de-Compostelle, en serez-vous plus avancé? Si vous insistez, je vous dirai qu'ils s'acheminèrent vers . . . oui, pourquoi pas . . . vers un château immense, au frontispice duquel on lisait: "Je n'appartiens à personne, et j'appartiens à tout le monde. Vous y étiez avant que d'y entrer, et vous y serez encore quand vous en sortirez" (XXIII, 42–43).

An architectural term as well as a typographical one, this frontispiece calls up the picaresque world Jacques and his master dwell in. But this minimal detail in the castle's description doubles its reference to the reality of a world outside the text by referring metaleptically to that other "world" that is the literary text. Designating a possible real place as well as the text, and all the intertexts *Jacques* comprises, from Cervantes, Sterne, and countless others to the great scroll where all is already written and already writing, the frontispiece states that whatever significance might be attributed to the castle depends on reading: "au frontispice duquel *on lisait* . . ." Reading is what determines our relation to the text and to the real, which is not to say that all is text and text alone, as certain pronouncements of structuralism have been taken to mean. Rather, reading is an act or mode of comprehension both cognitive and esthetic, relating at once to the text and to the reality of a world "outside" it. Perhaps the text reaches its limits in the gesture of pointing out that double relation, the duplicity or aporetic status of its language, which refers both to a world "outside" language and to itself, to the language through which that reference occurs. This aporetic status explains the apparently contradictory logic of what is written on the castle's frontispiece. For like this castle, language belongs to no one and to everyone, and if one "enters into" language, it is to discover there exists nothing "outside" with which to comprehend one's place "in" it. Like this castle, the book too belongs to no one and to everyone. The reader's place already exists there before the book is opened, the dialogical relation between text and reader preexisting any reading of any text. And thus aporetic logic proliferates: "Entrèrent-ils dans ce château?" asks the reader. "Non, car l'inscription était fausse, ou ils y étaient avant que d'y entrer," a statement that would make the inscription true. "Mais du moins ils en sortirent? – Non, car l'inscription était fausse, ou ils y étaient encore quand ils en furent sortis," which would also make the inscription true. Replacing the traditional logic of either/or, the text suggests the nondisjunctive logic of either/and, made possible by a metalepsis allowing Jacques and his master to exist in the same order of reality as text and reader. Just as Jacques leads his master, and the narrator leads the fictive reader, so too the text leads the real reader, doubling the reality of his or her world and doing so parodically, self-reflexively, and thus contesting any putative, regulative "outside" to the narratives of literature and its interpretation.

Diderot's novel self-reflexively ungrounds the extratextual reference upon which a realist reading is founded. Consequently, a reading attentive to the novel's self-reflexivity would seem to be fundamentally incompatible with the convention-bound referential readings it first received. Unnuanced and reductive, these readings were determined by the desire to contextualize *Jacques* by relating it to the immediate event of the French Revolution. However "naïve," these early readings are thus characteristic of all readings in that they contextualize the text by making it part of another narrative, thereby producing another story and another history, if not history itself. Despite the desire to break with the naïveté and errors of past interpretations, this narrativizing, historicizing imperative still functions in contemporary readings of Diderot's novel, even in the most formalist ones that seek to free the novel from extratextual determinism and interpretation from the constraints of history. As a brief discussion of the modern reception of Diderot's novel shows, a formalist theory of modern literature, far from ridding itself and literature from historical determinism, entangles itself all the more in the question of history. However better attuned to the inherent poetics of the literary text, the narrative of formalist theory cannot escape the contradictions of its own narrativizing imperative.

Beginning in the 1960s, *Jacques* was increasingly read as a novel of the twentieth century, not the eighteenth. Finding it a rich proving ground for structuralist literary theory, critics proclaimed it eminently modern, as much an "antinovel" or "new novel" as those of Beckett, Robbe-Grillet or Simon. Freeing *Jacques* from the evolutionary view of literary form, these critics read the novel not as an historical product but as a formal one, resulting solely from the potential of poetic form. This limit-text was heralded as exposing in all its arbitrary conventionality the mimetic assumption upon which realist esthetics (and ideology) are founded. Thus Diderot's novel could legitimately lay claim to a formal, esthetic truth precisely because it emptied the novelistic mirror of all but itself. It evacuated from the novel the world it was falsely taken to represent and thereby radically called into question any understanding of meaning, reality, and its representation that failed to reflect on the conventionally determined, socially motivated mechanisms governing such understanding.[18] As Lecointre and Le Galliot put it, "le roman de Diderot ne fait donc pas référence au réel, mais à l'art du réel . . . C'est bien la vérité que cherche Diderot, mais la vérité du et sur le roman."[19] With this shift in emphasis from the real to the art of its production as representation, from a "naïvely" mimetic reading to one that focuses on the text's formal properties and poetics, interpretation locates its own modernity in *Jacques*, which triumphantly inaugurates the liberating, even revolutionary event of literature. "Parce qu'il est le refus d'une 'mythologie' littéraire dont il dénonce toutes les valeurs signifiantes, *Jacques le fataliste*, seul parmi les romans du temps, rencontre une surprenante et moderne liberté" (p. clxiii). According to this view, Diderot's novel wins its freedom from the myth and the esthetic ideology of realism by parodying the real, not copying it. The novel displays its formal autonomy and poetic creativity by displacing reference to the real onto reference to the novel itself. In *Jacques*, just as no one narrative enjoys total regulative status with respect to any other, so too the text wins its freedom and its status as literature precisely by refusing to accord regulative status to any prior or successive text, be it a literary text such as Sterne's *Tristram Shandy* or the text of its own reading. Absolutely undetermined by any nonnarrative, extratextual principle, Diderot's novel would exemplify the liberation of modern literature from an extraliterary reality, insofar as the novel seems to claim that reality can occur only in the name of poetics.

In the modern reading of *Jacques* sketched out here, a general theory of narrative, poetics, and literature seeks to free Diderot's novel, and with it literature, from determination by the social and the historical. Such an approach does provide an effective critique of certain esthetic "mythologies," yet one must question its note of triumphant liberation, echoed moreover in numerous high structuralist readings of the novel in general. In arguing that the novel possesses the capacity to free itself from esthetic ideology, such readings assume that it exemplifies a kind of narrative able to situate all other narratives, that it contains a general theory or metanarrative (of the novel, of narrative, of literature) providing a standard for evaluating all possible readings. This desire for a general theory or metanarrative can hardly be satisfied, however, by a novel that undoes any hierarchical relation between narratives. Judged from this perspective, the modern reading of *Jacques* proclaims the modern liberation of literature in the name of a general theory in order all the better to dissimulate its own narrative desire to recount the story of literature's liberation. Unstated as well is the literary interpreter's desire for the freedom to disregard his or her place in history. "Nous avons peu le sens de la relativité historique, le goût de la distance et l'imagination du passé," claim Lecointre and Le Galliot. "Epris de synchronisme, notre temps est égocentrique: la modernité de *Jacques le fataliste* ne pouvait apparaître qu'à travers les thèmes et les formes . . . qui nous concernent et nous fascinent" (p. cxvii). Projecting these two readers' vision onto a collective readership, the statement suggests a modernity whose own self-reflexive fascination amounts to a phantasm of synchronic forms played out at the expense of diachrony. If the past is lost because it cannot be imagined, its place is taken by the imaginary reality of a continuous present moment to which these two readers' interpretation of *Jacques* refers. A critical fascination with form may free the text and its interpretation from prior mythologizing narratives, but not from the mythologizing notion of a metanarrative theory of form that can free itself from narrative determination. In Lecointre and Le Galliot's own narrative, poetic form signifies a highly determinate relation to history. For them, Diderot's novel signifies a literary modernity that in its refusal of social determination inscribes itself all the more in a social-political sphere. Certainly a new notion of literature and literary history emerges during the mid-twentieth century. It remains to be seen, however, whether the formalist mode of structuralist theory will have provided a stepping stone towards effectively articulating the relation between literature and the social, or set in place yet another myth of literature.

In any event, this discovery of a "surprising and modern freedom" in *Jacques*, the liberation from literary mythology and ideology, strangely reactivates a claim made by the eighteenth-century Enlighteners, and which is certainly one of Enlightenment's founding myths. Perhaps we are no freer to tell the story of literature's self-emancipation than the Enlighteners were to tell that of reason's freedom from ignorance and myth. In claiming that *Jacques* empties the mirror the novel was supposed to provide, a "modern" reading has not done away with the myth of referentiality. Rather, one referent has been replaced with another. The novel remains just as referential, although it now refers to itself as form, text, and literature.[20]

It has been claimed that twentieth-century interpretation has been unsuccessful in defining how Diderot's text is linked to history and society.[21] Without retreating from the insights afforded by a formalist perspective and the demystification it effectively produces, yet at the same time without closing off the question of the extratextual, one can articulate the linkage between literature and the social Diderot's novel establishes by reconsidering the twin questions of freedom and determinism. The roles played by Jacques and his master can be read as essentially narrative ones, comprehensible in terms of a general theory of narrative. They are also social roles, those of master and servant. The question then is whether the novel presents narrative relations as simply doubling social ones, which would justify collapsing the two orders, or whether they remain distinct yet related.

Throughout the novel Jacques appears to enjoy total freedom to tell his story when and as he wishes, a freedom structurally paralleled by the narrator's. Yet Jacques' narrative position is determined to a certain extent by his social one, for he apparently tells his story upon his master's orders. Jacques remains bound to the social hierarchy that determines his place and his actions. In one scene, however, he disobeys his master's order, explicitly refusing to go downstairs in the inn, to "descendre," in other words to keep to a position of social inferiority and subservience. The ensuing dispute between the two thematizes opposing views of what determines the reality of social relations. For the master, Jacques is and will always be "un Jacques," whose sole function is to serve a master. Representing a hierarchical and conventional understanding of social relations, the master's position alone determines what Jacques is and what his name signifies. Jacques responds, "Un Jacques! Un Jacques, Monsieur, est un homme comme un autre . . . C'est quelquefois mieux qu'un autre" (xxiii, 180). Arguing that he and any other "Jacques" are not only servants but people, Jacques proposes a more egalitarian view of things, one already common in eighteenth-century political theory.

Of more interest is Jacques' second comment, that a Jacques is sometimes better than others, which implies a different criterion for judging social relations and also a different temporality ("*sometimes* better"). Jacques does not rebel against the social hierarchy by seeking to take his master's place and become a master. The master's position is not one of freedom and autonomy but of severely limited mastery, for it depends totally upon servitude. As Jacques puts it, "vos ordres ne sont que des clous à soufflet, s'ils n'ont été ratifiés par Jacques." Diderot does not suggest, as Hegel would later in his discussion of the dialectical relation between lord and bondsman, that this consciousness of the servant's position frees him from his master's mastery, canceling it out yet preserving it as concept. This scene is not about mastery as a concept, the mastery that comes, for Hegel at least, from self-reflection and heightened self-consciousness. Rather, the scene reworks the concept of mastery. If the master defines social relations by means of a constative discourse, the scene also contains a performative discourse which contests the master's discourse, displacing its terms by showing how constative discourse ultimately depends upon a performative one. Only if Jacques obeys his master's orders do they become true performative statements, which is to say that Jacques represents a discursive performativity that determines the master's hierarchical definition of social relations. The master's conceptual, constative discourse can never be absolute, universal, unmediated. Jacques presses his master to recognize this state of affairs in the well-known stipulation scene where he announces that the knowledge of his master's dependency on him gives him the power and indeed requires him to abuse his privileges. Jacques' performative decree, "Stipulons," actualizes precisely the abusive power it refers to, yet it does not reverse the position of master and servant. This is why, when the master exclaims that such a decree makes Jacques' lot far better than his, Jacques does not argue; this is also why Jacques disagrees with his master's claim that he has but to change places with Jacques in order to preserve his mastery. "Savez-vous ce qui en arriverait? Vous y perdriez le titre, et vous n'auriez pas la chose." Jacques will continue to occupy the servant's position in a social hierarchy. But by defining his effective relation to that hierarchy in terms of a discursive performativity, he resituates that hierarchy and subjects it to different regulative principles. The master continues to possess the title, the socially recognized sign of power, but Jacques has "the thing," the ability to determine when and where that power will be played out, to stage the performance of power.

It is Jacques, then, who determines what the sign of power effectively signifies. Thus, he claims, it will always be said that "Jacques mène son maître." This does not mean Jacques becomes a master in his own right, that his servant's wiles and his narrator's skills have freed him from social determination. Rather, Jacques leads his master because of the discursive displacement of the social relation his performative discourse produces. The social is that linkage between individuals constantly performed in their language, in the discursive relations that situate them and with which they situate themselves and others. If Jacques' lot is better than his master's, it is because he alone reveals this contingency. Jacques does not free himself of this mediation any more than Diderot's novel does, for neither presents a general theory of anything, be it of literature or social relations. Neither exemplifies a conceptual discourse separate from all other discursive instances and possessing explanatory, regulative power with respect to them. What Jacques does represent is the performative power of language both to establish such hierarchies and to contest them. At the end of the stipulation scene, he announces once again in performative terms, "voilà qui est convenu." Jacques binds himself to his master, establishing a social relation between them that has been revealed to be a discursive one, a contractual agreement between two parties. This reworking of the social relation between Jacques and his master undermines the pregivenness of the social hierarchy, contesting any absolute authority that might be claimed for it. This critical displacement does not, however, free him from the social. In fact, the truly social link between the two is thematized in yet another of Jacques' performative statements: "que le reste de notre vie soit employé à faire un proverbe," namely, "Jacques mène son maître." Through another metalepsis, Jacques and his master will become a proverb. They enter (the) language, becoming like a proverb, a social text, one that presents the social relation, as all texts do, and that at the same time repeatedly contests any absolute determination by the social.

Does this mean that the novel, and with it literature, acquire absolute freedom with regard to the social? Clearly not, since any commentary on the novel, even the one the novel itself self-reflexively provides, situates the novel within yet another narrative, thereby establishing another discursive, social relation. This potentially interminable reinscription is thematized in the novel's ending, which contains no end of narrative perspectives and no end to narrative. Diderot's novel plays out a constant contest to narrate in a way that situates all other narratives; it also reveals that any such metaposition is a narrative one as well. Thus there exists no absolute narrator in *Jacques*, just as there is no general narrative that in theory would not be susceptible to being situated by yet another narrative. Commentary on Diderot's novel cannot escape playing out this struggle, whether it claims to remain "outside" the novel, anchored in a sociohistorical reality able to be comprehended independently of novelistic, narrative principles, or whether it collapses that reality into the text itself, making narrative "fictions" the sole manner of comprehending the real. In either case, this narrative struggle constitutes the stage upon which the real story of sociohistorical relations is performed.

Perhaps then *Jacques le fataliste* is a fundamentally political text, as the novel's eighteenth-century readers sensed, although not for the reasons they gave generally. One reader though does suggest how one might articulate the political nature of *Jacques*, a text Pierre-Louis Roederer characterizes in terms of "art." Writing in 1796, Roederer finds the novel somewhat free, although not immoral. He has greater difficulty defending the novel's form.

> Malgré la surcharge et l'interruption des événements, l'intérêt de chacun se soutient et le fil de tous se retrouve. L'auteur a poussé aussi loin qu'il est possible, l'art de tourmenter la curiosité sans l'affaiblir, et de s'en jouer sans la lasser; art qui suppose sans doute beaucoup d'esprit, mais au fond peu louable, et dont l'exemple même peut être dangereux: car il ne serait pas étonnant, vu notre inclination actuelle pour les choses bizarres, que mille romans ne se fabriquassent dans le cours d'une année sur ce modèle; qui pourrait répondre même qu'on ne portera pas l'imitation jusques dans l'art dramatique, et que quelque jour Phèdre n'interrompra pas son entretien avec Hipolite pour lui proposer d'aller voir *Caïus Gracchus*, et entendre la *marseillaise*![22]

For Roederer, Diderot's art is dangerously excessive. Because of the way it links literature to the real, the uncontainable metalepsis that characterizes narrative in *Jacques* invades the real to the point of altering our understanding of social reality. This metaleptical undoing of established hierarchies reveals them to be arbitrary and motivated, and thus thousands of other linkages are possible. The real danger posed by Diderot's text, then, is that it reveals narrative to be a social product, determined by "notre inclination actuelle," by a collective desire always set in a specific present moment. Diderot's art shows that narratives result from a social act and play out a social drama. The drama that fascinates Roederer, clearly present in the "bizarre" example he gives, plays out this invasion of metaleptical thought. The impossible linkage of Racine's *Phèdre* and Marie-Joseph Chénier's *Caïus Gracchus* of 1792 within the same reality undoes the closure of classical, eternalizing structures by interjecting reference to the unique and highly political event of the present, the revolution signified by "La Marseillaise" as well as the implicit reference to Gracchus Babeuf.

Roederer's unease concerning metalepsis helps us define the challenge Diderot's novel poses, and not only to eighteenth-century readers. Long after the events of the French Revolution, Diderot's reception continues to be haunted by the threat of metalepsis, the bizarre possibility that Diderot's reality coexists with our own. Depending on our "inclination actuelle," our interpretive desire, we either foreground this coexistence or deny it. We cannot do away with it though, insofar as the linkage between past and present, these two temporally heterogeneous texts and events, always occurs in the interpretive act, which in each instance constitutes social reality anew. The passionate readers of the Revolutionary period represented their own social reality by forging an image of Diderot, however partisan, and thereby linked their present moment to a past, however imaginary and phantasmic. Similarly, two early nineteenth-century editions of Diderot's complete works will present yet another Diderot and, in the process, other social narratives, albeit in essentially different ways.

Both the Brière edition of 1821 and the Paulin edition of 1830 portrayed a significantly different Diderot. The first contained a version of *Le Neveu de Rameau* supposedly based on an original manuscript (and not the French translation of Gœthe's *Rameau's Neffe*), and the second presented a number of important and previously unpublished texts, including *Le Rêve* and the more intimate writings, such as the correspondence with Falconnet and Sophie Volland. These two literary events are significant moments in the progressive revelation of the complete Diderot. Nevertheless, the hermeneutics of philology cannot help us evaluate the effect these editions were designed to produce. For like any interpretive act, an edition is never neutral. By virtue of the way it presents, frames, and comments upon its author's texts, an edition possesses an ideological function and status, which even the most stubbornly philological notion of completeness, accuracy, and truth cannot camouflage entirely. Consequently, we must consider these editions' portrayal of Diderot from a different and more contextual perspective.

By 1821 when the Brière edition appeared, the Jacobin spectre had almost completely been put to rest. Yet throughout the Empire and Restoration, discussing eighteenth-century literature remained more a political act than a literary one. La Harpe's and Barruel's acerbic denunciations of a "partie philosophique" composed of seditious and immoral sophists conspiring to overthrow royal order slowly gave way to a more comprehensive analysis that related literary and philosophical writings to the larger historical, social, and institutional context. Prosper de Barante, for example, in his highly influential *Tableau de la littérature française au 18e siècle*, seeks to "rattacher la littérature à tout l'ensemble de la société." "L'auteur de cet écrit," he adds, "ne sut voir dans les lettres qu'un symptôme de la maladie générale, un signe de l'état de dissolution."[23] Although Barante's medical metaphor of sickness harkens back to La Harpe and Barruel, he does not wish to quarantine the illness. Nor can it be, given that Barante views eighteenth-century literature as expressing the conflicts of the society that produced it. Critical of the agressively antireligious, at times anti-institutional position the philosophes adopted, Barante nevertheless argues that they were forced to do so because of an *Ancien Régime* that sought to prevent literature from having any effective social influence. This view of literature as being determined by social and political structures which it thus expresses will influence the generation of the 1830s as they seek to define the critical role of literature and art within a social and political context.

Against the backdrop of this emerging notion of literature, the Brière edition is an anachronism at best. At worst it encircles Diderot's texts with a kind of editorial and interpretive *cordon sanitaire* designed to preclude any meaningful reflection concerning the contemporary pertinence of Diderot's writing, especially regarding the critical function of literature developing at the time. Especially revealing is the place accorded to commentary by Diderot's disciple and first editor, Naigeon. The Brière edition reproduces Naigeon's introductions to Diderot's texts in more than half the cases. More significantly, the reading of all the texts is framed by Naigeon's 400-page *Mémoires historiques et philosophiques sur la vie et les ouvrages de D. Diderot*. Begun in 1784 and completed in 1795, the *Mémoires* not only are dated by 1821, they also date Diderot and his writing, inscribing them in the social and intellectual context of an eighteenth century with which a reader of the 1820s could scarcely have any affinity.

One example of Naigeon's antiquating portrayal is his definition of the intellectual's relation to the political order. His story of an unenlightened monarchy inimical to free speech replays the philosophes' own version of their combative relation to institutions of power and the critical distance they sought to achieve. At times the philosophes characterized this distance in terms of freedom from institutional and political orders, at others in terms of alienation. Yet they believed their critical stance always placed them outside such orders, at least in theory, Significantly, Naigeon does not hesitate to universalize this historically specific social configuration. "Diderot semble être parti d'un principe qui est vrai en général, c'est qu'en littérature, comme en politique, en morale et en philosophie rationnelle, les opinions communément reçues sont presque toujours fausses" (p. 169). By 1821, defining truth on such a principle had little if any regulative or critical force. Events of the preceding twenty-five years not only had brought destabilizing reversals in what was "commonly understood," they had rendered nonpertinent the notion, perhaps always ideal, of an oppositional yet effectively critical position exterior to political and institutional structures.

The *Mémoires* perform an equally antiquating act in the case of Diderot's materialism. Commenting extensively on *Le Rêve de D'Alembert*, Naigeon presents its intellectual debates in their most dated form, making Diderot's materialism seem to belong to an intellectually defunct world, impossible to relate to contemporary issues and social practices. As framed by the *Mémoires*, the most productive aspect of Diderot's materialism becomes literally unreadable.[24] The materialist practice of the *Encyclopédie* remains equally incomprehensible in terms of

Naigeon's own understanding of knowledge, which for him is derived primarily from medicine and physiology. My point here is not to condemn Naigeon for being intellectually ill-equipped to grasp the most pertinent aspects of Diderot's scientific texts, that is, the way they problematize knowledge as representation. I do want to suggest though that Naigeon's presentation of Diderot can be judged by considering how it blocks any effective engagement with the epistemological act on which Naigeon's own text is founded, the act of reading that results in "knowing" the text, or being able to present it and link it to a present moment. To say that Naigeon's text blocks such engagement with reading implies that it works to preclude a reading of Diderot in 1821, or today for that matter, that seeks to represent a present moment, to narrate an effective story of the present.[25] Naigeon's commentary should not be written off as being limited, misguided or even motivated, whether intentionally or ideologically. Rather, the *Mémoires* must be read emblematically in order to grasp how any portrayal of Diderot involves not only a hermeneutical act but also a social one that tells the story of its own present moment.

Where Naigeon's text does make Diderot's texts readable in a pertinent, contemporary way in 1821 is in the area of ethics. As if to parry before the fact the vitriolic attacks against Diderot's atheist materialism made immediately following the Revolution (and that would continue to be heard for decades), Naigeon adopts a strategy of humanization. Framing his discussion of the texts with an opening thirty-page biography, admittedly the most complete to that date, the *Mémoires* make understanding Diderot the writer dependent upon appreciating Diderot the man. Not surprisingly, the portrait sketched out is one of exemplary morality and virtue. Diderot may have written the *Supplément au voyage de Bougainville*, nevertheless he began his career by doing translation work in order to fulfill the "devoirs sacrés de père et d'époux" (p. 34). Diderot the prophet of immorality? "Tous les jours il se repentait d'avoir écrit *Les Bijoux indiscrets*" (p. 36). And taking on the question of atheism directly, Naigeon assures that "si Diderot ne croyait pas en Dieu, il croyait fermement à la probité, à la vertu, à cet intérêt puissant qu'ont tous les hommes à être justes, bienfaisants" (p. 36). With this strategy of moralizing humanization in place, the issue of atheistic materialism can adroitly be skirted, and rather ironically since Naigeon himself was hardly a devout believer. He presents *De l'interprétation de la nature*, for instance, as a highly technical and difficult to understand text, written primarily for other philosophes. While not entirely incorrect, this remark does sidestep Diderot's straightforward discussion of rational philosophy and the interpretation of a nature governed by internal and not divine principles. Similarly, Naigeon takes great pains to distance Diderot as much as possible from the atheism espoused by Saunderson in the *Lettre sur les aveugles* (just as Diderot himself attempted to do, albeit half-heartedly, in an almost apologetic letter to Voltaire, which Naigeon quotes without commentary). In sum, the Diderot portrayed by the *Mémoires* remains a materialist, one who even proposes explaining natural phenomena without recourse to divine principles. Yet this Diderot remains above all a paragon of virtue and morality. Naigeon's humanizing, moralizing portrayal aims to have Diderot's texts read as confirming not challenging an ethical order, and an essentially bourgeois one.

Naigeon's presentation of esthetic questions, both those Diderot addresses and those in terms of which his texts could be engaged, is consistent with his attempt to antiquate contemporary readings. Invariably, whether in his brief discussion of Diderot's dramatic theories or the more extensive treatment of the *Lettre sur les sourds et muets* – no mention is made of the *Salons* – Naigeon reads Diderot in the most classical, if not antiquarian, of terms. Consider the case of Diderot's theatrical theory. Already in 1760 Lessing had seized upon Diderot's *drame bourgeois* to free German theater from a stultifying imitation of classical forms and to make possible a more nationalistic and less French theater, one more expressive of the present social and historical moment. Yet Naigeon's outdated description of Diderot's theatrical theories could have been formulated as easily in the seventeenth century, at the height of the debate opposing Ancients and Moderns, as in the eighteenth.[26] Furthermore, Naigeon's remarks concerning style reflect his strategic attempt to insert Diderot in a tradition of writer-intellectuals in which writing is conceived above all as craft.[27] Such a strategy succeeds in the case of the earlier and more public texts. The later texts present more difficulty, for they contain "deux tons très disparates; un ton domestique et familier qui est mauvais, et un ton réfléchi qui est excellent" (p. 206). Is Naigeon referring simply to the difference between the polished and the unpolished phrase, or does he sense a more pervasive and troubling duality in Diderot's writing, and which far exceeds matters of style? In just which of the later works this double tonality occurs he does not say, but it seems that they are too intimate, reveal too much, touch too close to home. This is perhaps why the *Mémoires* make no mention of *Le Neveu de Rameau*, a text whose structuring principle is precisely that of "disparate tonality" and that subjects the classical notions of style and taste to a thoroughgoing ethical critique.

Significantly, Naigeon claims this troubling "tone" is so pervasive that not one of Diderot's manuscripts can be published as is, in other words without being taken over by an editor (such as Naigeon himself) "qui joigne à des connaissances profondes sur divers objets, un esprit juste, et surtout un goût très sévère" (p. 205). If only Diderot had followed his future editor's constant advice: "de relire, la plume à la main, tous ses manuscrits, d'en soumettre à l'examen le plus rigoureux les raisonnements, le style et les pensées, de n'y laisser aucune de ces expressions familières, aucune de ces petites négligences qui . . . échappent à l'écrivain le plus correct" (p. 412). Naigeon's excessive concern with style – "une des choses qu'on doit le plus soigner dans un ouvrage" (pp. 412–13) – belies his sense of something in Diderot's writing that resists the monumentalizing gesture of his disciple-editor, something that works against the desire to insert these texts in a tradition of writing in which esthetic practice is determined above all by "taste," that is, by rules and conventions reflecting a social hierarchy and designed to preserve it. In seventeenth-century France, the notion of the perfection of language and style was intimately linked to the accumulation of political power. Style was a way either to silence those discourses that could contest too directly the political discourse of absolutism, or, more effectively, to rechannel and neutralize them. In 1821, what Naigeon calls style harkens back to a relation between writing and the sociopolitical order that had already begun to disappear by the middle of the eighteenth century, as ideological notions such as "la cour," "l'honnête homme" or "le style noble" exercised less and less regulative power over increasingly contestatory discourses. Consequently, Naigeon's notion of style in the *Mémoires* works to disassociate Diderot's writing – at least as Naigeon would edit his texts – from the "prise de la parole" of Romantic writers, which they conceived of as an esthetic revolution against classicism but also as having an immediately political signification.

In sum, the place accorded to Naigeon's commentary in the Brière edition of 1821 gives the *Mémoires* an afterlife that robs Diderot's texts of theirs. To save Diderot, at times from himself, and above all to rescue him from an all too political reading, Naigeon turns his texts into cultural artifacts, unable to be linked to a contemporary critical practice in terms of either philosophy or literature. Remarkably untimely, the *Mémoires*' humanizing portrayal of Diderot reappears consistently throughout the history of his reception. The *Mémoires* also establish a principle whose regulative power will only increase during the coming 150 years, namely, that Diderot's text be framed by an editorial-interpretive discourse, the ideological function of which cannot be veiled, even by the most well-intentioned of appeals to philological reason. Jules Assézat's remark in the opening pages of his 1875 edition of the *œuvres complètes* is instructive in this regard. "Il est, avant tout, bien entendu que nous n'avons rien changé et que nous ne changerons rien au texte de Diderot. Il faut que l'homme se présente tel qu'il était, avec ses qualités et ses défauts" (AT I, vi–vii). The philological rigor of Assézat's edition successfully combatted a hostility manifested throughout the nineteenth century and into the twentieth by critics and historians such as Geruzez, Nisard, Taine, Faguet, and Brunetière. Even though this hostility was justified through an appeal to universal literary and ethical values, Diderot's most dismissive readers invariably linked him negatively to a present historical moment.[28] Diderot's nineteenth-century reception in general, and especially the one located within the university, sought to block out or defuse the perceived threat of something all too contemporary in his texts, something that could not be forgotten or ever successfully extirpated. Consequently, Diderot's portrayal by his most violently negative critics turns out to be a thoroughly phantasmic one. What is curious is that the editorial integrity of Naigeon's discipleship and Assézat's philological positivism, both designed to rescue Diderot, effectively block any effectively critical articulation of how these phantasmic portrayals function. No edition, however "complete" or "scientific" – a term reappearing constantly in Jean Varloot's description of the recent Hermann edition – can in and of itself provide a critical vantage point for comprehending the ideological mediation at work in any act of portraying Diderot. Where then might such a position exist?

The final episode in this genealogy of portrayals extends beyond the history of editions to consider Sainte-Beuve's portrayal of Diderot in three articles appearing in 1830 and 1831, and a fourth published in 1851. Whereas hostility or disinterest had for decades characterized Diderot's predominately politicized reception, Sainte-Beuve's essays extend the largely sympathetic judgment of Charles Nodier and Jules Janin. These essays also signal the beginnings of a more estheticizing reception and they contribute significantly to Diderot's Romanticization.[29] The key element of this estheticizing reception is the importance Sainte-Beuve attributes to the place of art in Diderot's writings as well as in literary criticism. His estheticizing portrayals employ a strategy for narrating the present moment that links esthetics and politics in the emerging and soon to be institutionalized discourse of literary criticism, a strategy that will long outlive the Romantic generation of 1830.

Sainte-Beuve's treatment of Diderot, characteristic of his critical method in general, starts from the assumption that before being described and analyzed, the object of literary history must first be constructed. Describing this creative, poetic moment in the critical enterprise, he writes:

On s'enferme pendant une quinzaine de jours avec les écrits d'un mort célèbre, poète ou philosophe; on l'étudie, on le retourne, on l'interroge à loisir; on le fait poser devant soi; c'est presque comme si l'on [faisait] . . . le portrait ou le buste de Byron, de Scott, de Gœthe . . . Chaque trait s'ajoute à son tour, et prend place de lui-même dans cette physiognomie qu'on essaie de reproduire . . . On sent naître, on voit venir la ressemblance; et le jour, le moment où l'on a saisi le tic familier, le sourire révélateur, la gerçure indéfinissable, la ride intime et douleureuse qui se cache en vain sous les cheveux déjà clairsemés – à ce moment l'analyse disparaît dans la création, le portrait parle et vit, on a trouvé l'homme.[30]

For Sainte-Beuve, to read is to portray. In the act of critical portraiture that constructs the author's image, the writer's creation is transformed through the critic's own poetic creativity. Sainte-Beuve accords literary criticism a heightened, nobler status, in that the critic can equal the artist by transforming "les écrits d'un mort" into a living, speaking portrait, a critical work of art. Significantly, the precondition of this poetic enterprise is a closing off – "on s'enferme . . ." – as if there existed a potential "opening" onto something the critic does not wish to contemplate or inject into literary criticism. We shall return to this curious precondition of Beuvian portraiture, especially since with time (and especially in the case of Diderot) such closure will be increasingly difficult to maintain.

Initially at least, the Beuvian desire to portray realizes its objective, a portrait. "[On] finit . . . par saisir tous les traits de cette figure forte, bienveillante et hardie, colorée par le sourire, abstraite par le front, aux vastes tempes, au cœur chaud, la plus allemande de toutes nos têtes" (p. 127). This "Germanic head" belongs above all to the author of the *Lettres à Sophie Volland* and the *Salons*, poet of feeling, analyst of the heart's inner secrets. Sainte-Beuve is one of the first to take Diderot seriously as an author. Not by chance moreover, this Diderot corresponds well to the image of the Romantic poet being elaborated in the 1830s. Clearly, a strikingly contemporary narrative is laid out in Sainte-Beuve's essay, which portrays its Diderot in order to articulate an emerging critical position. A sign of this is Sainte-Beuve's desire to distance Diderot, and more important the position he represents, from the political realm. Thus Diderot best exemplifies the "insurrection philosophique" of the eighteenth century, yet unlike the *Causeries*' Montesquieu, Raynal or Rousseau, "[il] s'occupe peu de politique" (p. 144). Biography and psychology may be the warp and woof of the critic's canvas, but this reference to a contestatory philosophical or intellectual position situated outside the political realm suggests that Sainte-Beuve's portrait has a frame as well. This framing desire removes the political from the picture in the name of a critical poetics, an exclusion that recalls the inaugural closure of the Beuvian method. The metaphor of the frame refers here to that part of the portrait that encloses it and separates it from what lies around it. The painting's outer border, the frame is so removed from what is essentially pictorial and esthetic that it seems a simple accessory. Indeed, the frame should ultimately appear invisible, as it shifts attention to what it contains. But frames never disappear. If they are not spoken of, it is because they are just not seen. They always remain though, materially relating the artwork to a background (not an exteriority) against which it is always set. In Sainte-Beuve's case, his esthetic framing of Diderot is doubled by the desire to frame out something else, which can be grasped by unpacking somewhat the curious national metonymy, "la plus allemande de nos têtes."

The term "German" was highly connotative in 1830, not only for Sainte-Beuve but also in the larger context of French Romanticism. Clearly, reference to beyond the Rhine played an essential role in formulating a Romantic theory of literature that could not be accommodated with French classicism. As far as Diderot is concerned, his Germanization by Sainte-Beuve can be read as an oblique reference to Diderot's German reception, which was markedly different from the immediately political reading in France, and with which Sainte-Beuve has no small affinity.

Thanks to Lessing, Diderot the dramatist was as well known in Germany as in France by 1830. Only in Germany however did Diderot the novelist, author of *Jacques le fataliste* and *Le Neveu de Rameau*, have an immediate impact on literary theory. Gœthe and Friedrich Schlegel, for example, seek to rescue Diderot the novelist from a politicized, moralizing reading. They present him not as a moralist or a philosophe but as an artist, praising him in terms of essentially esthetic values.[31] Yet Gœthe especially senses something in the social critique *Le Neveu* contains that an estheticizing reading cannot entirely defuse. "Ce dialogue éclate comme une bombe au beau milieu de la littérature française," he writes, "et il faut une extrême attention pour montrer comment elle porte et qui elle atteint."[32] To be sure, it was difficult to translate the explosive force of Diderot's satire of an *Ancien Régime* milieu into a German context. Yet in situating this bombshell squarely on French soil, does Gœthe express his concern over possible fallout across the Rhine? Must *Le Neveu* be translated with caution precisely because it portrays a highly civilized culture so perverse and corrupt that the sole truly lucid consciousness remaining is that of its own depravation, an insight that might strike dangerously close to home, touching even representatives of German culture, including Gœthe himself?

If Gœthe locates a destabilizing force in *Le Neveu*, Hegel attempts to comprehend it philosophically. Making strategic use of Diderot's text in the *Phenomenology*, Hegel presents it as the esthetic expression of a sociohistorical moment that coincides with a critical moment in the manifestation of consciousness to itself. Whereas for Gœthe and Schlegel, *Le Neveu* belongs to the domain of pure art, Hegel opens up the latter by linking the esthetic, the moral, and the cognitive, a linkage he finds already present in Diderot's text.[33] In annexing *Le Neveu*, inserting it into the text of speculative philosophy, Hegel provides a powerful way of comprehending the artwork as the concrete expression of an historicized consciousness. Thus for Hegel, the image of "pure culture" *Le Neveu* presents is that of monarchical, pre-Revolutionary France, and also of a self so alienated in what the Nephew calls "pantomime" that all moral values blur and the only truly lucid awareness is of general corruption and perversion. Representing the conflict between the noble and the base, the Nephew is literally torn apart in this struggle between two forms of consciousness. Yet the *zerissene Bewußtsein* he embodies is transformed into a truer self-consciousness in the act of conceiving of itself as free from the moral laws that could only perpetuate its enslavement. The notion of such a transformation makes it possible for Hegel to understand the Nephew's individual negation of morality as the simultaneous affirmation of self-identity and consciousness, which provides the basis for expressing a universalized concept of identity in fundamentally moral terms.[34]

The Hegelian reading of *Le Neveu* seeks above all to harmonize the forceful conflict Diderot's text stages. In the balance lies no less than philosophy's capacity to comprehend art critically, to master its destabilizing force by translating art's own self-reflexivity into the cognitive discourse of philosophy. This explains why Hegel can take what the Nephew presents – in his musical performance – as the artistic equivalent of what he represents in a moral sense.[35] But can what the Nephew presents in fact be represented? Is Hegel attempting valiantly to master something in Diderot's text (and the artwork) that cannot totally be made comprehensible? Analyzing the relation between philosophy and the esthetic in Hegel, Suzanne Gearhart argues that what Hegel must deny in *Le Neveu* is the double nature of art, which is both reflection and the expression of passion. "If the source of art is double, if art stems from passion/reflection, then it follows that passion never manifests itself directly, that is, without the mediation of reflection. But for the same reason, the artist never liberates himself from passion."[36] This principle must hold for all artists, even those who practice the philosophical art, which is to say Hegel himself. Gearhart locates the challenge to Hegel (and to philosophy) that *Le Neveu* poses in this text's presentation of

> art as a destabilizing force, art as productive of conflict and difference rather than unity and reconciliation ... [Art] is neither simply irrational or rational (beautiful or ugly, pleasurable or painful) and thus eludes the grasp of the philosopher who seeks to distinguish between a (rational) essence of art and the "irrational" or "sentimental" element that for Hegel remains inessential to art.

In the final line of *Le Neveu*, Rameau asserts, "Rira bien qui rira le dernier." In all his seriousness, Hegel may have the last word on Diderot's text, but Diderot quite possibly has the last laugh. Despite the strength of Hegelian reflection, this speculative discourse that powerfully situates art and expresses conceptually what it represents in the attempt to unify the conflicts it stages, such an end may in fact be a laugh. Laughter, a typically Diderotian form of passion, destabilizes the interpretive act, contesting it by playing it out in other modes, just as the Nephew mimics all possible players in the social comedy. The most powerful aspect of Diderot's art lies in its capacity to perform the interpretive act, thereby providing reflexive knowledge, yet at the same time marking the limits and limitation of any knowledge thus gained by presenting that act as performance, that is, as an esthetic act as much as a cognitive one.

Is it the complex problematic of the Hegelian reading that Sainte-Beuve senses in Diderot's "Germanity"? Quite probably not. And yet, in this earliest of critical evaluations of Diderot, one senses the desire to find in art the capacity to provide a way of comprehending a social reality, to locate there a socioesthetic consciousness that ultimately could guide historical transformations. Juxtaposing two moments in Diderot's reception in Germany with Sainte-Beuve's reading helps articulate the latter's critical insight, as well as its ultimate retreat from that insight, which is occasioned by the nature of the art Sainte-Beuve locates in Diderot.

In Sainte-Beuve's story of reading, he begins his act of portraiture by closing himself up for two weeks with Diderot's works. This closing off from everything outside the text, including the present moment, results in the most intimate knowledge of the author himself. Yet the knowledge derived from reading the texts of the past must provide a basis for comprehending and judging the present, and not solely in esthetic terms. Indeed, from the critical perspective Sainte-Beuve claims for himself, ethical judgment cannot be separated from esthetic judgment: "[le] point de vue littéraire et moral ... est celui que nous affectionnons" (p. 167). But as soon as

Sainte-Beuve proclaims the need for a kind of critical judgment that links the esthetic and the moral in order to comprehend the present moment, he retreats from this insight. Reflecting on his own position and profession, he reminds his readers that what "nous critiques littéraires" must always remember is "la marque éternelle de la grande littérature." What constitutes this "marque" Sainte-Beuve does not say; instead he affirms its eternal quality, its ability to withstand the ravages of time. "Les révolutions passent sur les peuples, et font tomber les rois comme des têtes de pavots; les sciences s'agrandissent et accumulent; les philosophes s'épuisent; et cependant la moindre perle, autrefois éclose au cerveau de l'homme, si le temps et les barbares ne l'ont pas perdu en chemin, brille encore aussi pure aujourd'hui qu'à l'heure de sa naissance." To keep these pearls glowing, he adds, "un portrait ne serait pas une puérilité . . . malgré ce qui a éclaté dans le monde et ce qui s'y remue encore" (pp. 143–44). Sainte-Beuve suggests that portraying great literary figures of the past requires the wisdom and judiciousness that comes with age and experience, a critical maturity all the more necessary given the violent vicissitudes of history. Significantly though, in describing this portraiture Sainte-Beuve employs the rhetorical figure of the litotes to characterize the critical act negatively, by what it is not ("un portrait ne serait pas une puérilité"). The litotes affirms through negation, and it is as if Sainte-Beuve could formulate the relation between art and the sociohistorical only through an essentially exclusionary notion of portraiture. The critical position suggested here is one from which art can be contemplated, but in order to negate, repress, and frame out a threatening and destabilizing linkage between art and all that is "outside" it.

I do not mean to suggest simply that Sainte-Beuve's critical position lacks any effective notion of art as mediation, as the esthetic expression of a socio-historical reality that critical reflection could in turn conceptualize (as the Beuvian or Romantic theory of literary history). Rather, what is striking in his critical portraiture is that in refusing such linkage in the artwork, he produces it all the more inevitably in his own critical narrative. Describing in impassioned detail the benefits of his critical portraiture of Diderot, he continues:

nous y avons gagné du moins, outre la connaissance d'un grand homme de plus, d'oublier pendant quelques jours l'affligeant spectacle de la société environnante, tant de misère et de turbulence dans les masses, un si vague effroi, un si dévorant égoïsme dans les classes élevées, les gouvernements sans idées ni grandeur, des nations héroïques qu'on immole, le sentiment de patrie qui se perd et que rien de plus large ne remplace, la religion retombée dans l'arène d'où elle a le monde à reconquérir, et l'avenir de plus en plus nébuleux, recélant un rivage qui n'apparaît pas encore. Il n'était pas tout à fait ainsi du temps de Diderot (pp. 143–44).

The picture of social history presented here is one so bleak that reading can offer no more than the chance to forget. Marked by conflict and the loss of measure and order, the present is so intractably present that even an escape into the future is impossible. If the present cannot be repressed though, it can be sublimated by Beuvian portraiture. Replacing the fallen heads of royalty with imaginary and timeless portraits of great writers, Sainte-Beuve seeks to place art outside the social and outside history. Yet in so doing he produces a narrative of nostalgia that does not escape the present, but rather produces it as an "affligeante spectacle." The pain Sainte-Beuve experienced in contemplating all that lies "outside" the work of art in "la société environnante" inscribes itself in the critical and poetic act of portraiture, suggesting that the critical knowledge he wishes to gain will never be pure.

One could argue that the knowledge of literature Sainte-Beuve does present is of an ideological order and not an esthetic one.[37] But the critical act can never rid itself thoroughly of ideology. Rather than dismiss Beuvian portraiture for expressing no more than ideology, one might read it as staging a perpetual conflict between desire and knowledge, and that occurs even in the attempt to comprehend the nature of their conflict. Given Sainte-Beuve's personal deception following the July Monarchy in 1830, and which only intensified after the revolution of 1848, he may indeed wish to "forget" the political. As it plays itself out though, this desire involves displacing and reinscribing the political more than effectively forgetting it. This is why in 1830–31 Sainte-Beuve ignores Diderot the philosopher, novelist, playwright, and polemicist, discovering instead a Diderot who originated modern journalistic criticism. For Sainte-Beuve, this discovery amounts to self-discovery, a way to portray himself and more importantly his profession. Thus, although Diderot may have been an atheist and a materialist, the matter is "trop délicate et trop épineuse pour que je l'aborde de près ou de loin" (p. 167). Moreover, "si l'*Encyclopédie* fut l'œuvre sociale et principale de Diderot en son temps et à son heure, sa principale gloire à nos yeux aujourd'hui est d'avoir été le créateur de la critique émue, empressée et éloquente" (p. 172). To a certain extent, rejecting Diderot the encyclopedist in favor of Diderot the *salonnier* suggests refusing politics in favor of art and esthetics. Yet Sainte-Beuve makes this strategic turn to Diderot's art criticism in 1851 following the upheaval of 1848 in order to discover an empassioned form of critical discourse that gives Diderot's writing far more forceful pertinence "today" than the discourse of Enlightenment encyclopedism. Sainte-Beuve may have overlooked the epistemological art of the *Encyclopédie*. Yet in turning to Diderot's esthetic writings, he finds there the basis for contemporary and effectively critical discourse. The knowledge Sainte-Beuve gains in reading Diderot, and the passions his portrayal stages, are those of the critical act itself.

At one point Sainte-Beuve expresses the desire to "[se représenter] Diderot tel qu'il était en effet." This desire to present Diderot "as he was in fact" shapes not only Sainte-Beuve's texts but all the countless others that constitute Diderot's aftermath, including the present one. Judged not in terms of their truth or falsehood, their authenticity or completeness, but rather as representations, these countless portrayals show above all the constitutive limit of critical knowledge. Diderot "en effet" can only be a representation, the effect produced by portraiture. Sainte-Beuve states, without entirely mastering, the paradoxical principle at work throughout Diderot's reception, namely, that the most authentic portrayals ("Diderot en effet") are also the most imaginary, produced by the desire to imagine an effective Diderot. Channeled into innumerable contexts, produced upon countless stages, the effects of representing Diderot have played themselves out for some two centuries. In the many instances of the "Diderot effect," we witness the interpretive act of symbolic representation, which orders time by narrativizing and historicizing it, presenting an imaginary bridge between Diderot and us, and a link among us, by joining the then of the Enlightenment and the now of the present moment. If these interpretive acts allow us to comprehend past and present, they do so by inscribing them within a symbolic representation. Any knowledge that Diderot's readers have gained results from an art that portrays him and his texts. And at the same time any effect such portrayal has had and can have also constitutes a form of knowledge of and for the present. Perhaps for some 200 years, in different contexts and with varying degrees of self-awareness, Diderot's readers have come to know no more, but to portray no less, than the act and art of interpretation.

CHAPTER 7

Interpreting Diderot: critical values, critical violence

Allegorical epilogue

In eighteenth-century fiction, drama, and art, the activity of reader and spectator acquires heightened significance as the esthetic object becomes part of a dialogical relation. But the esthetic object is not unique in this regard. The meaning and value of things in general becomes relative, since all objects susceptible to being known are related to the interpreting subject, the "comon center" as the encyclopedists put it. As a result, one story concerning the eighteenth-century Enlightenment would recount the emergence of a new and dialogical relation between subject and object, viewer and painting, reader and text, individual and world. The monological, authoritative discourse of a certain classicism and a certain classic subject gives way to a multiform discourse that is non-Cartesian, materialist and bourgeois, sentimental rather than tragic, novelistic rather than poetic. As it powerfully reopens the question of origins, meanings, and the authority of interpretations, the discourse of Enlightenment also confronts a crisis of its own making, which is its double bind. The encyclopedists masked that crisis by promoting practical and utilitarian knowledge, thus attempting to bypass the issue of whether Enlightenment in fact ungrounds all knowledge. And the philosophes worked to constitute systematic knowledge, seldom asking whether such synthesis could be maintained or at what price.

Diderot's role in this story is that of the steadfast skeptic with regard to such solutions. This skepticism involves far more than personal psychology though, for it is materialized in the most powerfully critical aspect of Diderot's writing, namely, the manner in which it turns interpretation back upon itself, revealing both the desire for knowledge behind all interpretation, as well as the artful practice of language that works to realize that desire. Thus, if the present study has helped define Diderot's place within philosophy, science, literature, esthetics or political theory, in short in all areas characterizing Enlightenment, it has been by tracing this turn back to the enabling conditions of interpretation, even at the risk of marking the latter's limits.

Few sensed as acutely as Diderot not only that interpretation is always dialogical, but also that interpretation is not secondary with respect to its object. However much the latter may appear to be the manifestation of Being, History, the Real or any other ground for knowledge, Diderot repeatedly stages the impossibility of moving beyond or outside interpretation. His texts play out innumerable situations in which there can be no end to interpretation, suggesting that what must be judged instead are interpretation's ends and its practical effects. Does this mean that interpretations are intrinsically neither true nor false? Perhaps, but Diderot does not bewail or rail against the loss of intrinsic truths. Nor does he rejoice in any supposed liberation from them. His tone is neither nostalgic nor revolutionary, neither apocalyptic nor anarchical. Instead, through his art of philosophizing he repeatedly experiments with interpretation in a manner that shows its value must be judged in the force of its effects. To make this point, I shall conclude by considering Diderot's comments on portraiture. This epilogue may be read as a critical allegory that pertains to the qustion implicit throughout this study, namely, on what basis can the interpretive act be judged?

To begin this critical allegory, let us recall that throughout the *Salons* Diderot writes both as a theoretician of art and as its spectator (just as he is a theoretician of knowledge and its practitioner). Thus, although he will judge paintings in terms of theoretical concepts such as pictorial imitation, the beautiful, the hierarchy of genres, art's moral and didactic function, etc., his text always plays out more than theoretical discourse can contain. As he attempts to reproduce in writing an image of what he has seen, description gives way to a narrative account of impressions of the present moment. Emphasis shifts from reproducing an object in order to pass esthetic judgment to producing an event occurring in and through writing. This event remains in excess, and manifest in this excess is what no purely formal theory can comprehend, namely, the particular effects of artworks once they become objects of intense desire for those who see, interpret, and write about them.

This general tension between esthetic theory and spectatorial practice leads to the dilemma Diderot initially confronts in judging portraits. Should they be evaluated in terms of their realism or their beauty, according to "le mérite de ressembler" or "celui du pinceau qui émerveille dans le moment, et qui éternise l'ouvrage" (XIII, 354), the truth of realism or the effect of *le faire*? In the 1763 *Salon* Diderot provides one answer to the imitation-effect dilemma posed by portraits. "Je conclus avec vous qu'il faut qu'un portrait soit ressemblant pour moi, et bien peint pour la postérité. Ce qu'il y a de certain, c'est que rien n'est plus rare qu'un beau pinceau, plus commun qu'un barbouilleur qui fait ressembler, et que quand l'homme n'est plus, nous supposons la ressemblance" (XIII, 354–55). The rule of imitation must hold now for those who have seen the model; in time though, once the model is dead and absent, this criterion will be supplanted by that of technique and expertise. It might seem that this temporal sleight of hand begs the question of any absolute principle for judgment more than it answers it. But perhaps Diderot is not in search of any such principle and is interested instead in what might possibly subtend it. The phrase "nous supposons la ressemblance" suggests that judging a portrait involves an act of supposition, a subpositioning or underlay that grounds critical judgment.

The nature of this act is made clearer in Diderot's comparison of how great artists paint portraits and the way Voltaire writes history: "Il agrandit, il exagère, il corrige les formes. A-t-il raison? a-t-il tort? Il a tort pour le pédant, il a raison pour l'homme de goût. Tort ou raison, c'est la figure qu'il a peinte qui restera dans la mémoire des hommes à venir" (XVI, 515). If elsewhere Diderot claims portraits must be faithful likenesses, here he qualifies that judgment as pedantic and antithetical to good taste. Yet another of his oversights? Perhaps, but the point to be made lies elsewhere. With a sweeping gesture – "tort ou raison" – Diderot turns to what lies beneath any esthetic theory that passes judgment in terms of absolute truth or falsehood. More important than judging what the portrait *is* – true to life or larger than life, a likeness or an embellishment – is what the portrait is capable of *doing*. A mimetic theory of art can neither explain nor contain the effects of portraiture, for what subtends the portrait, what we subpose there, is its figural capacity to work certain effects.

"Quand l'homme n'est plus, nous supposons la ressemblance ... C'est la figure ... peinte qui restera dans la mémoire des hommes à venir." In time the portrait always comes to take the place of its original in the latter's absence. The model is just remains and remains remembered, but only because of its place within representation. The issue here is not the mimetic function of portraiture but rather the portrait's status as an object invested by the desire to see. One might wish to define portraiture otherwise, in terms of absolute truth and resemblance, desiring somewhat nostalgically to recover a model still and always there beyond the portrait. But if imitation is what one *desires* to see, if seeing is determined by desire, then judging portraits in terms of their mimetic truth amounts to not seeing what in fact determines how they represent. This type of absolute judgment derives from the desire not to confront absence except insofar as it can be overcome and transcended by not seeing how it subtends esthetic judgment. If desire mediates this kind of judgment, effectively constituting its blind spot, can there occur a staging of desire – a portrayal of another sort – that involves an effectively critical act? With this question in mind, let us turn to the best known of Diderot's texts on portraiture, the 1767 *Salon* article on his own portrait by Michel Van Loo.

"Moi. J'aime Michel; mais j'aime encore mieux la vérité. Assez ressemblant" (XVI, 81). Viewing my portrait, I see an image of the subject who says "I." Yet this subject has become an object I must now call "me," the disjunctive pronoun repeating the disjunction staged by this viewing of the subject in representation. If the goal of portraiture is the truthful portrayal of its subject, then the portrait will always be less than true and will always represent something other than truth. Given that Diderot's evaluation of Van Loo's painting is determined at least initially by his own desire for truth ("mais j'aime encore mieux la vérité"), the portrait must inevitably turn up short.

Très vivant. C'est sa douceur, avec sa vivacité. Mais trop jeune, tête trop petite. Joli comme une femme, lorgnant, souriant, mignard, faisant le petit bec, la bouche en cœur ... Mais que diront mes petits-enfants, lorsqu'ils viendront à comparer mes tristes ouvrages avec ce riant, mignon, efféminé, vieux coquet-là? Mes enfants, je vous préviens que ce n'est pas moi (XVI, 81–82).

In one sense Diderot simply remarks that Van Loo's painting is not a good likeness and that others might be better. But portraits proliferate here beyond the frame of the canvas, as the term comes to stand metaphorically for future generations' "portrait of the author," imagined and produced in reading his "tristes ouvrages." Does Diderot suggest that these portraits too cannot be "me"? Does his disclaimer "ce n'est pas moi" answer not only Van Loo but also the constant critical imperative to portray him and his texts? If so, then to claim he is not captured in the portrait others (will) paint of him, and at the same time to affirm a critical principle involving both truth and desire ("j'aime la vérité"), Diderot must show why "this isn't me."

This explains why he discards the portrait by Van Loo only to remake it by producing his own portrait.

Mes enfants, je vous préviens que ce n'est pas moi. J'avais en une journée cent physionomies diverses, selon la chose dont j'étais affecté. J'étais serein, triste, rêveur, tendre, violent, passionné, enthousiaste. Mais je ne fus jamais tel que vous me voyez là ... J'ai un masque qui trompe l'artiste, soit qu'il y ait trop de choses fondues ensemble, soit que les impressions de mon âme se succédant très rapidement et se peignant toutes sur mon visage, l'œil du peintre ne me retrouvant pas le même d'un instant à l'autre, sa tâche devienne beaucoup plus difficile qu'il ne la croyait (XVI, 82–83).

Contained here is not one but a host of portraits, all constituting a "mask" the portraitist cannot comprehend. Like painting in general, portraiture represents by immobilizing; able to figure only the moment and not a succession of moments, it can never represent the ever-changing display of emotions that project themselves on the face. This is the mask that must deceive the artist, which has nothing to do with some supposed wish on Diderot's part to mystify or hide some innermost essence or aspect of being. The mask of temporal mobility cannot be removed. Thus, whoever desires to portray Diderot inevitably produces a mask of another sort, a death mask that eternalizes and idealizes. Portraiture is a static art of fatal immobilization, a deadly art. Unable to account for what causes this mobility of expression, which Diderot refers to as "la chose dont j'étais affecté," portraiture represents by blocking out the affective, by cutting off the subject represented from the time and context in which desires run their course and from the objects towards which they flow. This is precisely the type of portraiture Diderot counters by producing a portrait of his own. In the place of the static, affectless pictorial portrait, he produces an ever mobile, kaleidoscopic textual subject that could never be captured by the painter's brush.

But Diderot does not simply substitute one portrait for another. By occupying the double position of spectator of his pictorial portrait and writer of the discursive portrait, he makes the former into precisely "la chose dont j'étais affecté," an object of spectatorial affect. The effect of the pictorial portrait allows Diderot to display for himself a subject that could never have been represented once and for all, or could never be, at least not by the portraitist. Diderot inescapably plays out here his wish to outlive his portrait in the staging of his own desire.

But what of our own portrait of Diderot, especially the one produced here, which represents him as privileged spectator and self-portraitist? Making the self-reflexive aspect of this critical allegory more explicit, one must ask whether all discourse on portraiture is determined by the desire to see the self in representation, by our own desire for self-portrayal, which we have read in to, appropriated from, and produced through

Diderot's text? If so, then we are caught up in the same trap as Diderot, rewriting his text, just as he remakes Van Loo's portrait, but writing out of it what we would rather not see, namely, the mediation of truth by desire.

These are not the last words on portraiture however. Diderot digresses for a moment from his remarks on Van Loo's painting – although his entire article is perhaps one long digression expressing his desire to move away from the painting – by mentioning two other portrayals of himself. These effectively extend the critical allegory concerning portraiture and the desire to portray. The first story involves a painting by "un pauvre diable appelé Garant," who caught Diderot by chance. "Celui qui voit mon portrait par Garant, me voit" (XVI, 83). Having been portrayed though, Diderot begins to slip away once again, as the rest of the story relates. Grimm, it seems, had an engraving done of the portrait, which he refuses to let out of his hands. Diderot explains: "Il attend toujours une inscription qu'il n'aura que quand j'aurai produit quelque chose qui m'immortalise. 'Et quand l'aura-t-il?' Quand? demain peut-être. Et qui sait ce que je puis! Je n'ai pas la conscience d'avoir encore employé la moitié de mes forces. Jusqu'à présent, je n'ai que baguenaudé" (XVI, 83–84). Portrayed, Diderot has been dispossessed. His image now belongs to Grimm, the sympathetic friend but also the clever literary entrepreneur, who waits patiently for the moment he can frame Diderot with an inscription that will immortalize, eternalize, and monumentalize Diderot, capturing him once and for all.

To unpack this critical allegory, one might ask whether all Diderot's readers are in a sense Melchior Grimms, sympathetic but not disinterested, holding on to the image they themselves have made of Diderot, waiting for when it will be most valuable, when they can best benefit from packaging and marketing it. As for Diderot, the Diderot who refuses to be part of this inscription, he is always there warning "ce n'est pas moi." He escapes into dialogue, elsewhere and with another, postponing indefinitely the moment of his portrayal ("demain peut-être"). He resists any claim that we are the posterity able to judge with finality what he has produced by staging acts of judgment that are mediated by the desire to frame him.

But there is more. In a second allegory about portraiture, Diderot recalls one of the good portraits of himself he says he almost forgot to mention, a bust by Mlle Collot, a student of Falconnet, who himself also did a bust of Diderot. Both busts belong to Grimm, who replaced Falconnet's with Mlle Collot's. Diderot then recounts the following incident. "Lorsque Falconnet eut vu le buste de son élève, il prit un marteau et cassa le sien devant elle. Cela est franc et courageux. Ce buste en tombant en morceaux sous le coup de l'artiste, mit à découvert deux belles oreilles qui s'étaient conservées entières sous une indigne perruque" (XVI, 84). In the first story the immortalizing inscription Grimm awaits draws attention to the memorializing function of interpretation and to the motivating desire underlying it. Here though something else is at stake. Had Falconnet only admitted to having been outdone by another sculptor, he would have remained the portraitist, affirming the traditional values of portraiture and that only the best of portraits deserve to be passed on to posterity. But Falconnet's esthetic judgment takes the form of a violently critical act, which must be understood as well. He is still involved in portraying Diderot, for the outcome of this violence is the discovery of "deux belles oreilles." Yet his portraiture with a hammer is portraiture of a different sort. It is an act of critical judgment that destroys the work of art as such, that is, as finished production and organic whole, a work that in being preserved intact would somehow provide an escape from the contingency of the present.

Diderot's bust is in fragments, but the violence of Falconnet's act has revealed what was most unseen and could not be sensed except through the narrative staging of the critical act occurring in Diderot's text. For Falconnet the work of portraying Diderot is over, and it is now up to Mlle Collot, Grimm, and Diderot, in other words those before whom the critical act is performed, to respond and act in turn. Mlle Collot may have learned that the master portraitist still has something to teach after all, and Grimm may have wondered why he stocked up on images of Diderot, one of them now in pieces. As for Diderot, he inserts this story of a broken bust into the article on his own portrait. The violence of Falconnet's hammer blow is repeated, inscribed once again in the act of judging a portrait. Diderot tells us nothing of the motives behind Falconnet's act, or why he tells this story he supposedly almost forgot. All we know is that he qualifies it as "franc et courageux," effective and moral, which is perhaps his own Nietzschean way of philosophizing with a hammer that rewrites (in advance) the Kantian motto *sapere aude*.

This brief story from the *Salons* can stand allegorically for the longer story I have been telling concerning Enlightenment critique, its limits, and the manner in which Diderot's writing articulates the relation between them. Shifting attention from portrait to portrayal, from the product of portraiture to its production, this allegory refers to the event of the critical act of judgment. Just as Diderot admits his own desire ("j'aime mieux la vérité"), so too any story about the Enlightenment (including my own) doubtless springs from the desire for grounding truths and certitude. But can that desire be satisfied? Diderot presents no esthetic concept in terms of which the portrait could be judged a true likeness. Similarly, no vantage point or perspective supplied by theoretical discourse possesses the regulative force to guarantee that this or any representation of Enlightenment is truly accurate. The shards of Falconnet's bust can figure the portraits of Enlightenment, now irretrievably shredded, that have been passed down to us, beginning with those of the Enlighteners themselves. The story Diderot has helped me tell is thus one of destructive violence. It is also powerfully affirmative, which is what must also be grasped. Diderot relates here that in order to respond to the portraitist's claim to have represented him truly, he must reproduce, deframe, and destory the portrait, if not the very possibility of mimetic portrayal. What Diderot's story does not deny though is the power and effects of representation. He remakes a portrait of a different sort, representing in his story another kind of subject. The subject in question here at least is the one of stories of knowledge that help grasp the limits of knowledge, the subject of theory-fictions concerning the limits of theoretical discourse. These stories work to unseat, displace, and resituate other more masterful discourses. Inscribed in the story Diderot tells is the power of Enlightenment critique, which sought to do away with the absoluteness of prior representations of truth. Manifest in Diderot's manner, in his art of philosophizing, is the realization that this relation to truth must be ongoing and endlessly performative. Diderot refuses the interpretive imperative to decide what Falconnet's gesture means, to say nothing of this or any critical allegory. Instead he relates the event, replaying its effects and resituating their place in narrative. The artful manner of presenting events involving the imperative call to judge may, in Diderot's case, provide no sure ground for judgment. If Diderot cannot get beyond this situation, he does not retreat from it however. Through his art of philosophizing he recounts the desire to relate (truth), and in a self-reflexive practice that materially embodies this relation. As in the case of Enlightenment critique, what we come to know through this art of philosophizing may be no more than the artful practice whereby critical knowledge is produced. But we certainly come to know no less.

Notes

Introduction

1 Michel Foucault, "What is Enlightenment?", in *A Foucault Reader*, ed. Paul Rabinow (New York: Pantheon, 1984), p. 32.

2 "There can be no possible exercise of power without a certain economy of discourses of truth which operates through and on the basis of this association. We are subjected to the production of truth through power and we cannot exercise power except through the production of truth." Michel Foucault, *Power and Knowledge*, ed. Colin Gordon (New York: Pantheon, 1980), p. 93.

3 Reviewing Pierre Naville's *D'Holbach*, Maurice Blanchot succinctly describes the objectification and commodification of being occurring in Enlightenment materialism. "Obviously, if man is only a thing he can be modified scientifically . . . just as things are modified by adapting them to human needs and desires. However, one of the consequences of this taking possession of man, this appropriation of a being become thing, gravely affronts the encyclopedists: once man is no longer an existence but a thing, once he is no longer a subject but an object, it becomes both possible and legitimate to use him as one would use a thing, to make his work into a value expressed entirely by a price, a type of merchandise identical to all others. The materialist *Encyclopédie* made man into the absolute owner of the world, but it also subjected the owner to the common laws of that which is owned." *Journal des Débats*, 28–29 November 1943, p. 2.

4 Max Horkheimer and Theodor Adorno, *Dialectic of Enlightenment*, trans. John Cumming (New York: Seabury Press, 1972).

5 Alfred Cobban, *In Search of Humanity* (New York: George Braziller, 1960), p. 242.

6 Alfred Cobban claims that in refusing Enlightenment one "jettisons the whole rationality of social life." *In Search of Humanity*, p. 242. However, the consequences of this double bind are analyzed

more rigorously elsewhere. See for example Michel Foucault's discussion of the difficulty of analyzing madness in *Histoire de la folie* (Paris: Union Générale d'Editions, 1961). Jacques Derrida analyzes the position Foucault adopts, in "Cogito et histoire de la folie," *L'Ecriture et la différence* (Paris: Seuil, 1967).

7 The question "What is Postmodernism?", like Kant's question concerning Enlightenment, is perhaps best left unanswered, notwithstanding the innumerable recent attempts at synthesis, including Fredric Jameson, *Postmodernism, or, the Cultural Logic of Late Capitalism* (Durham: Duke University Press, 1991); Steven Connor, *Postmodern Culture* (New York: Basil Blackwell, 1989); and David Harvey, *The Condition of Postmodernism* (New York: Basil Blackwell, 1989). Insofar as the desire to answer the question of what postmodernism is inflects such works, one must ask whether they reveal the awareness that postmodernism itself (assuming such a phrase makes sense) could never ask such a question, except parodically.

8 See Gianni Vattimo, *The End of Modernity: Nihilism and Hermeneutics in Post-Modern Culture*, trans. Jon R. Synder (Baltimore: Johns Hopkins University Press, 1988). "Postmodern thought" is probably an oxymoron that reinjects the metaphysics postmodern practices upset. Vattimo coins the phrase *il pensiero debole* or "weak thought" to characterize how thinking takes place in postmodern terms.

9 "Apathie dans la théorie," in *Rudiments païens* (Paris: 10/18, 1977), p. 28. This attitude towards theory, or perhaps what Paul de Man calls its "resistance," is the hallmark of postmodernism. Cf. de Man's *The Resistance to Theory* (Minneapolis: University of Minnesota Press, 1980).

10 "Apathie dans la théorie," p. 29.

11 Theory-fictions work to undo the feint or disguise of theoretical discourses, which refuse or conceal their status as art. According to Lyotard, theoretical discourses must "dérober à la vue, à celle de leur audience, mais aussi à celle de leur propre autorité, l'artifice de leur discours, c'est-à-dire le fait reconnu, revendiqué par le poète ou le romancier que c'est l'ouvrage des mots qui *feint* ou façonne sa référence. *Non fingo* est leur article de foi le plus commun. C'est en vertu de lui que celui qui veut être philosophe doit se faire ignorer comme artiste, y compris de lui-même, qu'il doit déguiser le vouloir de feindre qui organise son discours en un vouloir-la-vérité de sa référence." "Dissertation sur une inconvenance," in *Rudiments païens*, p. 243.

12 See *La Condition postmoderne* (Paris: Minuit, 1979).

13 *Le Concentrique et l'excentrique: marges des Lumières* (Paris: Payot, 1980). Benrekassa discusses the possibility of ideological critique in a post-Hegelian age, pp. 11–27. See also his *La Politique et sa mémoire* (Paris: Payot 1983), pp. 11–34.

1 Representing knowledge: reading the Encyclopédie

1 In *The Business of Enlightenment* (Cambridge: Harvard University Press, 1979) Robert Darnton analyzes the complicated relation between cultural and economic production in the case of the *Encyclopédie.*

2 Among the numerous studies of the *Encyclopédie*, two representing this approach are Jacques Proust, *L'Encyclopédie* (Paris: Armand Colin, 1965); and John Lough, *Essays on the Encyclopédie of Diderot and D'Alembert* (New York: Oxford University Press, 1968).

3 "Le milieu du siècle où nous vivons paraît destiné à faire époque . . . dans l'histoire de l'esprit humain, par la révolution qui semble se préparer dans les idées," writes D'Alembert in *Sur la destruction des Jésuites, Œuvres* (Paris: 1805), v, 13. Diderot too proclaims, "nous touchons au moment d'une grande révolution dans les sciences," *Œuvres* (Paris: Hermann, 1970–), xix, 30.

4 Peter Gay, *The Enlightenment: An Interpretation*, 2 vols. (New York: Knopf, 1969). Michel Foucault forcefully argues against the illusion that these two entities are distinct. Foucault's entire project exemplifies the displacement required to analyze this conjuncture. His understanding of "discourse events" rejects the logic that relates them in temporal-causal terms such as origin, evolution, and end, a logic that seeks to "dissolve the singular event into an ideal continuity – as a teleological movement or natural process." "Nietzsche, Genealogy, History" (in *Language, Counter-Memory, Practice*, ed. Donald Bouchard [Ithaca: Cornell University Press, 1977]), p. 154.

5 This now familiar opposition was first elaborated programmatically by Roland Barthes in "From Work to Text" (1971), and in *Textual Strategies*, ed. Josué V. Harari (Ithaca: Cornell University Press, 1979), pp. 73–81, and also in *S/Z* (Paris: Seuil, 1970).

6 *Encyclopédie, ou dictionnaire raisonné des sciences, des arts et des métiers*, 17 vols. (Paris: Briasson, 1751–65), i, i.

7 For an analysis of the *Discours préliminaire*, see Walter Moser, "D'Alembert: l'ordre philosophique de ce discours," *MLN*, 91:4 (1976); and his "Les Discours dans le *Discours préliminaire*," *Romanic Review*, 67:2 (March 1976), 102–16. Cf. Robert Darnton,

"Philosophers Trim the Tree of Knowledge," *The Great Cat Massacre* (New York: Basic Books, 1983).

8 Wilda Anderson, *Between the Library and the Laboratory* (Baltimore: Johns Hopkins University Press, 1984).

9 See Ernst Cassirer, *The Philosophy of the Enlightenment* (1932), trans. Fritz C. A. Koelln and James P. Pettegrove (Princeton University Press, 1951), ch. 1. Aram Vartanian analyzes the continuity between Descartes and the Enlightenment in *Diderot and Descartes* (Princeton University Press, 1953).

10 Pierre Grosclaude's outdated *Un audacieux message: L'Encyclopédie* (Paris: Nouvelles Editions Latines, 1951) makes the *Encyclopédie* seem more revolutionary than it was. Jacques Proust provides a more balanced view in *Diderot et l'Encyclopédie* (Paris: Armand Colin, 1962).

11 See Louis Althusser, "Idéologie et appareils idéologiques d'Etat," in *Positions* (Paris: Editions Sociales, 1976). For an analysis of the ideological status of the *Encyclopédie*, see Bernard Groethuysen, "L'Encyclopédie," in *Tableau de la littérature française* (Paris: Nouvelle Revue Française, 1939), II, 343–49, and his *The Bourgeois: Catholicism vs. Capitalism in Eighteenth-Century France*, trans. Mary Ilford (1927; reprinted New York: Holt, Rinehart and Winston, 1968). See also Elinor Barber, *The Bourgeois in 19th-Century France* (Princeton University Press, 1955); and Lionel Gossman, *French Society and Culture* (Englewood Cliffs: Prentice-Hall, 1972).

12 See Jacques Proust, *L'Encyclopédie*, and *Diderot et l'Encyclopédie*.

13 Emerging as a discipline in the eighteenth century, this knowledge is called anthropology. See Michèle Duchet, *Anthropologie et histoire au siècle des Lumières* (Paris: Maspero, 1971). Martin Heidegger marks the metaphysical limits of such an anthropology in "The Age of the World Picture," in *The Question Concerning Technology and Other Essays*, trans. William Lovitt (New York: Harper, 1977), p. 153.

14 Jacques Derrida, *Psyché: inventions de l'autre* (Paris: Galilée, 1987), p. 42. For another analysis of invention, see Michel de Certeau, *L'Invention du quotidien* (Paris: 10/18, 1980).

15 Cf. Jacques Proust, "L'Image du peuple au travail dans les planches de l'*Encyclopédie*," in *Images du peuple au dix-huitième siècle* (Paris: Armand Colin, 1973), p. 68.

16 Diderot explicitly refers to several previous collections, including Ramelli's *Diverse et artificiose machine* (1588), Leupold's *Theatrum machinarum* (1723–27), and the *Description et perfection des arts et*

métiers that Colbert, minister of Louis XIV, had called upon the Académie Royale des Sciences to compile some hundred years earlier. See Robert Collison, *Encyclopedias: Their History Throughout the Ages* (New York: Hafner, 1964); Jean-Pierre Seguin, "Courte histoire des planches de l'*Encyclopédie*," in *L'Univers de l'Encyclopédie* (Paris: Les Libraires Associés, 1964), pp. 25–34; and Georges Huard, "Les Planches de l'*Encyclopédie* et celles de la *Description des arts et métiers* de l'Académie des Sciences," *Revue d'Histoire de Sciences et de Leurs Applications*, 4 (1951), 238–49.

17 The encyclopedic gaze visible in the plates resembles the clinical gaze Michel Foucault describes, which itself establishes structures of visibility and comprehensibility in its objects. "Le regard lisait souverainement un texte dont il recueillait sans effort la claire parole pour la restituer en un discours second et identique: donnée par le visible, cette parole, sans rien changer, donnait à voir. Le regard reprenait en son exercice souverain les structures de visibilité qu'il avait lui-même déposées dans son champ de perception." *La Naissance de la clinique* (1963; Paris: Presses Universitaires de France, 1978), p. 118.

18 See Guy Besse, "Aspects du travail ouvrier au XVIIIe siècle en France," in *Essays on Diderot and the Enlightenment*, ed. John Pappas (Geneva: Droz, 1974).

19 Roland Barthes, "Image, raison, déraison," in *L'Univers de l'Encyclopédie.*

20 Proust, "L'Image," p. 66.

21 "On a trop écrit sur les sciences: on n'a pas assez bien écrit sur la plupart des arts libéraux: on n'a presque rien écrit sur les arts méchaniques" (*Prospectus*, v, 99), hence the need to obtain information directly from workers and craftspeople themselves. The time-honored distinction between liberal and mechanical arts, based on whether what is involved is "l'ouvrage de l'esprit [ou] de la main," unfortunately results, Diderot adds, in the "[avilissement] des gens très estimables et très utiles," ("*Art*," v, 496).

22 In the article, "*Bas*," Diderot discusses the mercantilist principle and state protectionism of the weaving industry. See also de Jaucourt's article "*Industrie*."

23 Arthur Wilson, *Diderot* (New York: Oxford University Press, 1957), p. 360.

24 Georges Friedman, "L'*Encyclopédie* et le travail humain," *Annales de l'Université de Paris*, 22 (October 1952), 125.

25 The Industrial Revolution occurs much later in France than in England. Charles Ballot's *L'Introduction du machinisme dans l'industrie*

(Paris: F. Rieder, 1923), for example, locates the beginnings of the Industrial Revolution in France around 1780.

26 Readings of this article to which I am indebted include Christie V. MacDonald, "The Work of the Text: Diderot's *Encyclopédie*," *The Eighteenth Century*, 21:2 (Spring 1980), 128–44; and James Creech, "Chasing After Advances: Diderot's Article *Encyclopédie*," *Yale French Studies*, 63 (1982), 183–97.

27 Quoted in Sainte-Beuve, *Port-Royal*, 4th edn. (Paris: Hachette, 1878), 3,539. See Louis Marin's *La Critique du discours* (Paris: Minuit, 1975); and Michel Foucault's *Les Mots et les choses* (Paris: Gallimard, 1966).

28 Antoine Arnauld and Claude Lancelot, *Grammaire générale et raisonnée, ou la grammaire de Port-Royal* (1660) (1676; reprinted Stuttgart-Bad Cannstatt: Frommann, 1966), p. 5.

29 "L'on peut définir les mots, des sons distincts et articulés dont les hommes ont fait des signes pour signifier leurs pensées. C'est pourquoi on ne peut bien comprendre les diverses sortes de significations qui sont enfermées dans les mots, qu'on n'ait bien compris auparavant ce qui se passe dans nos pensées, puisque les mots n'ont été inventés que pour les faire connaître" (Arnauld, *Grammaire*, p. 27).

30 César Chesneau Du Marsais, *Véritables principes de la grammaire*, (Paris), p. xii.

31 Etienne Bonnot de Condillac, *Grammaire*, in *Œuvres philosophiques* (Paris: Presses Universitaires de France, 1947), I, 427.

32 Nicolas Beauzée, *Grammaire générale* (1767; reprinted Stuttgart-Bad Cannstatt: Frommann, 1974), pp. xxxiii-xxxiv.

33 See Ulrich Dierse, *Enzyklopädie: Zur Geschichte eines philosophischen und wissenschaftlichen Begriffs* (Bonn: Bouvier, 1977).

34 The "arbre des connaissances" is described as a continuous chain "par laquelle on peut descendre sans interruption des premiers principes d'une science ou d'un art jusqu'à ses conséquences les plus éloignées, et remonter de ses conséquences jusqu'à ses premiers principes; passer imperceptiblement de cette science ou de cet art à un autre; et, s'il est permis de s'exprimer ainsi, faire sans s'égarer le tour du monde littéraire" (v, 89). See Arthur O. Lovejoy, *The Great Chain of Being* (Cambridge: Harvard University Press, 1936), chs. 6–9.

35 "Les langues dans tous les temps sont à peu près la mesure des idées actuelles du peuple qui les parle . . . On n'invente des noms qu'à mesure qu'on a des idées à exprimer" (Turgot, "*Etymologie*"). As Diderot puts it, "la langue d'un peuple donne son vocabulaire,

et le vocabulaire est une table assez fidèle de toutes les connaissances de ce peuple ... Tout a son signe ... La langue est un symbole de cette multitude de choses hétérogènes: elle indique à l'homme pénétrant jusqu'où l'on était allé dans une science, dans les temps mêmes les plus reculés" (VII, 189–90).

36 Sylvain Auroux, *L'Encyclopédie, "grammaire" et "langue" au XVIIIe siècle* (Paris: Mame, 1973), p. 44.

37 Intellectual tastes change, for instance, shifting from mathematics to letters and the natural sciences (AT XIX, 452). More seriously, the sciences have their own finite temporality. "Il y a dans les sciences un point au delà duquel il ne leur est presque pas accordé de passer. Lorsque ce point est atteint, les monuments qui restent de ces progrès font à jamais l'étonnement de l'espèce entière" (VII, 187). For two studies focusing on the figures of catastrophe and the labyrinth to articulate the place of knowledge and history in Diderot's texts, see, respectively, Jeffrey Mehlman, *Cataract: A Study in Diderot* (Middletown: Wesleyan University Press, 1979), and Pierre Saint-Amand, *Diderot: le labyrinthe de la relation* (Paris: Vrin, 1984).

38 An opinion shared by Voltaire, who states with a rather bald conservatism, "il me semble que lorsqu'on a eu dans un siècle un nombre suffisant de bons écrivains devenus classiques, il n'est plus guère permis d'employer d'autres expressions que les leurs, et qu'il faut leur donner le même sens ou bien dans peu de temps, le siècle présent n'entendrait plus le siècle passé," *Œuvres complètes* (Paris: Garnier, 1877–82), XIX, 189. Antoine Rivarol makes explicit the politics of stylistics Voltaire suggests: "Les styles sont classés dans notre langue, comme les sujets dans notre monarchie. Deux expressions qui conviennent à la même chose, ne conviennent au même ordre de choses; et c'est à travers cette hiérarchie des styles que le bon goût sait marcher," *Discours sur l'universalité de la langue française* (1784), *Œuvres de Rivarol* (Paris: 1808), II, 62. One example of the gradual relaxation of this classical and conservative purism due in part to the fact that the court no longer possessed the power to provide a model for linguistic usage, is Paradis de Moncrif's *Dissertation qu'on ne doit ni ne peut changer une langue savante* (1742). See Alexis François, "La Langue postclassique," in Ferdinand Brunot, *Histoire de la langue française*, 2:2 (Paris: Armand Colin, 1932).

39 A well-made dictionary alone, Diderot suggests, might be enough to perfect logic and metaphysics (AT X, 39). This philosophical language is perhaps the language of metaphor. Referring in the *Lettre sur les sourds et muets* to poetic "hieroglyphs," figures

containing several meanings within one sign, Diderot notes, "si ces expressions énergiques étaient plus fréquentes, au lieu que la langue se traîne sans cesse après l'esprit, la quantité d'idées rendues à la fois pourrait être telle que la langue allant plus vite que l'esprit, il serait forcé de courir après elle" (IV, 158).

40 "Il n'y a point d'objets, soit dans la nature, soit dans le possible, que ces unités simples ne pussent représenter, des points, des lignes, des surfaces, des solides, des pensées, des idées, des sensations" (IV, 32–33). As Michel Serres puts it, "La géométrie donne à voir, domaine de l'intuition, l'algèbre donne à parler ou écrire, elle est le terrain du discours, ces deux variétés ont un voisinage commun, échangeur par où elles coulent de l'une à l'autre, le point de référence, lieu sans lieu mais lieu des lieux, zéro de la mesure et du logos, mais origine et possibilité de la parole et de l'écrit sur les phénomènes du lieu. Trou ponctuel par où les mots diffusent dans l'espace, par où les choses de l'espace, indéfiniment, vont se dire ou s'écrire. La représentation devient discursive par le point fixe, par lui le discours est représentable. En lui, l'âge classique se résout et condense." *Hermès III: la traduction* (Paris: Minuit, 1974), p. 189.

41 Like Descartes, Leibniz, and countless others, Diderot displays a fascination with a universal langage. "Un idiome commun serait l'unique moyen d'établir une correspondance qui s'étendît à toutes les parties du genre humain . . . Supposé cet idiome admis et fixé, aussitôt les notions deviennent permanentes; la distance des temps disparaît; les lieux se touchent; il se forme des liaisons entre tous les points habités de l'espace et de la durée; et tous les êtres vivants et pensants s'entretiennent" (VII, 189). Cf. James Knowlson, *Universal Language Schemes in England and France 1600–1800* (University of Toronto Press, 1975).

42 Early on, a certain Grammont claimed that "tout ce qui est antérieur au XIXe siècle, n'étant pas encore la linguistique, peut être expédié en quelques lignes" (quoted in Guy Harnois, *Les Théories du langage en France de 1660 à 1821* [Paris: Les Belles Lettres, 1929], pp. 9–10). Although this inflexible view has certainly changed, Thomas A. Sebeok's *Portraits of Linguists (1746–1963)* (Bloomington: Indiana University Press, 1966) includes no eighteenth-century French figures, and Georges Mounin's *Histoire de la linguistique* (Paris: Presses Universitaires de France, 1967) ennobles linguistics' origins by situating them in Greek philosophy's references to language.

43 Examples of this return, all of which displace language as a theoretical object by analyzing it in its practice, include Michel

Foucault's *Les Mots et les choses*; Louis Marin's *La Critique du discours*; Jacques Derrida's work on Rousseau (*De la grammatologie* [Paris: Paris: Minuit, 1967]) and on Condillac (*L'Archéologie du frivole* [Paris: Galilée, 1973]).

44 Throughout the eighteenth century, writes Sylvain Auroux, "la nature du signe linguistique n'est pensée que dans le déploiement patient des rapports qui unissent l'homme au monde, les hommes entre eux, et tout homme à lui-même." *La Sémiotique des encyclopédistes* (Paris: Payot, 1980), p. 34.

45 See for example René Bray, *La Formation de la doctrine classique en France* (Paris: Nizet, 1957); and Rensselaer Lee, "*Ut pictura poesis:* The Humanistic Theory of Painting," *The Art Bulletin*, 22:1 (1940), 197–269.

46 On the question of system and systematization in Diderot's thought, see Herbert Dieckmann, *Cinq leçons sur Diderot* (Geneva: Droz, 1959), ch. 2.

47 One example is the series of cross-references leading from "*Aius Locutius*" to "*Casuiste*" to "*Cas de conscience.*"

48 Proust, *Diderot et l'Encyclopédie*, p. 6.

49 According to Michel Foucault, the goal of the classical age's theory of language and representation is to achieve ultimate nomination, to "s'acheminer vers l'acte souverain de nomination, aller, à travers le langage, jusque vers le lieu où les mots et les choses se nomment en leur essence commune, et qui permet de leur donner un nom" (*Les Mots et les choses*, p. 133).

50 See Auroux, *La Sémiotique*; Ulrich Ricken, *Grammaire et philosophie au siècle des Lumières* (Villeneuve-d'Ascq: Publications de l'Université de Lille, 1978); and Daniel Droixhe, *La Linguistique et l'appel de l'histoire (1600–1800)* (Geneva: Droz, 1978).

51 "Quant à ce système général d'où l'arbitraire serait exclu, et que nous n'aurons jamais; peut-être ne nous serait-il pas fort avantageux de l'avoir; car quelle différence y aurait-il entre la lecture d'un ouvrage où tous les ressorts de l'univers seraient développés et l'étude même de l'univers? presqu'aucune" (VII, 211).

52 Wilda Anderson, *Between the Library and the Laboratory*, p. 43.

2 *Enlightenment critique and Diderot's art of philosophizing*

1 Dominic Lacapra, *Rethinking Intellectual History* (Ithaca: Cornell University Press, 1983). The most demanding questioning of the problem of history occurs in post-structuralism's efforts to reintroduce the history repressed by structuralism. See Geoff Bennington and Robert Young's introduction to *Post-Structuralism and the*

Question of History (Cambridge University Press, 1987, and Frederic Jameson's chapter on the New Historicism in *Postmodernism, or, the Cultural Logic of Late Capitalism* (Durham: Duke University Press, 1991).

2 Jacques Chouillet, *L'Esthétique des Lumières* (Paris: P.U.F., 1974), pp. 75–76.

3 Yves Benot, *Diderot: de l'athéisme à l'anticolonialisme* (Paris: Maspero, 1970), p. 93.

4 Georges Daniel, *Le Style de Diderot: légende et structure* (Geneva: Droz, 1986), p. 135.

5 "Une idée singulière se présente, un rapport bizarre distrait, et voilà la tête perdue, on revient de là comme d'un rêve: on demande à ses auditeurs: Où en étais-je? Que disais-je?" (AT XIII, 676). Diderot himself may bear the greatest responsibility for such a legend. Herbert Dieckmann's *Inventaire du fonds Vandeul et inédits de Diderot* (Geneva: Droz, 1951) first revealed the discrepancy between legend and writing process, and thus Diderot's readers' share in the perpetuation of such a legend.

6 See Robert Royalty Cru, *Diderot as a Disciple of English Thought* (1913; reprinted New York: AMS Press, 1966); Arthur Wilson, *Diderot* (New York: Oxford University Press, 1972); Franco Venturi, *La Jeunesse de Diderot*, trans. Juliette Bertrand (Paris: Skira, 1939).

7 J.-A. Naigeon, Diderot's first biographer, self-styled disciple, and earliest editor, calls the *Essai* "une traduction faite à sa manière." Article "Diderot," *Encyclopédie méthodique*, section "*Philosophie ancienne et moderne*," 2 (Paris: Panckoucke, 1792), p. 154. Diderot understood Shaftesbury's topic better than his language, argues Naigeon, as if to suggest that this "manner" were but a question of style. Naigeon argues that even outright errors in translation are amply counterbalanced by Diderot's mastery of the classical writer's skills. As I use the term, however, Diderot's manner involves far more than style.

8 Jean Starobinski, "Le Philosophe, le géomètre, l'hybride," *Poétique*, 21 (1975), 9.

9 Georges Daniel, *Fatalité du secret et fatalité du bavardage au 18e siècle* (Paris: Nizet, 1966), pp. 104–5.

10 Georges Poulet, *Etudes sur le temps humain* (Paris: Plon, 1950), p. 194.

11 A careful examination of how that self-knowledge is constructed and figured in Diderot's text (and in those of his readers) would go a long way towards placing the more idealizing of phenomenological readings on firmer ground. Passages such as the often-quoted

description of the genesis of the three dialogues grouped around *Le Rêve de D'Alembert* – "le plaisir de se rendre à soi-même un compte secret de ses opinions, les avait produits" (XVII, 221) – would have to be juxtaposed critically with other, less explicit references to language and writing. Consider the following: "Plusieurs fois, dans le dessein d'examiner ce qui se passait dans ma tête, de *prendre mon esprit sur le fait*, je me suis jeté dans la méditation la plus profonde me retirant en moi-même avec toute la contention dont je suis capable; mais ces efforts n'ont rien produit. Il m'a semblé qu'il faudrait être tout à la fois au-dedans et hors de soi . . . Mais il en est de l'esprit, comme de l'œil; il ne se voit pas. Il n'y a que Dieu qui sache comment le syllogisme s'exécute en nous . . . Un monstre à deux têtes emmanchées sur un même cou, nous apprendrait peut-être quelque nouvelle. Il faut donc attendre que la nature qui combine tout, et qui amène avec les siècles les phénomènes les plus extraordinaires, nous donne un *dicéphale* qui se contemple lui-même, et dont une des têtes fasse des observations sur l'autre (IV, 197–98, Diderot's emphasis).

Embodying epistemological and ontological unity, this bicephalous creature provides a perfect solution to the problem not only of thought ("comment le syllogisme s'exécute en nous") but also of self-knowledge. Both "within" and "outside" itself, this monstrous figure resolves all forms of opposition involving mind and body, contemplation and action, self and other. Although the strong desire to know the self produces the monster of Diderot's dream, the figure of the *dicéphale* substitutes for an impossibility: "il n'y a que Dieu qui sache." For Diderot the materialist though, such a God resembles nature, which too "knows" its exorbitant, monstrous workings far better than humans do. Finally though, cognition is less an issue in this supremely self-reflexive passage than language, which arguably is the monster in question. Like the *dicéphale*, one of whose heads views, speaks to and hears the other, language too refers to what is supposedly different from it, seemingly outside it, yet does so by referring simultaneously to itself. The opposition between inside and outside that appears comprehensible in the case of cognitive self-knowledge ("se retirer en soi-même") becomes far more problematic if we take this passage to refer to language. If anything is to be understood here, it is only by doing away with spatial models of cognition (inside/outside, "au-dedans et hors et soi"), perhaps even the entire visual metaphorics of self-knowledge and the space they are inscribed in, the space of "se voir," a metaphorics moreover upon which the vocabulary of phenomenology so heavily depends. Cognition may well be a referential issue and not a phenomenological one, a problem of determining to what monstrosities, including itself, language can refer, given its potential for combining anything. In Diderot's case, as *Le Rêve de D'Alembert* makes clear, the self made knowable is precisely such a monstrous combination of language. Teratology replaces phenomenology.

12 In "What Is An Author?", in *Textual Strategies* (ed. Josué V. Harari [Ithaca: Cornell University Press, 1979], pp. 141–60), Michel Foucault argues that the term author refers not to some objective, historically localizable person, but rather to an interpretive protocol, and a safeguard against the terrifying prospect of a subjectless history, that is, the emergence of events that do not stem from the will of a sovereign subject.

13 On the subject of intertextuality, see Julia Kristeva, *Semiotikè: recherches pour une sémanalyse* (Paris: Seuil, 1965), and *La Révolution du langage poétique* (Paris: Seuil, 1974); see also Mária Minich Brewer, "An Energetics of Reading," *Romanic Review*, 73:4 (1982), 489–504.

14 See *Diderot: Digression and Dispersion*, eds. Jack Undank and Herbert Josephs (Lexington: French Forum, 1984).

15 See Roland Barthes, "L'Ancienne rhétorique," *Communications*, 16 (1970), 172–229; Gérard Genette, "La Rhétorique restreinte," in *Figures III* (Paris: Seuil, 1972); and Pierre Kuentz, "Le 'Rhétorique' ou la mise à l'écart," *Communications*, 16 (1970). See also Paul de Man, "The Epistemology of Metaphor," *Critical Inquiry*, 5:1 (autumn 1978), 13–40; and Jacques Derrida, "La Mythologie blanche," in *Marges de la philosophie* (Paris: Minuit, 1972).

16 Herbert Dieckmann, *Cinq leçons sur Diderot* (Geneva: Droz, 1959), pp. 33–34.

17 Roger Kempf, *Diderot et le roman* (Paris: Seuil, 1964), p. 34.

18 See Jean-François Lyotard, "Dissertation sur une inconvenance," *Rudiments païens* (Paris: 10/18, 1977).

19 On the relation between literature and philosophy in the philosophical dialogue, see Maurice Roelens, "La Description inaugurale dans le dialogue philosophique aux 17e et 18e siècles," *Littérature*, 18 (May 1975), 51–62; his "Le Dialogue philosophique, genre impossible," *CAIEF*, 24 (May 1972), 43–58; and my "The Philosophical Dialogue and the Forcing of Truth," *MLN*, 98:5 (1983), 529–43.

20 Montaigne withdraws to his tower to write the *Essais*, and Descartes to his *poêle* in Holland to invent the *cogito*; the Princesse de Clèves flees from Paris for the country where she reveals her desire for Nemours; Alceste in Molière's *Le Misanthrope* retreats to

a social "desert" to remake a more authentic society. The 1694 *Dictionnaire de l'Académie* defines a philosopher as "celui qui s'applique à l'étude des sciences, et qui cherche à connaître les effets par leurs causes et par leurs principes . . . On appelle aussi philosophe un homme sage qui mène une vie tranquille et retiré, hors de l'embarras des affaires . . . Il se dit quelque fois absolument, d'un homme qui par libertinage d'esprit se met au-dessus des devoirs et des obligations ordinaires de la vie civile."

21 See Jacques Chouillet, "Le Mythe d'Ariste, ou Diderot en face de lui-même," *Revue d'Histoire Littéraire*, 64:4 (1964), 565–88; and "Le Personnage du sceptique dans les premières œuvres de Diderot," *Dix-Huitième Siècle*, 1 (1969), 195–211.

22 Herbert Dieckmann argues, for example, that allegory is used in the *Promenade* "not to veil, but to *unveil* and accentuate the absurdity of certain beliefs and rites . . . [Diderot] does not use poetic metaphors and symbols which we have to decipher; rather he disguises ironically in order to show up the hidden real meaning" ("Diderot's *Promenade du sceptique:* A Study in the Relationship of Thought and Form," in *Studien zur europäischen Aufklärung* [Munich: Wilhelm Fink Verlag, 1974], p. 207). The real allegory Dieckmann deciphers thus involves self-representation through art as symbolic form. In this "first attempt to give literary expression to his ideas," Diderot establishes an esthetic distance between himself and his ideas, literary form providing a means of "objectivation, distancing and disguise." Even in this most unspontaneous and least personal of texts, Dieckmann locates a "hidden real meaning" in its portrayal of a writer constantly refining the formal, technical means of expressing his ideas, the most intimate aspect of himself.

23 For a general discussion of *De l'interprétation*, see Herbert Dieckmann, *Cinq leçons*; Ernst Cassirer, *Philosophy of the Enlightenment*; and Suzanne Pucci, *Diderot and A Poetics of Science* (New York: Peter Lang, 1986).

24 Jean Luc, *Diderot* (Paris: Editions Sociales Internationales, 1938), p. 107.

25 "What it is to be is for the first time defined as the objectiveness of representing, and truth is first defined as the certainty of representing, in the metaphysics of Descartes." Martin Heidegger, "The Age of the World Picture," in *The Question Concerning Technology and Other Essays*, trans. William Lovitt (New York; Harper, 1977), p. 127. On representation in Descartes, see Jean-Luc Nancy, *Ego Sum* (Paris: Flammarion, 1979); and Dahlia

Judovitz, *Subjectivity and Representation in Descartes* (New York: Cambridge University Press, 1988).

26 It has been suggested that Diderot characterizes *De l'interprétation* as a series of thoughts so as to engage the eighteenth-century reader who might be put off by a drier, more imposing genre such as the treatise. This reference to spontaneous thought has also been read as Diderot's characteristic refusal to make his writing – or his thinking – fit the mold of preconceived ideas and preestablished systems; he prefers instead a suppler mode of inquiry, which allows him to explore the complexity of issues to the point of paradox, thus postponing the moment of final synthesis even at the risk of making resolution impossible. Diderot's own comments concerning his writing provide a certain justification for this interpretation. In the *Lettre sur les sourds et muets*, he writes that "[il] s'occupe plutôt à former des nuages qu'à les dissiper, et à suspendre les jugements qu'à juger" (IV, 162). Elsewhere, he claims, "on doit exiger de moi que je cherche la vérité mais non que je la trouve . . . qu'ai-je à craindre, si c'est innocemment que je me trompe" (AT I, 140). Most commentators take such statements at face value, allowing themselves the luxury of paraphrase and a retracing of the author's intellectual quest, concerning themselves with, as Roland Mortier puts it, the "acheminement vers la recherche de la vérité plutôt que . . . le caractère de la vérité atteinte" ("Diderot et le problème de l'expressivité," *CAIEF*, 13 [June 1961], 283).

9 The matter of judgment and the art of phrasing sensation

1 Jean-Claude Bonnet, *Diderot: textes et débats* (Paris: Librairie Générale Française, 1984), p. 79.

2 *Réfutation suivie de l'ouvrage d'Helvétius intitulé "De l'homme,"* in *Œuvres philosophiques* (Paris: Garnier, 1964), p. 565.

3 Diderot, *Œuvres philosophiques*, p. 559.

4 Jean Mayer, *Diderot, homme de science* (Rennes: Imprimerie Bretonne, 1959), pp. 24–25.

5 Commentators of *Le Rêve* have become increasingly aware of the crucial entwining of "form" and "content" in Diderot's writing, which I would rather call his experimentation with the materiality of thought. See Herbert Dieckmann, "Die künstliche Form des *Rêve de D'Alembert*," in *Studien zur französischen Aufklärung* (Munich: Wilhelm Fink, 1974), pp. 155–202; Jean Starobinski, "Le Philosophe, le géomètre, l'hybride," *Poétique*, 21 (1975), 8–23;

Jean-Pierre Seguin, *Diderot, le discours et les choses* (Paris: Klincksieck, 1978); and Wilda Anderson, *Diderot's Dream* (Baltimore: Johns Hopkins University Press, 1990). These studies help reformulate the more traditional characterization of the literary-poetic in Diderot's writing according to the opposition between form and content, text and idea, in sum the material and the idea.

6 Jacques Proust, "Diderot et la philosophie du polype," *Revue des Sciences Humaines*, 54:182 (1981), 21–22.

7 "L'Article *Jouissance* et l'idéologie érotique de Diderot," *Dix-Huitième Siècle*, 12 (1980), 31.

8 Analyzing Cartesian thought as representation, Marian Hobson writes, "Chez Descartes l'œil, le point qui est le foyer de l'opposition théâtre/hors théâtre, c'est le Cogito." She adds, quoting Jacques Derrida, "il est le point où s'enracine la possibilité de penser la totalité en lui échappant . . . c'est-à-dire en excédant la totalité, ce qui n'est possible – dans l'étant – que vers l'Infini ou le néant." "Du *theatrum mundi* au *theatrum mentis*," *Revue des Sciences Humaines*, 167 (1977), 385.

9 "Mais quand il dit, *cela est beau*, il ne juge pas, il rapporte seulement le jugement de ceux qui voient . . . La beauté pour un aveugle n'est qu'un mot, quand elle est séparée de l'utilité; et avec un organe de moins, combien de choses dont l'utilité lui échappe" (IV, 19).

10 D. J. Adams, *Diderot, Dialogue and Debate* (Liverpool: Francis Cairns, 1986), p. 130.

11 For a discussion of the eighteenth-century inversion question, see Gérard Genette, *Mimologiques: voyage en Cratylie* (Paris: Seuil, 1976).

12 The most rigorous analyses of these slippages, and one that powerfully challenges any stabilizing knowledge that might contain them, are found in Paul de Man's reading of Rousseau in *Blindness and Insight* and *Allegories of Reading*. De Man repeatedly displays interpretation's inability to know in fact what "nature" refers to in Rousseau, arguing that inability stems from the essence of metaphor in general and not from any particular way an individual writer may have used it.

13 Diderot's theory of the "sublime de situation" is sketched out in the *Bijoux indiscrets*, ch. 38, "Entretien sur les lettres."

14 Louis Marin, "1674: On the Sublime, Infinity, Je Ne Sais Quoi," in *A New History of French Literature*, ed. Denis Hollier (Cambridge: Harvard University Press, 1989), pp. 341–42. See also Samuel Monk, *The Sublime: A Study of Critical Theories in XVIII-Century England* (New York: Modern Language Association of America,

1935); Théodore A. Litman, *Le Sublime en France (1660–1714)* (Paris: Nizet, 1971); Neil Hertz, *The End of the Line: Essays on Psychoanalysis and the Sublime* (New York: Columbia University Press, 1985).

15 The Port-Royal grammarians recognized that affectivity is an integral part of language, and thus that reason cannot be taken as the sole norm of syntax. "Les expressions figurées signifient, outre la chose principale, le mouvement et la passion de celui qui parle" (quoted in Ricken, *Grammaire*, p. 99). Whereas they sought to circumscribe that affectivity through a regulative rhetoric however, Diderot unleashes it, in order to consider its effects all the better.

16 See Marian Hobson, "La *Lettre sur les sourds et muets* de Diderot: labyrinthe et langage," *Semiotica*, 16:4 (1976), 291–327.

17 Jacques Chouillet notes the influence on Diderot of Condillac's break with general grammar, exemplified by Condillac's differentiating between "real thought" and "discursive thought." *La Formation des idées esthétiques de Diderot, 1745–1763* (Paris: Armand Colin, 1973), p. 171.

18 There may well be an "artistic" side to Condillac's text, which a "frivolous" reading might uncover. See Jacques Derrida, "L'Archéologie du frivole," introduction to Condillac's *Essai sur l'origine des connaissances humaines* (Paris: Galilée, 1973). Condillac the philosopher seeks to systematize and control this art, whereas Diderot the artist-philosopher works to unleash its effects.

19 Addressing himself to the painter, Diderot writes in the *Salons*, "Touche-moi, étonne-moi, déchire-moi, fais-moi tressaillir, pleurer, frémir, m'indigner d'abord; tu récréeras mes yeux après si tu peux" (XIV, 389). Elsewhere, he formulates the relation between vision and the imagination as follows: "Le champ de l'imagination est en raison inverse du champ de l'œil" (XVI, 343).

20 "La pensée est énergie en même temps que langage. La pensée qui s'exprime est une énergie qui se libère." For Diderot, Chouillet claims, "la pensée reste l'élément premier; le geste et le discours sont tous deux nécessaires pour en libérer l'énergie." Chouillet, *La Formation*, pp. 186ff.

21 Roland Barthes, *L'Empire des signes* (Geneva: Skira, 1970). See especially Madeleine V. David, *Le Débat sur les écritures et l'hiéroglyphe aux XVIIe et XVIIIe siècles* (Paris: S.E.V.P.E.N., 1965).

4 *Critical narratives: Diderot's* Salons

1 For examples of such descriptions, see Rémy Saisselin, *Taste in Eighteenth-Century France* (Syracuse University Press, 1965); Michael Levey, *Rococo to Revolution: Major Trends in Eighteenth-Century Painting* (New York: Praeger, 1966); Robert Rosenblum, *Transformations in Late Eighteenth-Century Art* (Princeton University Press, 1967); Arnold Hauser, *The Social History of Art*, 3 vols. (New York: Knopf, 1952); and Michael Fried, *Absorption and Theatricality: Painter and Beholder in the Age of Diderot* (Berkeley: University of California Press, 1980).

2 "Permettez que je rompe un peu la monotonie de ces descriptions et l'ennui de ces mots parasites, *heurté, empâté, vrai, naturel, bien colorié, bien éclairé, chaudement fait, froid, dur, sec, moelleux*, que vous avez tant entendus, sans ce que vous les entendrez encore, par quelque écart qui nous délasse" (XIV, 125). Cf. "La Langue de la peinture" in Ferdinand Brunot, *Histoire de la langue française*, VI, part I (Paris: Armand Colin, 1930).

3 See for example Fredric Jameson, *The Prison-House of Language* (Princeton University Press, 1972).

4 Arnold Hauser, *The Social History of Art*, II, 502.

5 Analyzing the social origins of the academicians and collaborators of the *Encyclopédie* identified by Jacques Proust, Daniel Roche shows that the Enlightenment, at least that of the *Encyclopédie* project, did not involve a monolithic power shift from aristocracy to bourgeoisie. Rather, existing élites joined with a *bourgeoisie de talents* (and not an industrial-commercial bourgeoisie) to assume a new role of intellectual leadership. "Encyclopédistes et académiciens: essai sur la diffusion sociale des Lumières," in *Livre et société dans la France du XVIII*[e] *siècle*, II (Paris: Mouton, 1970), pp. 73–92.

6 The emergence of such a subject is one of the leitmotivs of Simon Schama's *Citizens: A Chronicle of the French Revolution* (New York: Knopf, 1989).

7 For an exhaustive analysis of this shift in esthetic judgment, see Marian Hobson, *The Object of Art* (Cambridge University Press, 1982).

8 Barthes, "The Discourse of History," in *Structuralism: A Reader*, ed. Michael Lane (London: Cape, 1970), pp. 145–55.

9 Norman Bryson, *Vision and Painting: The Logic of the Gaze* (London: Macmillan, 1986), p. 14. As Nelson Goodman puts it, "realistic representation . . . depends not upon imitation or illusion or information, but upon inculcation," *Languages of Art: An*

Approach to a Theory of Symbols (Indianapolis: Bobbs-Merrill, 1968), p. 38.

10 Louis Althusser, "Idéologie et appareil d'Etat," *La Pensée* (1970). Paul de Man characterizes ideology as the confusion of linguistic entities for natural ones. As de Man's analyses consistently show, any knowledge one might have of these natural entities – prior to reading – is highly problematic. See *The Resistance of Theory* (Minneapolis: University of Minnesota Press, 1986).

11 Bryson, *Vision and Painting*, p. 14.

12 Typical of this approach are T. M. Mustoxidi, *Histoire de l'esthétique française, 1700–1900*, (1920; reprinted New York: Burt Franklin, 1968); Raymond Bayer, *Histoire de l'esthétique* (Paris: Armand Colin, 1961); David Funt, *Diderot and the Esthetics of the Enlightenment* (Geneva: Droz, 1968).

13 See for example Louis Marin, *Etudes sémiologiques: ecritures, peintures* (Paris: Klincksieck, 1971); Jean-François Lyotard, *Discours, figure* (Paris: Klincksieck, 1971); Jacques Derrida, *La Vérité en peinture* (Paris: Flammarion, 1978).

14 The *salonnier* need not adopt Diderot's position. Roger de Piles, for example, commenting on Rubens and other masters, dismisses the role of description in the discourse of the connoisseur. "Je suppose qu'on ait assez veu de leurs Tableaux pour s'en estre fait une idée, et la disposition entr'autres que je demande à ceux qui se donneront la peine de lire ce discours, c'est qu'ils ayent un peu goûté Rubens par le veuë de ses plus beaux Ouvrages," *Dissertation sur les ouvrages des plus fameux peintres* (1681; reprinted Franborough: Gregg, 1968), pp. 23–24.

15 Other (and less interesting) explanations could be given for the slackening off of description following the watershed 1767 *Salon:* Diderot's increased awareness of painting's technical complexity; language's inability to account for it; advancing age (the last *Salon* was written when he was sixty-eight); loss of interest; and a decline in the quality of the artworks exhibited. See Gita May, *Diderot et Baudelaire, critiques d'art* (Geneva: Droz, 1957); Michael T. Cartwright, "Diderot critique d'art et le problème de l'expression," *Diderot Studies*, 13 (1966), 13–267; and August Langen, "Die Technik der Bildbeschreibung in Diderot's *Salons*," *Romanische Forschungen*, 61 (1948), 324–87. The most complete study to date of Diderot's art criticism is Else Maria Bukdahl, *Diderot, critique d'art*, 2 vols. (Copenhagen: Rosenkilde and Begger, 1980, 1984).

16 "Le beau spectacle! La belle et grande poésie! Comment vous transporterai-je au pied de ces roches qui touchent le ciel? Comment vous montrerai-je ce pont de grosses poutres soutenues

en dessous par des chevrons, et jeté du sommet de ces rochers vers ce vieux château?" (XIV, 156–57).

17 Cf. Lester G. Crocker, *Two Diderot Studies: Ethics and Esthetics* (Baltimore: The Johns Hopkins Press, 1952); and Aram Vartanian, *Diderot and Descartes* (Princeton University Press, 1953).

18 "Chaque art a ses avantages; il semble qu'il en soit d'eux comme des sens. Les sens ne sont qu'un toucher; tous les arts qu'une imitation" (*Entretiens sur le Fils naturel*, AT VII, 172). "Que ces arts qui ont pour objet d'imiter la nature ... sont des arts longs, pénibles et difficiles!" (*Salon de 1767*, XIV, 22). Marie-Luise Roy has argued, somewhat rigidly, that two of the pillars of French classical esthetics, the imitation of nature and the formula *ut pictura poesis*, are nodal points in terms of which can be defined the essential unity of Diderot's entire esthetic theory (*Die Poetik Denis Diderots* [Munich: Wilhelm Fink, 1966]).

19 Concerning Vernet's landscapes Diderot writes: "Ses fabriques, ses édifices, les vêtements, les actions, les hommes, les animaux, tout est vrai. De près il vous frappe, de loin il vous frappe plus encore. Chardin et Vernet, mon ami, sont deux grands magiciens" (XIV, 135). "[Vernet] a volé à la nature son secret: tout ce qu'elle produit, il peut le répéter" (XIII, 388). And Vien's *Saint Germain* depicts the universal truth of "things themselves": "Je n'y trouve rien qui me transporte, mais tout m'en plaît et m'arrête. Il y règne d'abord une tranquillité, une convenance d'actions, une vérité de disposition qui charment ... Les natures ne sont ici ni poétiques, ni grandes; c'est la chose même, sans presque aucune exagération. Ce n'est pas la manière de Rubens; ce n'est pas le goût des écoles italiennes. C'est la vérité qui est de tous le temps et de toutes les contrées" (XIII, 234–35).

20 Norman Bryson opens *Vision and Painting*, his critique of art historical theory, with a similar scene of deception. Seeking to best his rivals, Pliny recounts, Zeuxis painted grapes so lifelike that birds flew down to eat them. Parrhasius won the competition however by painting a curtain, whose naturalness deceived even Zeuxis into asking to have the curtain drawn back. Bryson comments upon the anecdote, suggesting that it "sum[s] up the essence of working assumptions still unquestioned[:] ... the rivalry between technicians for the production of a replica so perfect that art will take the palm from nature" (p. 1). We should note as well the notion of nature as absence and lack that this theory of (pictorial) representation implies, and the correlative constraint such a notion places on the theoretician to produce through theoretical argument that absence as negativity. Cf.

Jean-François Lyotard, "Beyond Representation," trans. Jonathan Culler, *The Human Context*, 7:3 (1975), 495–502.

21 It is (self-)deceptively simple to misunderstand this type of illusion and decry those who entertain it as indulging in something tantamount to critical skepticism or even philosophical nihilism. See Timothy Murray, "Consenting with Hassan, Graff (and Now Booth), *Boundary 2*, 12:3 (1984), 215–34.

22 See Martin Jay's discussion of vision and its place in contemporary French philosophy and theory, "In the Empire of the Gaze," in *Foucault: A Critical Reader*, ed. David Couzens Hoy (New York: Blackwell, 1986), pp. 175–203.

23 *Œuvres esthétiques* (Paris: Garnier, 1968), p. 792.

24 Michael Fried, *Absorption and Theatricality*, pp. 104–5.

25 This term is commonly translated in English as domestic drama, which nicely captures the way representations of eighteenth-century bourgeois consciousness privilege new spaces in order to reconfigure relations of order and authority. See Peter Szondi, "*Tableau* and *Coup de théâtre:* On the Social Psychology of Diderot's Bourgeois Tragedy," *New Literary History*, 11:2 (winter 1980), 323–41.

26 A sampling of such scenes includes the following: Greuze's *Un père de famille qui lit la Bible à ses enfants, Un écolier qui étudie sa leçon, L'Aveugle trompé, Le Baiser envoyé*; Chardin's *Philosophe occupé à ses lectures, Le Dessinateur, Une jeune fille qui récite son Evangile*; Van Loo's *Saint Augustin disputant contre les Donatistes*; and Vien's *Ermite endormi*.

27 Fried uncovers far more than a simple formal structure, yet his work raises the same question posed by any formalism or structuralism, namely, the specific and historically localizable nature of the subject before whom and at whose behest these innumerable forms and structures are deployed. Sharon Willis argues (more tellingly in Fried's case than Diderot's) that "in relying on and reinforcing notions of an autonomous subject which necessarily transcends its object, but without interrogating these categories, Fried repeats Diderot's critical gesture." "Lettre sur des taches aveugles: a l'usage de celles qui voient," *L'Esprit Créateur*, 24:1 (1984), 90. See Jack Undank's rich, eloquent, and critical response to Fried, "Between the Eye and the Word: Eighteenth-Century Readers and Viewers," *Boundary 2*, 10 (spring 1982), 319–41. "Fried, without being fully aware of it, exposes the lasting, modern repercussions of absorptive behavior in a movement toward reflexivity. The remarkable lesson to be learned from his still unravelling story is profoundly sublimated ... The artist

whose driving motive Fried interprets selectively and exclusively through the choice or position of absorbed figures, eventually – as if these figures had all along merely embodied their creator's desire – becomes the artist who solipsistically represents himself in the act of representing" (p. 329).

28 See Ian J. Lochhead, *The Spectator and the Landscape in the Art Criticism of Diderot and His Contemporaries* (Ann Arbor: UMI Research Press, 1981).

29 See Jay Caplan, *Framed Narratives: Diderot's Genealogy of the Beholder* (Minneapolis: University of Minnesota Press, 1985).

30 "On s'arrête devant un Chardin, comme d'instinct, comme un voyageur fatigué de sa route va s'asseoir, sans presque s'en apercevoir, dans l'endroit qui lui offre un siège de verdure, du silence, des eaux, de l'ombre et du frais" (XVI, 174).

31 Ultimately genre painting receives the following disparaging comment: "Cette peinture qu'on appelle de genre devrait être celle des vieillards ou de ceux qui sont nés vieux; elle ne demande que de l'étude et de la patience, nulle verve, peu de génie, guère de poésie, beaucoup de technique et de vérité, et puis c'est tout" (XIV, 118).

32 Jacques Chouillet, *L'Esthétique des Lumières* (Paris: Presses Universitaires de France, 1974), p. 9.

33 Lyotard, "Beyond Representation," p. 497.

34 For an analysis of the developing notion of the socially didactic function of art, see James A. Leith, *The Idea of Art as Propaganda in France, 1750–1799* (University of Toronto Press, 1965).

35 See Elizabeth de Badinter, *The Myth of Motherhood*, trans. Roger DeGaris (London: Souvenir, 1981); and Peggy Kamuf, *Fictions of Feminine Desire* (Lincoln: University of Nebraska Press, 1982).

36 Cf. Paul Hoffmann, "La Beauté de la femme selon Diderot," *Dix-Huitième Siècle*, 17 (1977), 283–89.

5 *Embodying knowledge*

1 Evelyn Fox Keller, *Reflections on Gender and Science* (New Haven: Yale University Press, 1985) p. 18.

2 Jack Undank writes of Diderot's desire "to overcome distance, to ratify an understanding, to appropriate an alien consciousness by some supplementary physical act." *Diderot: Inside, Outside, and In-Between* (Madison: Coda Press, 1979), p. 3. Georges Daniel notes that the act of bringing together, linking, and uniting "fut la principale ambition de Diderot: sa volonté et sa volupté," *Le Style de Diderot* (Geneva: Droz, 1986), p. 345. Although both readers

imply a kind of libidinal energetics ("desire," "volupté"), Undank more forcefully displays its effects on what he calls "consciousness."

3 See Jacques Derrida, "La Mythologie blanche," *Marges de la philosophie* (Paris: Minuit, 1972).

4 This is the epistemological and sociopolitical operation the Enlightenment performed upon the body, a practice still continuing today. Michel Foucault traces its genealogy in *La Naissance de la clinique* (Paris: Presses Universitaires de France, 1963).

5 See Maurice Merleau-Ponty, "L'Entrelacs – Le Chiasme," in *Le Visible et l'invisible* (Paris: Gallimard, 1964).

6 James Creech, *Diderot: Thresholds of Representation* (Columbus: Ohio State University Press, 1986), pp. 26–27. Creech notes in passing the similarity between Diderot's "theoretical fable" and the story Rousseau tells about writing, both ring and writing figuring a process of representation that holds the promise of remedying precisely the malady, the lack, the absence, it brings about.

7 Jean-François Lyotard, *The Differend: Phrases in Dispute*, trans. Georges Van den Abbeele (Minneapolis: University of Minnesota Press, 1988), p. xi.

8 Michel Foucault, *Histoire de la sexualité*, I, *La Volonté de savoir* (Paris: Gallimard, 1976), p. 101. Foucault's embodying metaphors merit scrutiny: "Comme si ce fantasque animal que nous logeons avait de son côté une oreille assez curieuse, des yeux assez attentifs, une langue et un esprit assez bien faits, pour en savoir fort long, et être tout à fait capable de le dire, dès qu'on le sollicite avec un peu d'adresse. Entre chacun de nous et notre sexe, l'Occident a tendu une incessante demande de vérité: à nous de lui arracher la sienne, puisqu'elle lui échappe; à lui de nous dire la nôtre, puisque c'est lui qui la détient dans l'ombre" (p. 102). Need one ask whether – and if so why – Foucault's common discourse ("our society," "we," "the question of what we are," "our body," etc.) elides precisely the difference Diderot's text makes manifest, the *différend* it phrases?

9 See Michèle Duchet, *Anthropologie et histoire au siècle des Lumières* (Paris: Maspero, 1971); and Michel de Certeau, *L'Ecriture de l'histoire* (Paris: Gallimard, 1975), especially "Ethno-graphie: L'Oralité, ou l'espace de l'autre," pp. 215–48.

10 I am not suggesting Foucault disregards the literary, poetic, esthetic status of Diderot's tale, for he grants strategic importance not only to particular artworks but more generally to literature, a transgressive "counter-discourse." On the relation between

Foucault's critical project and "the esthetic," see David Carroll, *Paraesthetics: Foucault, Lyotard, Derrida* (New York: Methuen, 1987).

11 "Il n'y a qu'une sorte de causes, à proprement parler," he affirms, "ce sont les causes physiques" (IX, 258). See Elisabeth de Fontenay, "A propos de Diderot," *Cahiers Renaud-Barrault*, 98 (1979), 47–60, and her *Diderot, ou le matérialisme enchanté* (Paris: Grasset, 1981).

12 "C'est qu'il est difficile de faire de la bonne métaphysique et de la bonne morale sans être anatomiste, naturaliste, physiologiste et médecin" (AT II, 322). In *Jacques*, the Master remarks on "une chose assez singulière, c'est qu'il n'y a guère de maximes de morale dont on ne fit un aphorisme de médecine, et réciproquement peu d'aphorismes de médecine dont on ne fît une maxime de morale" (XXIII, 268).

13 Henri Lefebvre, *Diderot, ou les affirmations fondamentales du matérialisme* (Paris: L'Arche, 1949), p. 137.

14 Immanuel Kant, "What is Enlightenment?", in *Philosophical Writings* (New York: Continuum, 1986), pp. 268–69.

15 D'Holbach, *Essai sur les préjugés*, in Dumarsais, *Œuvres* (Paris: Pougin, 1797), VI, 43–353.

16 *Examen de l'Essai sur les préjugés* (1770), quoted in Diderot, *Œuvres politiques*, ed. Paul Vernière (Paris: Garnier, 1963), p. 140.

17 The *Encyclopédie* defines paradox as "une proposition absurde en apparence, à cause qu'elle est contraire aux opinions reçues, et qui, néanmoins, est vraie au fond, ou du moins peut recevoir un air de vérité."

18 Diderot, *Œuvres politiques*, p. 140.

19 See for example Ernst Cassirer, *The Philosophy of the Enlightenment*, who refers to "the whirlpool of [Diderot's] dialectic"; and Lester Crocker, *Diderot's Chaotic Order* (Princeton University Press, 1974).

20 Yvon Belaval, *L'Esthétique sans paradoxe de Diderot* (Paris: Gallimard, 1950); Francis Pruner, *L'Unité secrète de "Jacques le fataliste"* (Paris: Minard, 1970); Daniel Mornet, "La Véritable signification du *Neveu de Rameau*," *Revue des Deux Mondes*, 40 (August 1927), 881–908; Jean Catrysse, *Diderot et la mystification* (Paris: Nizet, 1970); Roger Lewinter, *Diderot ou les mots de l'absence* (Paris: Editions Champ Libre, 1976).

21 Rosalie Colie, *Paradoxica Epidemica: The Renaissance Tradition of Paradox* (Princeton University Press, 1966), provides a helpful introduction to the question of paradox, pp. 3–39.

22 Philippe Lacoue-Labarthe, "Diderot, le paradoxe et la mimésis," *Poétique*, 43 (1980), 270.

23 See Lacoue-Labarthe, "L'Imprésentable," *Poétique*, 21 (1975), 53–95.

24 See Jacques Roger, *Les Sciences de la vie dans la pensée française du XVIIIe siècle* (Paris: Armand Colin, 1963).

25 The dreaming D'Alembert exclaims, "Suite indéfinie d'animalcules dans l'atome qui fermente, même suite indéfinie dans l'autre atome qu'on appelle la Terre . . . Tout change, tout passe, il n'y a que le tout qui reste" (XVII 128).

26 "Si j'avais voulu sacrifier la richesse du fond à la noblesse du ton, Démocrite, Hippocrate et Leucippe auraient été mes personnages; mais la vraisemblance m'aurait renfermé dans les bornes étroites de la philosophie ancienne et j'y aurais trop perdu," *Lettres à Sophie Volland* (Paris: Minuit, 1950), II, 226.

27 See Michel Foucault's discussion of Descartes' fear, in *Histoire de la folie*.

28 See Jacques Chouillet, "La Poétique du rêve dans les *Salons* de Diderot," *Stanford French Review*, 8:2–3 (1984), 245–56.

29 *Mlle. de l'Espinasse:* Ma foi, Docteur, j'entendais si peu de ce que j'écrivais, il parlait si bas, cet endroit de mon papier est si barbouillé que je ne le saurais lire. *Bordeu:* J'y suppléerai, si vous voulez (XVII, 123).

30 *Cahiers*, p. 50. Commentators have pointed out that none of the characters speak for Diderot, and that none in fact are spokespersons for the scientific-philosophical positions the text elaborates. Georges Daniel, for instance, refers to Diderot's "vision *chorale* de la réalité" ("Autour du *Rêve de D'Alembert*: Réflexions sur l'esthétique de Diderot," *Diderot Studies*, 12, [1969], 21). Jean Starobinski relates this polyphony to the question of truth in Diderot's texts: "la vérité est un bien commun; elle est généralisable; l'énoncer, c'est aussitôt la communiquer, tenter de lui assurer la reconnaissance universelle; à la limite, elle n'est plus la parole de l'autre, elle devient le discours de tous, dont seule peut se distinguer la voix du génie qui le premier aura su en faire la découverte" ("Diderot et la parole des autres," *Critique*, 296 [1972], 14). Starobinski does not question whether this "universal discourse" can possibly be a conflictual one.

31 Jean Mayer, *Diderot, homme de science* (Rennes: Imprimerie Bretonne, 1959), pp. 24–25.

32 Yvon Belaval, "Le Matérialisme de Diderot," in *Europäische Aufklärung*, eds. Hugo Friedrich and Fritz Schalk (Munich: Wilhelm Fink, 1967), p. 10.

33 Aram Vartanian, "Diderot and the Phenomenology of the Dream," *Diderot Studies*, 8 (1966), 218.

34 Ilya Prigogine and Isabelle Stengers, *La Nouvelle alliance: métamorphose de la science* (Paris: Gallimard, 1979), p. 91.

35 *Lettres à Sophie Volland*, II, 224–26.

36 Diderot refuses the term "soul" for the "centre commun de toutes les sensations, là où est la mémoire, là où se font les comparaisons," preferring a more sensationalist explanation of thought: "chaque brin n'est susceptible que d'un certain nombre déterminé d'impressions, de sensations successives, isolées, sans mémoire. L'origine est susceptible de toutes, elle en est le registre, elle en garde la mémoire ou une sensation continue, et l'animal est entraîné dès sa formation première à s'y rapporter soi, à s'y fixer tout entier, à y exister" (XVII, 175).

37 Jean-Claude Bonnet suggestively characterizes Diderot's writing as one through which he "dresse partout un petit théâtre, pour une vertigineuse mise en scène de soi, et construit un espace labile de métamorphoses, où la fragmentation délibérée du sujet, semblable à l'éparpillement de la vie même, rejoint les préoccupations scientifiques et l'inspiration matérialiste" (*Diderot*, p. 185).

38 Bordeu's most striking examples of physical monstrosity all display the same paradoxical logic of either/and: the patient whom François de la Peyronie trephined to treat a brain abcess and who "vécut et mourut alternativement" as la Peyronie injected a liquid into the brain and suctioned the liquid away; or the Siamese twins of Rabastens joined at the back, one with her head up, the other down, one who lost consciousness as the other regained it. Abnormalities made normal by Bordeu's explanation to Julie, these monstrous bodies embody a nondisjunctive, paradoxical logic which for Diderot is that of nature itself.

39 Julie's statement is far more radical than another in the *Eléments de physiologie*, which conflates sexual difference but in the name of the masculine. "Clitoris semblable au pénis de l'homme. Il est très sensible. Il a des muscles, un gland, un prépuce, des corps caverneux, un frein, les mêmes mouvements ("*Matrice*," XVII, 416).

40 In his exhaustive stylistic analysis, Georges Daniel shows how all Diderot's texts are characterized by the phenomenon of reversibility, as personal idiosyncrasy, rhetorical technique, and world view. "La tendance la plus consistante de Diderot [est] de montrer les choses comme indéfiniment réversibles et non comme définitivement renversées." "Du fait . . . des procédés d'écriture, la dialectique de Diderot se donne à lire comme un interminable mouvement pendulaire dépourvu de finalité." *Le Style de Diderot*, pp. 328, 306.

41 Aram Vartanian plays out this drama, reading *Le Rêve* as an

"indirect reflection of Diderot's class consciousness and political outlook." "The *Rêve de D'Alembert:* A Bio-Political View," *Diderot Studies*, 17 (1973), 41–64.

42 In precisely these terms Diderot describes the *génie* in *Le Paradoxe sur le comédien:* "La sensibilité n'est guère la qualité d'un grand génie... Ce n'est pas son cœur, c'est sa tête qui fait tout... Toutes les âmes chaudes occupent le théâtre, tous les hommes de génie sont au parterre; les premiers s'appellent des fous, les seconds s'appellent des sages" (AT VIII, 368).

6 Portraying Diderot: the aftermath

1 *Eloge philosophique de Denys Diderot* (Paris: An X [1803]).

2 See J. Th. de Booy and Alan J. Freer, *"Jacques le fataliste" et "La Religieuse" devant la critique révolutionnaire (1796–1800)* (*SVEC*, 33) (Geneva: Institut et Musée Voltaire, 1965). The newspaper *L'Eclair* mentions a "déchaînement universel contre Diderot" in October 1796, and a letter in *La Quotidienne* in the same year calls him the "fondateur de la secte philosophique." "Les jacobins, les dignes élèves [de ces charlatans de tolérance et d'humanité], n'ont fait que mettre en pratique les préceptes qu'ils tenaient de cette secte impie et anti-sociale, qui a conçu, combiné et réalisé la révolution française" (quoted in de Booy, p. 179).

3 See Herbert Dieckmann, "Three Diderot Letters, and *Les Eleuthéromanes*," *Harvard Library Bulletin* (1952), 69–91.

4 See V. P. Volguine's introduction to the *Code de la nature* (Paris: Editions Sociales, 1953), pp. 7–30.

5 Naigeon expresses indignation that "des hommes sanguinaires et féroces autoris[ent] du nom de Diderot leurs monstrueuses extravagances; lui attribu[ent] publiquement, et cit[ent] en faveur de leur opinion, un livre qu'il n'avait jamais ouvert" (*Préface*, pp. v–vi).

6 Barruel, *Mémoires pour servir à l'histoire du jacobisme.* Jean-François de La Harpe in his *Cours de littérature* still associated Diderot with *Le Code de la nature* in 1799.

7 Among these early "portraits" are Grimm's description in the *Correspondance littéraire*, Meister's eulogy, "A la mémoire de Diderot," *Correspondance littéraire*, 14 (1786), 460–68, and the *Mémoire pour servir à l'histoire de la vie et des œuvres de M. Diderot* by his daughter, Marie-Angélique Vandeul. Along with comments by Mme. Necker, the *abbé* Galiani, Marmontel, and others, these portraits created a truly legendary Diderot, which hostile reactions only aggravated. As Georges Daniel rightly notes, these

portrayals' "mythological ingredients" were first provided by Diderot himself (*Le Style de Diderot*, pp. 1–2).

8 These symbolic representations are certainly not specific to the Revolution and are but one moment in the long history of entwined power and representation in monarchical France. See Mona Ozouf, *Festivals and the French Revolution*, trans. Alan Sheridan (Cambridge: Harvard University Press, 1988); François Furet, *Interpreting the French Revolution*, trans. Elborg Forster (Cambridge University Press, 1981); Maurice Agulhon, *Marianne into Battle: Republican Imagery and Symbolism, 1789–1800*, trans. Janet Lloyd (Cambridge University Press, 1981); Lynn Hunt, *Politics, Culture, and Class in the French Revolution* (Berkeley: University of California Press, 1984); Marie-Hélène Huet, *Rehearsing the Revolution*, trans. Robert Hurley (Berkeley: University of California Press, 1982).

9 Jean-François de La Harpe, *Cours de littérature ancienne et moderne* (Paris: Firmin Didot, 1851), III, 255.

10 "D'ailleurs, son esprit ressemblait à ces estomacs chauds et avides qui dévorent tout et ne digèrent rien, et ce ne sont pas ceux des hommes sains" (p. 373).

11 Quoted in de Booy, *Jacques le fataliste*, p. 40.

12 See Georges May, *Le Dilemme du roman au dix-huitième siècle* (Paris: Presses Universitaires de France, 1963).

13 For L.-S. Mercier, "les mœurs de la queue du XVIIIe siècle s'y reflètent avec la netteté d'une miniature parfaite et sous des couleurs plus vives, plus saillantes les unes que les autres," producing a series of portraits in which Mercier finds "le dard du serpent [qui] se pose tour-à-tour au milieu de ce terrible miroir, au-dessus de chaque personnage; il les indique, les laisse voir à nu: le vice y montre à la fois toutes ses têtes, et telle est leur difformité que ceux qui s'y reconnaîtront rougiront et auront peur d'eux-mêmes; et c'est là sans doute le véritable point moral de cette espèce de roman" (quoted in de Booy, *Jacques le fataliste*, p. 106).

14 *La Décade philosophique, littéraire et politique* might dismiss *Jacques* as "une suite de caprices, de boutades," (quoted in Simone Lecointre's and Jean Le Galliot's edition of *Jacques* [Geneva: Droz, 1976], pp. lxxxi–lxxxii), but already the text's fictive reader retorts to the narrator, "Et votre *Jacques* n'est qu'une insipide rhapsodie de faits, les uns réels, les autres imaginés, écrits sans grâce et distribués sans ordre." And if *Le Journal littéraire* calls Diderot's novel "une mauvaise singerie de *Candide*," just as other

critics called it a bad imitation of Sterne's *Tristram Shandy*, *Jacques* marks its intertextuality in far more extensive and interesting terms.

15 Lecointre and Galliot, *Jacques*, p. lxxxi.

16 "Lorsqu'on fait un conte," begins *Ceci n'est pas un conte*, "c'est à quelqu'un qui l'écoute." Diderot's biographical, psychological interpreters have taken this statement to refer to his penchant for dialogue and his need for an interlocutor, either real or imagined. From the perspective of discourse analysis, however, one would argue that all speech and writing are always dialogical, inevitably addressed to another, even in the refusal or denial of its own dialogical status. The question raised by *Jacques* is slightly different, however, for it is whether all discourse is not in fact narrative.

17 Vivienne Mylne, *The Eighteenth-Century French Novel: Techniques of Illusion* (University of Manchester Press, 1965).

18 See Thomas Kavanaugh's *The Vacant Mirror*, which represents the most exhaustive attempt to read *Jacques* through the prism of structuralist literary and linguistic theory.

19 Lecointre and Galliot, *Jacques*, pp. xlvii–xlviii.

20 In a 1973 critical review of analyses of *Jacques*, Maurice Roellens finds that despite their similarities all derive from "une sorte de vague obédience hégélienne" that reduces form to the expression of the Idea, whether that of deterministic materialism or of the novel and literature. "*Jacques le fataliste* et la critique contemporaine," *Dix-Huitième Siècle*, 5 (1973), 126.

21 Roellens, *Jacques le fataliste*, p. 127.

22 De Booy, *Jacques le fataliste*, p. 135.

23 Preface (1822), 7th edition (Paris: Charpentier, 1847), pp. 3–4.

24 Georges Benrekassa, *Le Concentrique et l'excentrique*, p. 334.

25 One example of how Naigeon evacuates the *Encyclopédie*'s critical force is his discussion of Diderot's article "*Encyclopédie*": "article conçu, écrit partout de verve, et qui, soit par l'étendue et la variété des connaissances qu'on y remarque, soit par la profondeur des idées, soit par les vues générales, utiles et neuves qu'il offre sur une foule d'objets divers . . . soit même par l'énergie, l'élégance, et le coloris du style, me paraît très supérieur au discours préliminaire de D'Alembert" (p. 78). While Naigeon does quote or paraphrase some of the article's more interesting passages, at least half his commentary concerns stylistic and linguistic questions disassociated so completely from their philosophical, esthetic, and above all practical context that in 1821 they must have resembled intellectual folklore.

26 "Plus j'y réfléchis, et plus je suis convaincu que Diderot n'a fait qu'étendre, exagérer le système dramatique des Anciens, et rapprocher l'art de la nature" (p. 171).

27 In the *Pensées philosophiques*, for example, "on y trouve des paragraphes d'une éloquence forte et persuasive, des raisonnements serrés, précis; et partout le talent, cet art si difficile et si rare de colorer agréablement tous les objets, et de leur donner en quelque sorte de la vie et du mouvement" (p. 42).

28 Nisard's explicit reference following the Revolution of 1848 to "une certaine morale qui a eu cours ces dernières années" is given as an explanation of why Diderot is so favorably received by "une certain classe de lettrés, outre son désordre dont l'attrait n'est pas médiocre pour les gens qui ne goûtent pas l'ordre" (quoted in Jacques Proust, *Lectures de Diderot* [Paris: Armand Colin, 1974], p. 77). And Faguet's critical characterization of Diderot's populism says far more about Faguet's attitude towards populist socialism than about any eighteenth century.

29 The delayed, sporadic, and piecemeal publication of the *Salons* helped make Diderot's Romanticization possible. Public editions of new *Salons* appeared in 1795, 1798, 1813, and 1819; only in 1857 would the remaining five *Salons* be published.

30 Charles-Augustin Sainte-Beuve, *Les Grands écrivains français* (Paris: Garnier, 1927), pp. 141–42.

31 Gœthe refers to Diderot's ability to "assembler les éléments les plus hétérogènes de la réalité en un tout idéal" (quoted by Roland Mortier, *Diderot en Allemagne (1750–1850)* [1954; Geneva: Slatkine, 1986], p. 223). This ideal esthetic totality – Gœthe refers here to *Jacques* – cannot be judged according to traditional literary norms, which it resists, for it is unique and unprecedented, in short a work of art. Schlegel too finds in *Jacques* a play of contrasts and oppositions that he characterizes in terms of the Romantic notion of *Witz* and irony. Diderot's novel expresses "la plénitude du Witz entièrement débarrassée de tout immixtion sentimentale. Il est conçu avec intelligence et exécuté d'une main sûre; j'ose, sans exagération, l'appeler une œuvre d'art" (Mortier, *Diderot en Allemagne*, p. 234).

32 Mortier, *Diderot en Allemagne*, p. 260.

33 "Hegel does not recognize a necessity for different 'rules' when dealing with the aesthetic, the moral, and the cognitive. In fact, the only distinctions between the moral, aesthetic, and cognitive spheres allowed by Hegel are the ones that determine their relative privileges and subordination. The aesthetic is the 'Aufhebung' of the moral because it reconciles what in morality can be

thought only in terms of opposition, because it makes concrete what, in morality, is abstract. The cognitive is in turn the sublation of the aesthetic, because the cognitive provides the aesthetic with the concept – its own concept – of the beautiful it is incapable of providing for itself. The essential themes of the *Aesthetics* – the triumph of art over morality and the essentially conceptual nature of art – are already implicit in Hegel's reading of *Le Neveu.*" Suzanne Gearhart, "The Dialectic and its Aesthetic Other," *MLN*, 101:5 (1986), 1053–54. On Hegel's annexation of Diderot, see also James Hulbert, "Diderot in the Text of Hegel," *Studies in Romanticism*, 22:2 (1983), 267–91.

34 Rameau repeatedly resists all Moi's arguments based on universal moral values in the name of a lucid awareness of who and what he is, and a resolute refusal to lie to himself: "Il faut que Rameau soit ce qu'il est; un brigand heureux avec des brigands opulents; et non un fanfaron de vertu, ou même un homme vertueux, rongeant sa croûte de pain, seul, ou à côté des gueux" (XII, 121). Explaining this inability to return to the Bertin house from which he had been ejected for having told the truth, namely, that all the guests there were as much perverse social parasites as he, Rameau exclaims, "moi! moi enfin! j'irais! . . . tenez, monsieur, cela ne se peut . . . Je me sens là quelque chose qui s'élève et qui me dit, Rameau, tu n'en feras rien. Il faut qu'il y ait une certaine dignité attachée à la nature de l'homme, que rien ne peut étouffer" (XII, 91–92).

35 "The content uttered by spirit and uttered about itself is, then, the inversion and perversion of all conceptions and realities, a universal deception of itself and of others. The shamelessness manifested in stating this deceit is just on that account the greatest truth. This style of speech is the madness of the musician 'who piled and mixed up together some thirty airs, Italian, French, tragic, comic, of all sorts and kinds . . .' " G. W. F. Hegel, *The Phenomenology of Mind*, trans. J. B. Baillie (New York: Harper and Row, 1967), p. 543. Hegel is quoting here from *Le Neveu.*

36 Suzanne Gearhart, "The Dialectic and its Aesthetic Other," pp. 1063–64.

37 As Roger Fayolle puts it, for Sainte-Beuve "il s'agit de déguiser une morale, représentative des intérêts et des privilèges d'une classe sociale, en une science révélatrice des caractères universels et immuables du Monde et de l'Homme: je juge, mais ce que mon jugement désigne, ce n'est pas le bien, c'est le vrai. Fallacieuse confusion des ordres où nous retrouvons la faiblesse congénitale de notre enseignement de la littérature: l'œuvre est belle parce

qu'elle est vraie; et quelle est cette vérité-là, sinon la conformité à un certain ordre de valeurs morales, à une certain conception du bien?" *Sainte-Beuve et le XVIIIe siècle, ou comment les révolutions arrivent* (Paris: Armand Colin, 1972), p. 13.

Index

Cambridge Studies in French

Also in the series (* denotes out of print)

1 J. M. COCKING
Proust: Collected Essays on the Writer and his Art

2 LEO BERSANI
The Death of Stéphane Mallarmé

*3 MARIAN HOBSON
The Object of Art: The Theory of Illusion in Eighteenth-Century France

4 LEO SPITZER, translated and edited by DAVID BELLOS
Essays on Seventeenth-Century French Literature

5 NORMAN BRYSON
Tradition and Desire: From David to Delacroix

6 ANN MOSS
Poetry and Fable: Studies in Mythological Narrative in Sixteenth-Century France

7 RHIANNON GOLDTHORPE
Sartre: Literature and Theory

8 DIANA KNIGHT
Flaubert's Characters: The Language of Illusion

9 ANDREW MARTIN
The Knowledge of Ignorance: From Genesis to Jules Verne

10 GEOFFREY BENNINGTON
Sententiousness and the Novel: Laying Down the Law in Eighteenth-Century French Fiction

*11 PENNY FLORENCE
Mallarmé, Manet and Redon: Visual and Aural Signs and the Generation of Meaning

12 CHRISTOPHER PRENDERGAST
The Order of Mimesis: Balzac, Stendhal, Nerval, and Flaubert

13 NAOMI SEGAL
The Unintended Reader: Feminism and Manon Lescaut

14 CLIVE SCOTT
A Question of Syllables: Essays in Nineteenth-Century French Verse

15 STIRLING HAIG
Flaubert and the Gift of Speech: Dialogue and Discourse in Four 'Modern' Novels

*16 NATHANIEL WING
The Limits of Narrative: Essays on Baudelaire, Flaubert, Rimbaud and Mallarmé

17 MITCHELL GREENBERG
Corneille, Classicism and the Ruses of Symmetry

*18 HOWARD DAVIES
Sartre and 'Les Temps Modernes'

19 ROBERT GREER COHN
Mallarmé's Prose Poems: A Critical Study

20 CELIA BRITTON
Claude Simon: Writing the Visible

21 DAVID SCOTT
Pictorialist Poetics: Poetry and the Visual Arts in Nineteenth-Century France

22 ANN JEFFERSON
Reading Realism in Stendhal

23 DALIA JUDOVITZ
Subjectivity and Representation in Descartes: The Origins of Modernity

24 RICHARD D. E. BURTON
Baudelaire in 1859

25 MICHAEL MORIARTY
Taste and Ideology in Seventeenth-Century France

26 JOHN FORRESTER
The Seductions of Psychoanalysis: Freud, Lacan and Derrida

27 JEROME SCHWARTZ
Irony and Ideology in Rabelais: Structures of Subversion

28 DAVID BAGULEY
Naturalist Fiction: The Entropic Vision

29 LESLIE HILL
Beckett's Fiction: In Different Words

30 F. W. LEAKEY
Baudelaire: Collected Essays, 1953–1988

31 SARAH KAY
Subjectivity in Troubadour Poetry

32 GILLIAN JONDORF
French Renaissance Tragedy: The Dramatic Word

33 LAWRENCE D. KRITZMAN
The Rhetoric of Sexuality and the Literature of the French Renaissance

34 JERRY C. NASH
The Love Aesthetics of Maurice Scève: Poetry and Struggle

35 PETER FRANCE
Politeness and its Discontents: Problems in French Classical Culture

36 MITCHELL GREENBERG
Subjectivity and Subjugation in Seventeenth-Century Drama and Prose: The Family Romance of French Classicism

37 TOM CONLEY
The Graphic Unconscious in Early Modern French Writing

38 MARGERY EVANS
Baudelaire and Intertextuality: Poetry at the Crossroads

39 JUDITH STILL
Justice and Difference in Works of Rousseau: Bienfaisance and Pudeur

40 CHRISTOPHER JOHNSON
System and Writing in the Philosophy of Jacques Derrida

41 CAROL A. MOSSMAN
Politics and Narratives of Birth: Gynocolonization from Rousseau to Zola